BRAKE SYSTEMS

OEM & RACING BRAKE TECHNOLOGY

MIKE MAVRIGIAN & LARRY CARLEY

HPBooks

HPBooks
are published by
The Berkley Publishing Group
A member of Penguin Putnam Inc.
375 Hudson Street
New York, New York 10014

First Edition: October 1998

© 1998 Mike Mavrigian & Larry Carley
10 9 8 7 6 5 4 3 2 1

Library of Congress Cataloging-in-Publication Data

Mavrigian, Mike.
    Brake System : OEM & racing brake technology / Mike Mavrigian &
Larry Carley. -- 1st ed.
    p.   cm.
    Includes index.
    ISBN 1-55788-281-9
    1. Automobiles--Brakes. 2. Automobiles, Racing--Brakes.
    I. Carley, Larry W.   II. Title
    TL269.M39   1998   98-25879
    629.2'46--dc21   CIP

Cover design by Bird Studios
Book design and production by Michael Lutfy
Interior photos by the authors unless otherwise noted
Cover photo by Rich Chenet

CONTENTS

I would like to thank all the aftermarket brake suppliers who provided technical input and photos for this book. Special thanks goes to Wagner Brakes and Raybestos (Brake Parts Inc.).

I would also like to thank the original equipment vehicle manufacturers and their suppliers for granting us permission to use their illustrations.—Larry

A special thanks to the following racing brake systems experts for their input and advice. The racing information in this book would not have been possible without their cooperation and guidance.

Mark Wood, Reb-Co/Outlaw Brakes; Warren Gilliland, The Brake Man; Tilton Engineering; Jeff Ocasek and Vinod Vemparala, Hawk Brakes; John Dillon, Baker Racing; Aerospace Components; Sierra Brakes; Wilwood; AP Racing.—Mike

ACKNOWLEDGMENTS

This book was written in an attempt to cover the vast spectrum of brake system technology, both on the OEM side and the racing side. Whether you're trying to diagnose a brake problem, just want to reline or repair your brakes, or need the latest information on racing brake components and tuning, this book is a good place to start.

Because good brakes are absolutely essential for safe driving, and critical to racing success, it's important to understand how they work, what can go wrong with them, and how to diagnose and fix common brake problems. On the OEM side, most shop manuals don't provide this kind of information. A manual will tell you the step-by-step procedures for disassembling, replacing or adjusting various components, but little else. If you want more background information or a detailed explanation about how something works or how to diagnose problems you usually have to look elsewhere. That was one reason for publishing this book.

Another was to provide up-to-date information on today's electronic antilock brake systems (ABS). ABS and traction control are either standard equipment or optional on many of today's vehicles, so it's essential to know how ABS can affect brake performance on your vehicle as well as brake diagnosis and repair work. Some ABS-equipped vehicles, for example, require special bleeding procedures if air gets inside the brake lines.

The second section of this book talks about high performance and racing brake systems and components, such as calipers, rotors, pads, hydraulics and racing brake cooling. The purpose of this section is designed to give you some basic background to help you select the proper components for your racing brake systems.

About Do-It-Yourself Oem Brake Repairs

Most brake repairs you can do yourself using ordinary hand tools. But if you don't feel comfortable doing your own brake work, or you don't have the tools that may be required for more advanced repairs or diagnosis, you should seek out a competent professional who has the necessary skills and tools to fix your brakes. Look for someone who is Automotive Service Excellence (ASE) certified in brakes. Shops that employ certified technicians display the blue and white ASE logo. Also, try to find a shop that participates in the Motorist Assurance Program (MAP). This is a voluntary program that requires repair facilities to adhere to a strict Code of Ethics, provide a written estimate to customers, and to follow prescribed inspection and repair guidelines.

If you are doing your own brake work, then read the sections in this book that pertain to the components you'll be working on, as well as the chapters on basic troubleshooting and service. If your vehicle has antilock brakes, read those chapters, too, as well as any that pertain to your particular vehicle. Reading this material will help you better understand the components you're working on as well as what you're doing.

INTRODUCTION

SECTION I

OEM BRAKE SYSTEMS

BRAKING

HISTORY

Brake systems have come a long way since the early days of the automobile. Hydraulic brakes weren't invented until 1918, so cars of that era typically used mechanical band brakes on the transmission or rear wheels only.

The brakes on today's cars and trucks have come a long way from those that brought the vehicles of a generation ago to a halt. The basics of hydraulics haven't changed, but friction materials have, as have many of the components in today's brake system. Composite rotors have replaced one-piece cast iron rotors, new master cylinder and caliper designs have been introduced, and electronic antilock brakes and traction control are standard equipment or optional on most new cars and trucks.

To better understand the brakes on today's vehicles, we need to consider how brake systems evolved. Prior to the 1920s, all brake systems were mechanically operated rather than hydraulic. Rods or cables connected to the brake pedal were used to tighten band brakes around the flywheel, driveshaft or a wheel drum, or to rotate a cam or wedge that pushed a set of brake shoes outward against the inside of a drum. So on most vehicles, only the rear drive wheels had brakes. The few vehicles that did have front brakes used a hollow flexible steel "Bowden" cable

to operate the brake drums. Four wheel braking was better than two wheel braking, but required a complex arrangement of equalizer yokes and pulleys to even out the braking forces so the rear wheels wouldn't lock up and skid when the brakes were applied.

HYDRAULIC BRAKES

The invention of hydraulic brakes in 1918 by Malcom Loughead proved to be a real breakthrough because hydraulics allowed the brakes to be applied by fluid pressure. Because fluids are incompressible, force applied by a piston to a fluid will be transmitted equally to pistons located at each wheel brake. This eliminated the rods, levers and cables that were previously needed to work the brakes, which greatly simplified the job of providing balanced four-wheel braking. Hydraulics also reduced the amount of pedal effort required to stop the vehicle, which made for easier braking and safer driving.

In 1920, Duesenberg became the first production vehicle to offer hydraulic brakes. Chrysler was the

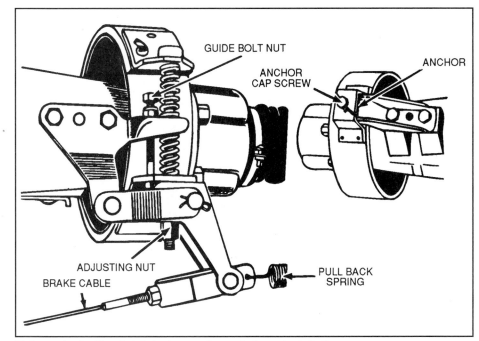

Early mechanical band style brake on a transmission output shaft.

next in 1924, and soon all the vehicle manufacturers offered hydraulic brakes.

POWER BRAKES

The next big innovation in brakes came with the addition of power-assisted braking. Cadillac was the first to offer vacuum assisted power brakes in 1930. The original "Master-Vac" power brake booster that became the predecessor to today's vacuum boosters was patented in the 1950s by Bendix. A popular option in the 1960s, it became standard equipment on most vehicles by the mid-1970s partly because everybody wanted it and partly because disc brakes were becoming more common. Today power brakes are standard equipment on nearly all cars and light trucks.

DISC BRAKES

Disc brakes were another major innovation in the evolution of today's brake systems. Though primitive disc brakes were used as early as 1898 on an electric-powered car, disc brakes didn't really catch on until the late 1960s and early 1970s in this country. The Europeans were using disc brakes on sports cars in 1956 (Triumph and Jaguar), but it was 1965 before disc brakes were first offered here (standard on the '65 Corvette and optional on the '65 Mustang GT).

As vehicles were becoming heavier and more powerful in the 1950s and 1960s, the limitations of drum brakes were becoming more apparent. Brakes generate a tremendous amount of heat which requires lots of cooling to prevent fading. Drum brakes don't cool as well as discs because their enclosed design allows cooling only on the outer surface. Another limitation of a drum is that it can trap water if a vehicle is driven through a puddle. If water gets inside the drum, it acts like a lubricant and prevents the shoes from grabbing.

Using a disc rather than a drum has several advantages. One is that a disc brake cools better. The flat faces of the exposed rotor provide a more open surface for cooling, and the addition of fins or vents between the faces of the rotor increase its ability to dissipate heat even more. A rotor also won't trap water like a drum making it a safer design for wet weather driving. A disc brake is also lighter than a drum, which saves weight and bulk, and disc brakes are self-adjusting which eliminates the need for self-adjusters or periodic adjustment.

As disc brakes were adopted, most vehicles only used them up front where they provided the most good. Using drums in the rear saved cost and allowed the use of a simpler (less expensive) parking brake. Even today, most domestic as well as many import vehicles still use the front disc/rear drum arrangement because it provides the best compromise between cost and performance. Four wheel disc brake systems tend to be limited to sports models and high-end luxury sports sedans.

ANTILOCK BRAKES

The next major improvement in the evolution of today's brakes came with the arrival of electronic antilock brake systems (ABS). The addition of ABS to a brake system adds a significant margin of safety by minimizing wheel lockup and skidding when braking on wet or slick surfaces or when stopping suddenly on dry pavement. ABS allows you to maintain steering control when braking hard so you can steer your way around obstacles and out of trouble. It also helps to keep the vehicle straight and stable during a panic stop, which reduces the chance of getting sideways. That's why ABS has become standard or optional on most vehicles today.

These Duesenberg IIs are a modern replica of the original, which was one of the first production cars of its day to come equipped with hydraulic brakes.

The origins of ABS date back to shortly after World War Two when ABS was originally developed for heavy aircraft. The first "modern" electronic ABS system for automotive use was invented by the Robert Bosch Corp. and offered on certain European Mercedes-Benz and BMW models in 1978. Other European vehicle manufacturers soon followed suit and the option quickly grew in popularity. In 1985, the first ABS-equipped BMWs and Mercedes produced for the U.S. market came ashore, starting the rush to ABS on this side of the Atlantic Ocean. That same year, Ford become the first domestic vehicle manufacturer to offer an ABS system, with General Motors jumping on the ABS bandwagon the following year. By 1990, 25% of all new cars and light trucks were equipped with ABS as either standard or optional equipment, and by 1995 ABS was available on over 90 of all new vehicles.

As ABS evolved, traction control capabilities were added. This allowed the ABS system to monitor and prevent wheel spin when accelerating on wet or slippery surfaces, too. Traction control proved to be especially helpful on performance cars with wide tires which were notorious for poor wet weather traction.

Traction control works something like an electronic limited slip differential. When the wheel speed sensors detect wheel spin, the brakes are applied to the wheel with the least traction so engine power will go to the wheel with the most traction. If both wheels are spinning, both are braked to maintain traction. Some traction control systems also employ various "power reduction" strategies to reduce engine power when the drive wheels start to spin. The system may momentarily reduce engine power by retarding spark timing, disabling one or more fuel injectors or reducing the throttle opening.

STABILITY CONTROL

The latest twist in the ongoing evolution of brakes is to use the ABS/traction control system to assist steering. It's called "Vehicle Dynamics Control" (VDC) and is the brainchild of the Robert Bosch Corp.

Vehicle Dynamics Control is the "next generation" antilock brake system. VDC combines the basic functions of ABS and traction control with the unique ability to brake any of the vehicle's four wheels individually as needed to provide "corrective" steering to improve steering control and vehicle stability. Thus, the VDC system uses the brakes to help straighten out a vehicle that is in danger of going out of control.

Let's say you're driving down an unfamiliar road at night and suddenly encounter a sharp left turn. You enter the turn going too fast and the rear end starts to slide to the outside. You're in danger of losing control. If you hit the brakes, the rear wheels may lock up causing the car to spin out of control, even if you have ABS. Countersteering may not save you either if the rear wheels are already starting to lose traction and slide to the outside.

In a situation like this, the VDC system would sense the problem as it starts to develop. It would immediately react by braking the right front wheel at the first sign of instability to help straighten out the car so you could regain control. If additional braking were needed at other wheels, that would be done too until the vehicle was back under control.

Brake steering is the same basic principle that's used in farm tractors and dune buggies. Rear wheels are braked individually so the vehicle can turn sharply. If the left rear brake is applied, the vehicle steers sharply to the left. Apply the right rear brake and

In the late 1960s, disc brakes began to appear on American performance cars such as this '67 Camaro SS350 as an extra cost option or standard equipment. The first cars to get them were the '65 Mustang GT and Corvette.

the vehicle veers right. VDC uses the same principle but in a different way. It brakes wheels individually as needed to maintain and restore steering control and directional stability, and it's all done automatically without any driver input.

Unlike ABS which is only active when braking, or traction control which only comes into play when accelerating, VDC is on guard all the time. You don't even have to hit the brakes because VDC will sense when the vehicle is becoming unstable and react before you can. It's almost like having an expert driver in the back seat overseeing your every move, ready to assist if assistance is needed.

Of course, VDC can't idiot-proof a vehicle. Nor can it overcome the basic laws of physics. If a vehicle enters a corner going way too fast, VDC can't magically make it stick to the road. But it can help the driver regain

control if there is any hope of doing so.

VDC is primarily a safety aid, not a system for enhancing handling performance. Even so, VDC adds something which no driver can do regardless of how skilled they are, which is to use individual wheel braking to help stabilize and steer a vehicle when it is being pushed to the limits of adhesion.

The heart of the VDC system is a "yaw rate" sensor. This device, which was originally developed to help guide military missiles to their targets, senses changes in motion about the vehicle's vertical axis to detect understeer, oversteer and fishtailing. The yaw sensor uses a solid state piezoelectric element to monitor the rotational motions of the vehicle so the VDC system can intervene if the vehicle starts to become unstable.

The VDC control module also monitors the driver's steering inputs

via a steering angle sensor on the steering column. This tells the control module which way the driver is steering the vehicle so it can determine if the vehicle is responding normally. Additional inputs from the four wheel speed sensors allow the control module to compare relative wheel speeds. This also tells the control module if there's a speed differential between the inside and outside wheels (which occurs when turning). If the data inputs from all the sensors fail to follow the VDC program maps, it tells the control module that the vehicle is starting to lose its grip and that help is needed to regain control.

The first production vehicles to offer the new VDC system were the 1996 Mercedes "S" Class and E420 models. A similar but not as sophisticated system called "Dynamic Stability Control (DSC)," also by Bosch, was offered in 1995 on V12-

powered BMW 750iL and 850Ci models.

LOOKING AHEAD

What comes next in brake innovations is anybody's guess. One thing's for sure: the evolution of today's brake systems will continue to keep pace with changes in vehicle technology and design, and the public's ongoing demand for safety.

Automatic braking systems that self-engage to prevent accidents and/or minimize collision damage are being developed that activate when sensors detect an object or vehicle in the path of your vehicle. If you don't react fast enough to the emergency, the system reacts for you. The same system might also be designed to reduce the risks of tailgating. Follow the vehicle ahead too closely and your vehicle would automatically slow down until you were following at a "safe" distance.

Automatic braking might also become part of an overall collision avoidance system that would monitor the road ahead and automatically attempt to steer you around or away from obstacles or oncoming vehicles in your path.

The technological challenges that

The arrival of antilock brake systems in 1985 on Mercedes and BMWs marked the beginning of a whole new era in brake technology. But the latest stability control systems are taking brake technology to new heights. The car on the left can't navigate the sharp turn, understeers and skids. But the car on the right is held safely on course by a Bosch Vehicle Dynamics Control (VDC) system. The system senses steering inputs and vehicle yaw to employ individual wheel braking to counter the effects of understeer or oversteer.

seem insurmountable today may not be tomorrow. Anything is possible. After all, electronic ABS and traction control might have seemed pretty far-fetched back in the 1960s.

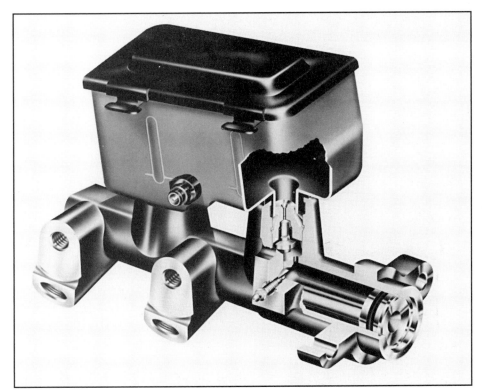

The master cylinder is what provides the "oomph" to apply the brakes when you step on the pedal. This one happens to be an aftermarket replacement unit that has a bleeder screw to make bleeding trapped air out of the piston cavity easier.

The master cylinder is the heart of the hydraulic system. It converts the force exerted on the brake pedal into hydraulic pressure that applies the brakes. Depressing the brake pedal moves a push rod in the master cylinder. Mounted on the push rod are a pair of pistons (primary and secondary) in tandem (one after the other) that exert force against the fluid in the master cylinder bore. This creates pressure, which along with the fluid that's displaced by the pistons is routed through the brake lines to each of the wheel brakes.

Because brake fluid is incompressible, it acts like a liquid linkage between the master cylinder and each of the wheel brakes. Any increase in pressure that is created in the master cylinder is instantly transferred to each of the brakes. So as the pistons in the master cylinder push against the fluid, it flows through the brake lines and pushes the caliper pistons outward to apply the disc brakes and the wheel cylinder pistons outward to apply the drum brakes.

When the brake pedal is released, the spring-loaded piston assembly in the master cylinder returns to its rest position. The fluid that was displaced by the pistons is pushed back to the master cylinder as the disc brake pads and drum brake shoes retract. The fluid returns to the fluid reservoir through the "compensating ports" which are nothing more than small openings between the master cylinder bore and fluid reservoir just ahead of each of the pistons.

FLUID RESERVOIR

The fluid reservoir supplies the master cylinder with brake fluid and stores excess fluid for the brake system. It may be an integral part of the master cylinder casting as in the case of a "unitized" master cylinder, or it may be a separate component

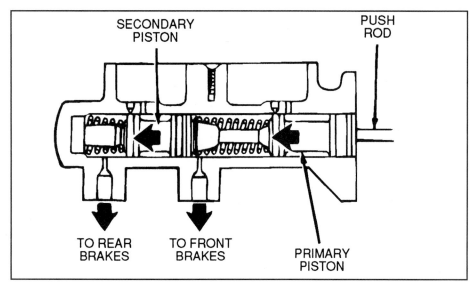

When pressure is applied at the brake pedal, the pistons inside the master cylinder push fluid to the front and rear brake circuits, or in the case of front-wheel drive cars to each pair of diagonally opposed wheels (left front and right rear, and right front and left rear).

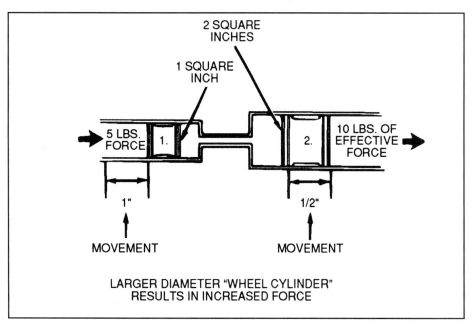

The amount of hydraulic pressure that's generated by the master cylinder depends on the size and displacement of the pistons as well as the pedal ratio. Pressure may range from a few hundred psi up to 1,000 psi or higher. The pistons in the wheel cylinders and calipers are usually larger in diameter than those in the master cylinder to multiply the force generated.

Many fluid reservoirs today also contain a fluid sensor to monitor the fluid level. When the level drops too low, it closes a contact switch and illuminates a warning light.

Reservoir Tips

Two things to keep in mind about your fluid reservoir:

1. Keep it full—but don't overfill. The level must be maintained at the full mark because it will drop as the brake linings wear. If it gets too low, air can be drawn into the master cylinder. Air is compressible and will reduce hydraulic pressure, creating a soft and/or low brake pedal. Don't fill the reservoir to the brim because a little space is needed to allow for fluid return after braking as well as changes in fluid volume that result from temperature changes.

2. Keep anything that doesn't belong in the reservoir out. If any substance other than the specified brake fluid (usually DOT 3) is accidentally dumped into the fluid reservoir (such as motor oil, hydraulic oil, power steering fluid, automatic transmission fluid, etc.), you'll have a major disaster on your hands. Anything with oil or petroleum distillates in it can attack and ruin the rubber elements in the brake system. To rid the system of such contamination, it may be necessary to disassemble, rebuild or replace the master cylinder, calipers and wheel cylinders in addition to replacing the fluid and flushing all the lines.

Dirt is another contaminant you don't want in your brake fluid. Dirt will act like an abrasive in the master cylinder and can also plug up the compensating ports or other metering valves.

(usually translucent plastic) that is attached to a "composite" master cylinder. The plastic reservoir may be mounted on the master cylinder and held in place by a pair of O-rings, or it may be remote mounted and attached by rubber hoses (as is the case with some import applications).

Most late model cars have composite master cylinders because the translucent plastic reservoir allows the fluid level inside to be checked without having to open the reservoir filler caps. Being able to see the fluid level inside makes it easier to notice any loss of fluid. And not having to open it for inspection helps keep moisture and dirt out of the system.

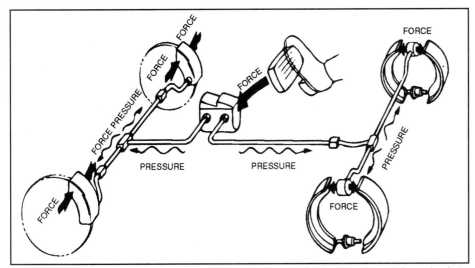

Stepping on the brake pedal creates hydraulic pressure that is distributed to all four wheels to apply the brakes.

DUAL MASTER CYLINDER

Since 1967, all master cylinders have been divided into two separate hydraulic circuits each of which has its own fluid reservoir and piston. Such units are called "dual" master cylinders because they are essentially a two-in-one design.

The danger with a single-piston, single circuit master cylinder is that a leak anywhere in the brake system will cause the brakes to fail. A leak in a rear wheel cylinder will affect all four brakes, not just the rear brake, because all share the same hydraulic system.

A dual master cylinder, on the other hand, provides redundancy by splitting the brakes into two separate hydraulic systems. This greatly improves safety because there will always be one brake circuit to stop your vehicle should a leak develop in a hose, caliper or wheel cylinder.

With most rear-wheel drive (RWD) vehicles, the hydraulic system is split front-to-rear with one half of the master cylinder operating the front brakes and the other half operating the rear brakes.

On front-wheel drive (FWD) cars, the brake system is usually split diagonally. The left front and right rear brakes are on one circuit while the right front and left rear brakes are on the other. This arrangement is necessary because the front brakes do about 80% of the braking. FWD cars typically have a higher proportion of their weight over the front wheels, and

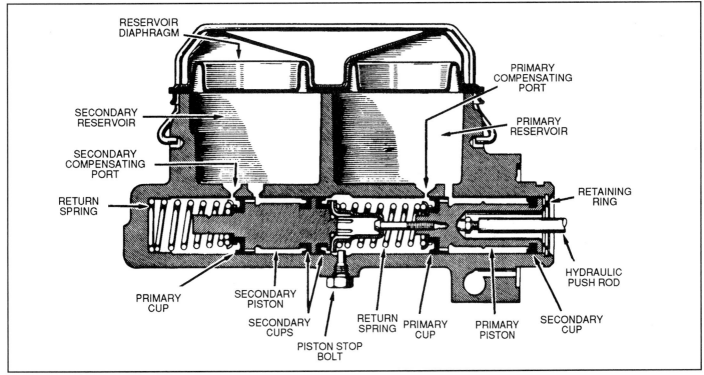

This is typical of an older style dual master cylinder. The casting contained two reservoirs, a primary reservoir for the front brakes and a secondary reservoir for the rear brakes. Splitting the hydraulics into two separate circuits meant at least one would remain functioning in the event of a leak.

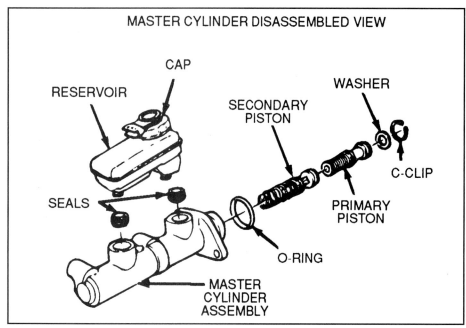

MASTER CYLINDER DISASSEMBLED VIEW

This is a typical design for a modern master cylinder. A plastic reservoir is attached to a lightweight aluminum cylinder assembly. The see-through reservoir eliminates the need to open the cap and expose the fluid to possible contamination when you check the fluid level.

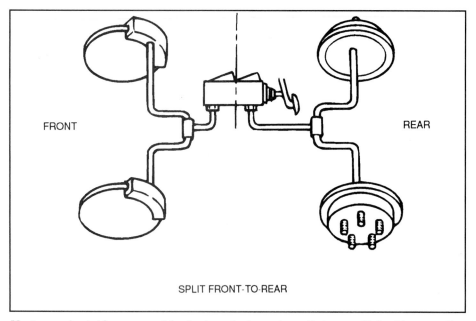

SPLIT FRONT-TO-REAR

Most rear-wheel drive cars and trucks have brake systems that are split front-to-rear. One piston in the master cylinder supplies the front brakes while the other supplies the rear brakes.

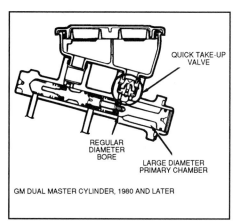

GM DUAL MASTER CYLINDER, 1980 AND LATER

GM quick take-up master cylinder. The stepped bore diameter causes fluid pressure to rise more rapidly as the pistons move forward.

delivers a larger volume of fluid when the brake pedal is initially depressed. This allows the caliper piston seals to retract the pistons when the brakes are released so the pads don't drag against the rotors. With other designs, the rotor has to kick out the pads so they don't rub. The drawback with this design is that the caliper pistons have to travel further when applied, so the master cylinder must provide more fluid volume to move the pistons.

PROPORTIONING VALVES & BRAKE BALANCE

To reduce hydraulic pressure to the rear brakes so the rear brakes don't lock up when the brakes are applied, a "proportioning valve" is required. This valve is required because of differences in weight distribution front-to-rear as well as the forward weight shift that occurs when brakes are applied.

What we're really talking about here is "brake balance" or "brake bias," which refers to the difference in the amount of hydraulic pressure channeled to the front and rear wheels. The front brakes on most rear-wheel drive vehicles normally handle about 60 to 70% of the brake

the front wheels do the driving. If a FWD brake system were split front-to-rear and there was a failure in the front circuit, the rear brakes alone might not be able to bring the vehicle to a safe stop.

Quick Take-Up Master Cylinder

Many late model vehicles have a special kind of master cylinder called a "quick take-up" master cylinder. This design reduces brake drag for improved fuel economy. The master cylinder has a stepped bore that

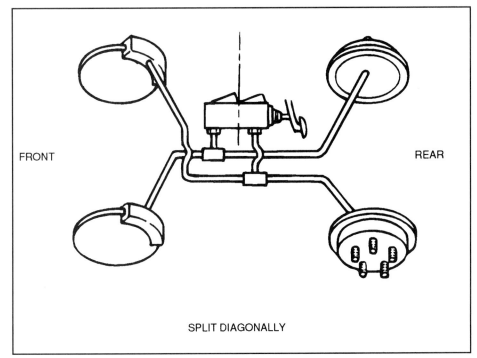

FRONT

REAR

SPLIT DIAGONALLY

With front-wheel drive, the hydraulic system is usually split diagonally with the left front and right rear brake sharing one circuit, and the right front and left rear brake sharing the other circuit. This is necessary because the front brakes (which do more work) are also the drive wheels. If both front brakes shared a common circuit and failed, the rear brakes alone might not be able to stop the vehicle safely. So splitting the system diagonally means at least one front brake will remain operational should one side of the system fail.

tighter against itself. Because of this, drum brakes are "self-energizing" and require little additional pedal effort once applied.

Disc brakes, on the other hand, are not self-energizing. It takes increased pedal effort to squeeze the pads against the rotor. In a vehicle that has front disc brakes and drums in the rear, therefore, the drums generate increasingly greater amounts of friction with little additional pedal effort while the discs require increased effort just to maintain the same amount of friction. So the proportioning valve splits the applied pressure so each brake receives just the right amount.

Inside the proportioning valve is a spring-loaded piston that determines how much pressure goes fore and aft. Each valve is calibrated for a specific application by the vehicle manufacturer, so it's important to make sure you get the correct replacement valve for your vehicle if the original valve is defective. The calibration of the proportioning valve is fixed and cannot be adjusted.

load. But on front-wheel drive cars, minivans, pickups and sport utility vehicles (most of which tend to be nose heavy), the percentage handled by the front brakes is much higher—more like 80 to 90%! Consequently, the front brakes need a higher percentage of the total hydraulic force that's applied to keep all four brakes properly balanced.

If the front-to-rear brake force isn't balanced correctly by the proportioning valve, the rear brakes may receive too much brake force causing them to lock up and skid when the brakes are applied.

The other reason for using a proportioning valve to reduce hydraulic pressure to the rear brakes has to do with the design of the brakes themselves. When hydraulic pressure is applied to the wheel cylinder inside a drum brake, the shoes are pushed

outward against the drum. When the shoes make contact, the rotation of the drum tries to drag them along. But since the shoes are anchored in place, the drum only pulls the shoes up

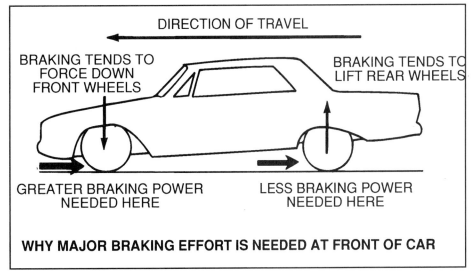

DIRECTION OF TRAVEL

BRAKING TENDS TO FORCE DOWN FRONT WHEELS

BRAKING TENDS TO LIFT REAR WHEELS

GREATER BRAKING POWER NEEDED HERE

LESS BRAKING POWER NEEDED HERE

WHY MAJOR BRAKING EFFORT IS NEEDED AT FRONT OF CAR

A proportioning valve is needed in a brake system to reduce pressure to the rear brakes. This is necessary to offset the forward weight transfer that occurs when braking. With front-wheel drive cars and minivans, the difference is even greater because the front wheels are also the drive wheels.

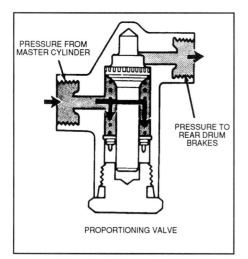

A proportioning valve uses a spring-loaded piston to reduce pressure to the rear brakes.

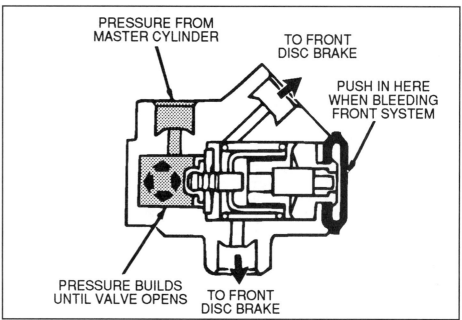

Metering valves are used in brake systems with front discs and rear drums to delay pressure to the front brakes until the rear brakes start to apply.

Load Sensing Proportioning Valves

Some vehicles have "load sensing" proportioning valves that change rear brake metering to compensate for changes in vehicle loading and weight shifts that occur during braking. This type of proportioning valve has an adjustable linkage that connects to the rear suspension or axle. As the vehicle is loaded, ride height decreases and pressure to the rear brakes is increased. This type of proportioning valve can be found on many minivans, pickups and even some passenger cars (Ford Tempo/Mercury Topaz, and Ford Taurus/Mercury Sable to name a few).

Load sensing proportioning valves are adjustable, and must be adjusted correctly if they are to properly balance the rear brakes to the vehicle's load. The valve linkage is adjusted with the suspension at its normal height (wheels on the ground) and the vehicle unloaded. The adjustment bracket or linkage is then adjusted according to the vehicle manufacturer's instructions, which typically involves adjusting the linkage to a certain position or height.

Load sensing proportioning valves are also calibrated to work with stock springs. Any modifications you might make that would increase the load carrying capability (helper springs, overload or air assist shocks for example) of your vehicle may adversely affect the operation of the valve. Modifications that make the suspension stiffer reduce the amount of deflection in the suspension when the vehicle is loaded. This, in turn, prevents the proportioning valve from increasing rear brake effort as much as it normally would, which can have an adverse affect on overall braking.

A defective proportioning valve or one that is not adjusted properly can also upset brake balance. So if the rear brakes on your vehicle seem to be overly aggressive (too much pressure to the rear brakes), or if your vehicle seems to take too long to stop (not enough pressure to the rear brakes), the problem may be the proportioning valve.

Testing a proportioning valve requires two hydraulic pressure gauges that read up to 2000 psi. Install one gauge immediately behind the valve and the other ahead of the valve. When pedal pressure is applied, the first gauge will show the output pressure from the master cylinder and the second will show the reduced pressure to the rear brakes. If the valve fails to reduce pressure according to specs, it needs to be replaced. Or, if it is a load-sensing type, it needs to be adjusted.

METERING VALVE

Another device called a "metering" or "hold-off" valve is used in vehicles that have front disc brakes and rear drum brakes to compensate for physical differences between the two different types of brakes. The metering valve holds off or delays the application of hydraulic pressure to the front disc brakes until the rear drums start to work. This is necessary because disc brakes don't have return springs, and consequently start to apply as soon as hydraulic pressure

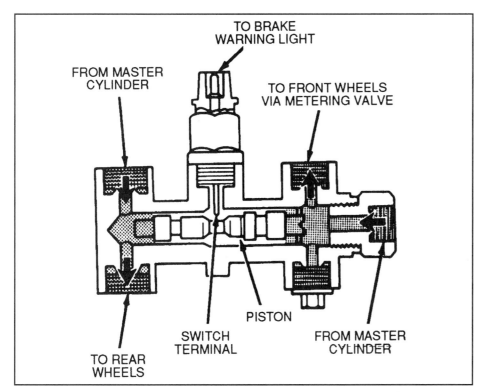

The pressure differential valve uses a sliding piston to detect loss of pressure in either side of the hydraulic system. The piston works a switch that activates the brake warning light.

to the front brakes.

PRESSURE DIFFERENTIAL VALVE & BRAKE WARNING LIGHT

Located between the front and rear (or diagonally split) brake lines in your brake system is a "pressure differential valve." This valve contains a switch that illuminates the brake warning light to warn you in case either side of your brake system loses pressure.

The valve has a piston that remains in a neutral position as long as pressure on both sides of the hydraulic system are equal. A loss of fluid on either side causes the piston to slide to one side when the brakes are applied, which completes the electrical circuit to illuminate the brake warning light. The valve is self-centering on most applications, but must be reset on others if a problem has occurred.

reaches the calipers. But the shoes inside the rear drum brakes have to overcome the resistance of the return springs before they engage the drum. The metering valve (or valves) is usually located in the hydraulic lines

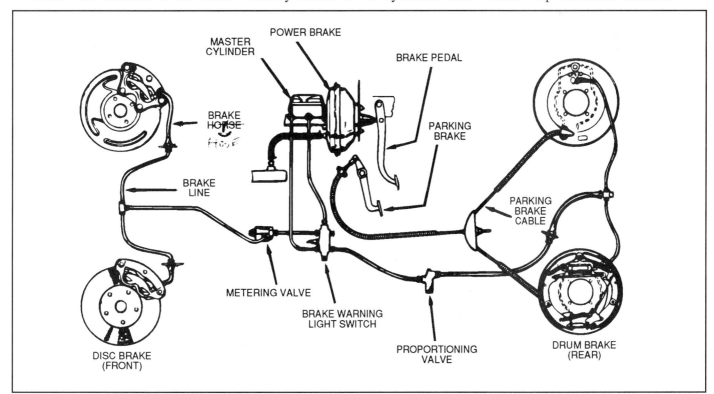

This drawing shows how the brake lines and various valves might be configured in a typical rear-wheel drive brake system.

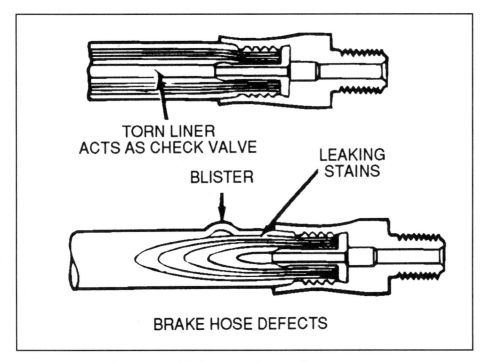

TORN LINER
ACTS AS CHECK VALVE

BLISTER

LEAKING
STAINS

BRAKE HOSE DEFECTS

A brake hose should be replaced if it shows any of these defects.

Does a brake warning light always mean trouble? No, because the light is also designed to come on when the parking brake is applied. This is to remind you to release the parking brake before driving. If the light remains on after releasing the parking brake, the parking brake switch may need adjustment. If the light comes on while driving or when you apply the brakes, though, it means trouble. The brake system either has a leak or the fluid level in one side of the master cylinder is low. Either way, the cause should be immediately investigated and repaired because your vehicle may not be safe to drive.

COMBINATION VALVES

On many vehicles, a "combination valve" is used that contains a pressure differential valve, proportioning and/or metering valve. The combination valve performs the same function as these other valves in a single unit.

BRAKE LINES & HOSES

The arteries of the brake system are the steel lines and flexible rubber hoses that route hydraulic pressure to each brake when you step on the brake pedal. The lines and hoses must withstand pressures that can range from a few hundred pounds per square inch up to almost 2000 psi! If a line or hose can't take the pressure and blows, all braking ability in the affected brake circuit will be lost. That means at least a 50% reduction in braking in a vehicle with a diagonally split system (most front-wheel drive cars), and as much as an 80% reduction in a system that's split front to rear (most rear-wheel drive cars and trucks) if the front brakes are lost.

Leaks

A slow leak in a brake line or hose is almost as bad as a sudden failure because over time enough fluid may be lost to allow air to enter the hydraulic system. Air in the fluid is bad because air is compressible. This increases the amount of pedal travel that's necessary to apply the brakes, and may increase it to the point where the pedal hits the floor before the brakes apply.

The first indication of a leak in a brake line or hose may be a low fluid level in the master cylinder reservoir. Other clues may include wet spots on the driveway, dampness on the back of a drum brake, or a brake warning light that comes on.

If you suspect a leak, check the master cylinder fluid level. If low it may indicate leakage somewhere in the system so give your brake system a thorough inspection. If you can't find any obvious leaks around the master cylinder, calipers, wheel cylinders or brake hoses, line connections, etc., the fluid could be leaking at one of two places. There could be a leak in a steel brake line that isn't visible from underneath the vehicle such as in a line that runs inside a frame rail, rocker panel, inside the floorpan or trunk. Or the fluid could be disappearing into the engine through a leak in the power brake vacuum booster. Check the inside of the brake booster vacuum hose. If you find fluid, the booster diaphragm is leaking, allowing intake vacuum to siphon brake fluid into the engine. The booster needs to be rebuilt or replaced.

When inspecting steel brake lines, look for wetness around connections or areas where the line bends or curves sharply. Stains or excessive corrosion may indicate past leaks. Also check for chafing, loose or missing support clips, kinks, dents or damaged armor (the spring-like wire that may be wrapped around a line to provide added protection against road hazards).

Because they are steel, the brake lines are vulnerable to both internal and external rust. External rust can be a problem on brake lines that are routed inside the vehicle if water leaks allow water to puddle around the lines. Water leaking around the rear and side windows, or from the rear wheel housing finds its way into the area where the brake lines are routed, puddles and eventually rust the lines. Lines routed under the chassis normally have a protective coating to ward off corrosion.

Inspection & Maintenance

Rubber hoses also need to be carefully inspected not only if you suspect a leak, but anytime you're doing brake work on the vehicle or are under it for other maintenance or repairs. Flexible hoses are especially vulnerable to damage because they're in a much more exposed location. They can be damaged by foreign objects tossed up by the tires, rubbing, over-extension, or careless use of J-hooks if somebody tows your vehicle and snags a brake line. Rubber hoses also tend to harden with age. The loss of flexibility may cause the hose to crack, split or break. So if you see cracks, any indication of leakage or other damage, the hose needs to be replaced.

Rubber hoses should be checked for bulges or swelling that would indicate internal damage or deterioration. Rubber hoses have an expansion resistant inner lining that is not supposed to give under pressure. If the inner liner leaks, fluid will force its way under the outer liner causing a bubble or blister to appear when the

brakes are applied. Have a helper depress the brake pedal while you observe each hose. If you see a bubble or blister rise on any part of the hose or if the hose appears to swell, it needs to be replaced.

A word of caution about brake hoses: Never allow a caliper to hang by its hose when doing brake work. Always hang it from a piece of wire so the weight of the caliper can't damage the hose.

Although it doesn't happen very often, sometimes internal damage or deterioration in a rubber hose allows a small flap of material to lift up and plug the line. This prevents brake pressure from reaching the wheel causing a brake pull when the brakes are applied.

The same thing can also happen to steel brake lines. Debris in the brake fluid or a crushed or kinked line can block the passage of hydraulic pressure to the brakes. In some cases, pressure will get through but when the brakes are released the blockage prevents pressure from releasing back to the master cylinder causing the brake to drag.

Replacing Steel Brake Lines

When replacing a damaged steel brake line, it's absolutely essential to use "approved" double-walled welded steel tubing because of the high pressure the line must hold. Never use any other type of tubing (copper or aluminum tubing, for example). It's also important to replace the original brake line with one of the same size. Installing a larger or smaller diameter line may alter the brake balance in the affected circuit and upset the braking characteristics of the vehicle. Tubing diameters are commonly 3/16 in. (4.8 mm), 1/4 in. (6.4 mm) and 5/16 in. (7.9 mm).

The ends of the steel brake lines are either double flared or use an ISO (International Standards Organization) flare. The ISO flare is designed to deform when the fitting is tightened which creates a more uniform seal and lessens the danger of over-tightening. One type of flare is not interchangeable with another. The replacement line must have the same kind of flare as the original to seal properly.

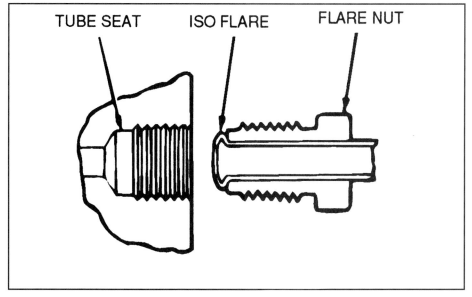

TUBE SEAT   ISO FLARE   FLARE NUT

ISO flare fitting for a steel brake line.

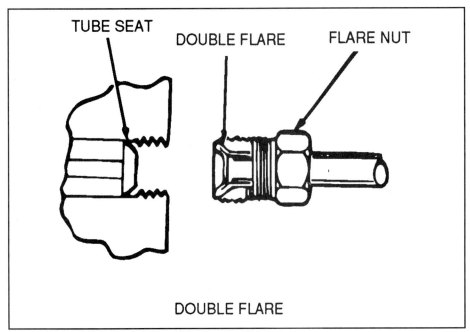

TUBE SEAT   DOUBLE FLARE   FLARE NUT

DOUBLE FLARE

Double flare fitting for a steel brake line.

Replacing Hoses

When replacing a rubber brake hose, make sure the new one is exactly the same length. Too long a hose may rub against the suspension or other parts, while too short a hose may be pulled tight and break (as when turning or when the suspension undergoes full jounce/rebound).

Most hoses have a male fitting on one end and a female fitting on the other end. Disconnect the female end first. Remove the clip or jam nut that holds the female end down, then unscrew the male end. If a hose fitting has a copper gasket, throw the old gasket away and use a new one. Copper gaskets take a set and may not seal tightly if reused.

To install the new hose, use the reverse procedure. Screw on the male end first, then the female end last. It's a good idea to draw a straight line on the hose to help you avoid twisting it (which can weaken or tear it). Check the position of the hose for interference to make sure it clears the suspension during jounce/rebound and has sufficient length to handle full suspension and steering travel. If you have to reposition the hose, never adjust the male end after the female end is tight as doing so can twist the hose. Loosen the female end, then the male end, reposition the hose, then retighten the male and female ends.

Many replacement brake lines come with preformed ends so all you have to do is match the flare and bend to shape (carefully so you don't kink the pipe!). On lines that lack preformed ends, you'll have to use the appropriate tool to make the flare. Don't forget to slip the fittings on the line before forming the ends! Also, if the old line has armor around it, armor should be installed on the replacement line.

Replacement steel lines should be routed along the same path as the original. If the line passes through sheetmetal, it should be protected against chafing with a rubber or plastic grommet. Replacement brake lines must be located away from the exhaust system because heat can make the brake fluid boil (which can lead to brake fade). The lines must also be clear of all suspension members (springs, control arms, etc.).

Before a metal line is installed, make certain that the line is clean inside and free from any metal chips, dirt or other foreign material that could form an obstruction. Then start the male fitting into the female threads in the cylinder or hose connection by hand so as not to cross-thread the fitting. The fitting should then be tightened using a flare wrench to the manufacturer's suggested specifications.

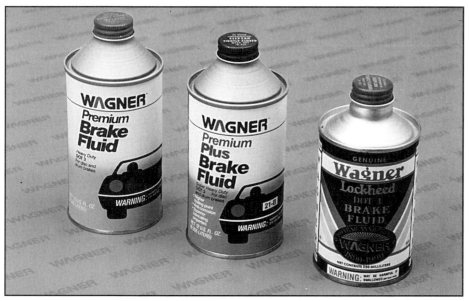

Brake fluid is the most critical component of your brake system. It must be maintained and serviced properly. Always use the correct brake fluid specified by the manufacturer. Courtesy Wagner.

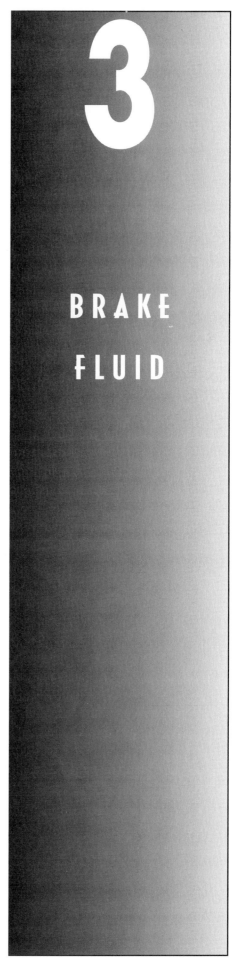

Brake fluid is the lifeblood of your brake system. So it's important to not only maintain the proper fluid level in the master cylinder but to also maintain the fluid itself.

The health and longevity of the brake system depends as much on the condition of the fluid that's in it as the engine depends on regular oil changes. Yet compared to the other vital fluids under the hood, brake fluid is probably one of the most neglected.

When was the last time you read anything in an owner's manual about changing the brake fluid for preventative maintenance? Few car makers say it's necessary to change the brake fluid except when the brakes are relined. But most brake experts say replacing the fluid every two years for preventative maintenance could significantly extend the life of the hydraulic and ABS components in today's brake systems.

FLUID CONTAMINATION

The fluid needs to be changed periodically because brake fluid is "hygroscopic," meaning it absorbs moisture. DOT 3 and 4 brake fluid is made from polyglycol which is "anhydrous" (contains no water). So when fresh brake fluid is exposed to the air, it starts to absorb moisture like a sponge soaks up water. Leaving the lid off a master cylinder reservoir or a can of brake fluid overnight can be enough to contaminate the fluid. That's how fast it picks up moisture.

But brake fluid is supposed to absorb moisture. By absorbing any moisture that enters the hydraulics and dispersing it throughout the system, the fluid prevents the formation of water droplets or slugs of water that could boil at high temperature or freeze at low temperature. This also prevents the concentration of water that might lead to localized corrosion. Such corrosion can eat pinholes through steel brake lines or attack the calipers, wheel cylinders or master cylinder. In fact, one of the reasons why conventional brake fluid is polyglycol-based rather than mineral- or petroleum-based is so it can absorb and disperse moisture. But that ability also creates problems.

After a year of service, the brake fluid in the average vehicle contains about two percent water. After 18 months, the level of contamination

17

When adding brake fluid, do not leave the fluid reservoir open any longer than necessary to limit the exposure to air in the system.

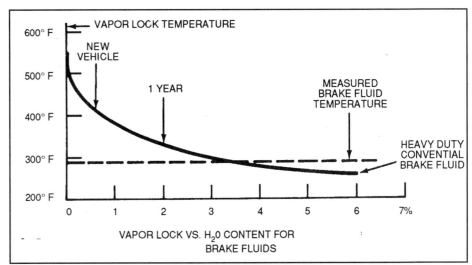

DOT 3 and 4 brake fluids absorb moisture over time, which lowers the temperature at which the fluid will boil and vapor lock.

can be as high as three percent. And after several years of service, it's not unusual to find brake fluid that contains as much as seven to eight percent water.

Where does all this water come from? It penetrates the hydraulic system through microscopic pores in the rubber hoses and seals, past tiny air leaks around the seals, and through the fluid reservoir every time it's opened for inspection (which is a good reason not to unnecessarily open fluid reservoirs with transparent sides).

As the fluid soaks up and disperses the invading moisture, the buildup of water lowers the fluid's boiling point. The higher the level of contamination, the more the boiling point is reduced. Only three percent water lowers the boiling point of a conventional DOT 3 fluid by 25%. DOT 4 fluid, which soaks up moisture at a slower rate, suffers even more when it reaches the same level of contamination. Three percent water in a DOT 4 fluid lowers its boiling point as much as 50%!

Water contamination is bad news because it increases the danger of vapor pockets forming at elevated temperatures, particularly in the calipers where temperatures are usually the highest. If the fluid starts to boil, it can "vapor lock" the hydraulics by increasing the distance the brake pedal must travel before hydraulic pressure can compress the vapor and apply the brakes.

Normally, there's enough safety margin designed into the brake system so the fluid won't get hot enough to boil. But in a front-wheel drive vehicle with semimetallic disc brakes, operating temperatures are considerably higher than a comparable rear-wheel drive application. The safety margin can quickly evaporate under severe or prolonged braking conditions, especially if the vehicle has unvented rotors and badly contaminated fluid.

Moisture contamination also increases the viscosity of the fluid, making it more sluggish in cold weather. And because the moisture is dispersed throughout the fluid, it promotes internal corrosion and pitting of metal surfaces. That's why even new cars show evidence of pitting and corrosion in the caliper bores, wheel cylinders and master cylinder after a couple of years. It's like a cancer that eats away at the inside of the brake system, and the only way to keep it under control is to replace the contaminated fluid on a regular basis.

TYPES OF BRAKE FLUID

When adding or changing the brake fluid in your vehicle, always use the type of fluid specified by the vehicle manufacturer. You can find this information in your owners manual, or on a label on the master cylinder itself.

Brake fluids are classified by their physical properties, and must meet certain minimum standards within each category that have been established by the U.S. Department of Transportation (DOT). The three basic classifications for brake fluid are: DOT 3, DOT 4 and DOT 5.

DOT 3 Brake Fluid

This category requires a minimum "wet" (moisture saturated) boiling point of 284 degrees F. and a "dry" (new) boiling point of 401 degrees F. DOT 3 fluid is the type commonly specified by most vehicle manufacturers. It is glycol-based and absorbs moisture, which lowers its boiling point over time and promotes internal corrosion in the brake system.

DOT 4 Brake Fluid

This category is for "heavy-duty" glycol-based brake fluids that have a higher wet boiling point of 311 degrees F. and a dry boiling point of 446 degrees. This type of fluid is sometimes specified for performance vehicles or those subject to high brake temperatures. DOT 4 is often used in European imports, and also Corvettes.

DOT 5 Brake Fluid

This category is for silicone-based fluids that do not absorb moisture and have a minimum boiling point of at least 500 degrees F. DOT 5 fluids contain purple dye to distinguish them from ordinary glycol-based DOT 3 and 4 fluids. Because DOT 5 fluid does not absorb moisture, it may be used in vehicles that are stored for long periods of time or driven infrequently, to protect the brake system against corrosion. Silicone is also chemically inert, nontoxic and won't damage paint like conventional brake fluid. But DOT 5 silicone brake fluid is NOT recommended for any vehicle equipped with antilock brakes because it tends to absorb air and foam when cycled rapidly through small orifices.

DOT 5 fluid is quite expensive, costing three to five times as much as DOT 3 or 4 fluids. But it has some other drawbacks, too. One is that it doesn't mix with conventional DOT 3 or 4 glycol-based brake fluids. If a brake system containing conventional

The fluid at left is new, the fluid at right is how it will look after 2 years of normal service. Courtesy Wagner.

brake fluid is drained and refilled with DOT 5 silicone, the residual glycol fluid that remains in the system will form slugs that may concentrate moisture. If the fluid gets hot enough, the concentrated slugs may boil and cause loss of pedal. The slugs may also concentrate corrosion. To maximize the corrosion protection benefits of silicone, therefore, the brake system must be completely drained of glycol fluid (a very difficult task) or factory filled with silicone.

BRAKE FLUID SERVICE

Some general cautions when working with brake fluid:

• Always use the type of brake fluid that's specified by the vehicle manufacturer (usually DOT 3 but sometimes DOT 4).
• Avoid contact with DOT 3 and 4 brake fluids. It can cause eye and skin irritation, and may be harmful or fatal if swallowed.
• Be careful not to splash or spill DOT 3 or 4 brake fluid on painted finishes. It acts like a solvent and attacks the paint. If you do spill, don't wipe. Flush immediately with water.
• Use only fresh brake fluid from a sealed container. Never reuse old fluid or brake fluid from an open or unmarked container.

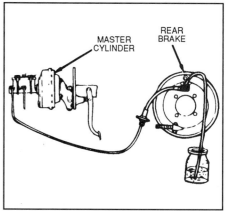

When bleeding the brakes, loosen (but do not open) the bleeder valve at the wheel cylinder or caliper. Slip one end of a piece of clear plastic tubing over the bleeder valve and place the other end of the tubing in a clear glass or plastic jar. Then open the bleeder valve and gently push the brake pedal to the floor to bleed the brake line. Let the pedal rise slowly and repeat until you see no bubbles in the fluid coming from the bleeder valve. Then close the valve and repeat for each wheel. Don't forget to check the fluid level in the master cylinder so it doesn't get too low and reintroduce air into the system.

• Don't leave brake fluid containers open. Close the lid immediately after use to keep out moisture. The same goes for the master cylinder fluid reservoir. Don't leave it open unless you are adding fluid or bleeding the brakes.

Bleeding The Brakes

Anytime the brake system is opened for repairs or to replace a hydraulic component such as a caliper, hoses, wheel cylinder, etc., the system should be bled to purge all the air from the lines. Air is compressible so you don't want any in the fluid. So you may have to bleed the entire brake system even if you only opened or replaced a single line. Air bubbles can quickly migrate through the system, so in most cases you can plan on bleeding all four brakes.

A time-saving trick that can eliminate the need to bleed all four brakes is to clamp off the rubber hose

Small rubber caps are often used to keep dirt out of bleeder valves. Don't forget to replace these after you've bled the brakes.

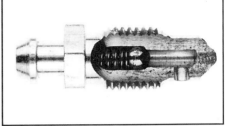

The Speed Bleeder by Russell Performance Products replaces the stock OEM bleed screw to make it easier to bleed brakes with one person. The check ball system allows for bleeding without having to tighten then reopen the screw after pumping up. With the Russell Speed Bleeder, open the screw, attach a hose, pump the brakes until all air is purged from the wheel cylinder, close valve, and move on to the next wheel. Courtesy Russell Performance Products.

to the brake prior to opening the line to replace a caliper or wheel cylinder. The clamp will prevent air from backing up through the open line. When you're done, just remove the clamp and bleed the one line.

When bleeding the brakes (or changing the brake fluid), any of the following techniques can be used: manual bleeding, gravity bleeding, pressure bleeding or vacuum bleeding.

Bleeder Screws—Regardless of which method you use, the hardest part of bleeding the brakes is loosening the bleeder screws without breaking them off. If it's been years since the brakes were last bled, chances are the bleeder screws will be difficult to loosen. Apply penetrating oil and allow it to soak overnight. The careful application of heat with a propane torch may help loosen stubborn screws. Using a six-point bleeder socket or wrench is also a good idea to prevent rounding off the tiny screw.

If a screw twists off, you have two options: forget it and move on to the next one, or replace it. If you can bleed the other lines and get a firm pedal, it may not be necessary to replace the broken bleeder screw. But if there's air in the line and the pedal remains soft or won't come up, then you'll have to replace the broken screw. This usually requires removing and replacing the caliper or wheel cylinder unless you can get the base of the broken screw out with a reverse-twist extractor bit. Drilling out the broken screw and retapping the hole is also possible but also requires removal and/or disassembly of the caliper or wheel cylinder so you don't end up with bits of metal inside the hydraulic system.

Manual Bleeding—With this procedure you use the brake pedal to push fluid through the lines. The "bleeder screws" on the calipers and wheel cylinders are opened one at a time (in the specified sequence, usually starting with the brake furthest

away from the master cylinder). A "bleeder hose" is then attached to the bleeder screw and immersed in a container partially filled with brake fluid. The pedal is then slowly depressed to push fluid through the line to remove air. When the fluid emerging from the bleeder screw is clear (no bubbles or discoloration), the bleeder screw is closed to prevent air from being drawn back into the line. Check the fluid level in the master cylinder after bleeding each brake to make sure it doesn't run low and allow air to be drawn back into the system. Then move on to the next brake in the sequence until all have been bled.

Surge Bleeding—A variation on manual bleeding is called "surge" bleeding. This procedure is sometimes needed to remove trapped air pockets in wheel calipers and wheel cylinders. The basic idea with this technique is to surge the fluid through the system so it will entrap the air. You'll need a helper because it's a two-person job. You start by having your helper pump the brake pedal very hard and rapidly for about ten strokes. As he finishes the last stroke and holds the pedal down, you immediately open the bleeder screw and let the fluid escape while your helper maintains pressure. You then close the bleeder screw and repeat until there are no bubbles in the fluid.

Master cylinders can sometimes be tricky to bleed because air can become trapped in the bore, especially in vehicles where the master cylinder is mounted at an upward angle with respect to the firewall. Raising the rear of the car with a jack so the master cylinder is level can prevent air from being trapped in the front of the master cylinder while it is being bled.

Bench Bleeding—If the master cylinder is being replaced, it should always be "bench bled" off the car before it is installed. This is done by filling the fluid reservoir and attaching return hoses from the outlet ports to recycle the fluid back into the reservoir as the push rod is stroked.

ABS Bleeding—On some vehicles with antilock brakes, a special procedure must be followed to remove air from the ABS hydraulic modulator. Those that require a special procedure bleeding typically usually need a "scan tool" to cycle the ABS solenoids in the modulator. The scan tool is plugged into the vehicle's onboard diagnostic connector to operate the solenoids. Scan tools are pretty expensive, so if your vehicle requires this type of bleeding procedure you may have to take it to a professional.

Gravity Bleeding—This is a method of bleeding the brakes that allows fluid to dribble out of the open bleeder screws by gravity. It's a slow process and rarely used except in some import applications that require it because of metering valve arrangements that prevent normal manual or power bleeding procedures.

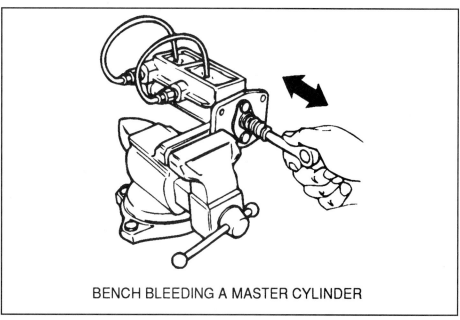

BENCH BLEEDING A MASTER CYLINDER

If you're replacing a master cylinder, it's a good idea to bench bleed it before installing it with a setup like this. Getting all the air out of the master cylinder will also make it faster and easier to bleed the individual brake lines once the unit has been installed.

Pressure Bleeding—The preferred technique used by most professional automotive technicians because it's the fastest way of getting the job done. Pressure bleeding (also called "power bleeding") uses a pressurized tank of fluid to force the old fluid out of the system. The pressure bleeding equipment is filled with the appropriate fluid, attached to the master cylinder reservoir with an adapter and pressurized with shop air. When the brake bleeder screws are opened, the fluid is forced through the lines. On some brake systems with metering valves, the metering valve must be held open so the pressurized fluid will pass through the valve. Special tools and clips are available for this purpose.

Vacuum Bleeding—A less common but equally effective technique for bleeding the brakes. This process requires a special vacuum tool that uses shop air to create a vacuum siphon to pull fluid through the lines and out of the bleeder screws. Vacuum bleeding does not require special adapters for the master cylinder nor do metering valves have to be held open.

Bleeding Sequence

The sequence or order in which the individual brakes are bled is very important to get all the air out of the system. The sequence varies from one vehicle to another, so always refer to the bleeding sequence specified by your vehicle manufacturer. You'll find this information in a shop manual.

The most common procedure on hydraulic systems that are split front-to-rear (most rear-wheel drive cars and trucks) is to do the rear brakes first, then the fronts, starting with the wheel furthest from the master cylinder. With systems that are split diagonally (most front-wheel drive cars and minivans), the sequence is often right rear, left front, then left rear and right front.

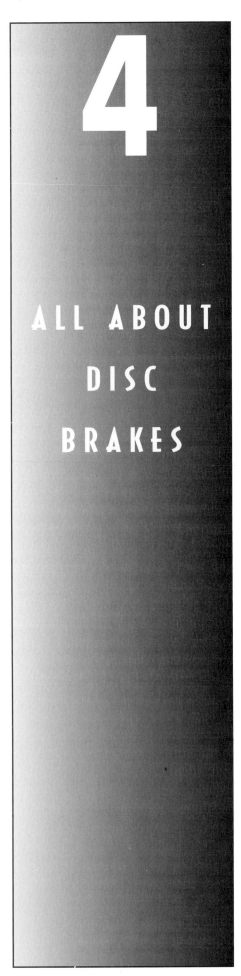

Disc brakes come in a wide variety of configurations. Courtesy Wagner Brakes.

Disc brakes may be used either on the front wheels only or on all four wheels. Four-wheel disc brake systems are the best, but are usually only found as standard equipment or offered as an option on sports, performance or luxury vehicles because of the added cost.

Disc brakes provide a number of important advantages over drums, including better cooling, better fade resistance, little or no wet fading due to road splash, and reduced weight and complexity. Disc brakes are also self-adjusting. But disc brakes require more pedal effort than drum brakes, which means power brakes are usually necessary when a vehicle is equipped with disc brakes.

DISC BRAKE CONVERSIONS

Disc brake conversion kits for older cars (Mustangs, Camaros, etc.) as well as trucks are available from various aftermarket suppliers for upgrading brake performance. Such a kit would be recommended if you were swapping a V8 for a stock six-cylinder engine, adding a performance cam, manifold, carburetor and headers to a stock V8 engine, or dropping in a larger displacement, more powerful engine for some serious street or drag racing. After all, when you add more go power you may also need to add more stopping power.

Most disc brake conversion kits provide all the parts needed to make the changeover including knuckles and spindles, calipers, pads, rotors, hoses and hardware. The parts in the kit may be new OEM parts, reproduction OEM parts, remanufactured parts, aftermarket parts or any combination thereof. Some of these kits are based on factory disc brake options that were available for the same or a later model year vehicle, while others are engineered from scratch because disc brakes were not available.

Going with a kit takes the guesswork out of converting drums to discs because you don't have to figure out which parts you need, compile a list of part numbers, and then waste a lot of time calling suppliers and dealers, and searching junkyards for

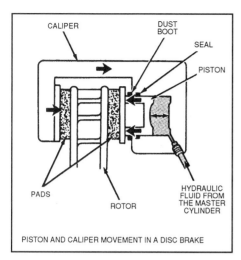

PISTON AND CALIPER MOVEMENT IN A DISC BRAKE

When hydraulic pressure is applied to the piston in a floating caliper, the piston pushes the inboard shoe out against the rotor. This causes the caliper to slide sideways until the outer pad contacts the rotor. When pressure is released, the piston seal helps retract the piston as runout in the rotor kicks the pads away. Courtesy Brake Parts, Inc.

what you need. It also eliminates the danger of mismatched parts if you try to cobble together a disc brake conversion using parts from other vehicles. Besides, it's nearly impossible to find all the parts you might need for a disc brake swap in a salvage yard today because (1) disc brakes were a scarce option on most of the older vehicles, and (2) most of these older vehicles have already been cannibalized for parts (all the good parts have already been stripped). So if you want to upgrade to disc brakes, chances are you'll have to go with a kit.

If you're converting an older vehicle that has drum brakes to disc brakes, you may also have to install a vacuum booster between the master cylinder and brake pedal. Some kits include a booster while others require the booster to be purchased separately.

DISC BRAKE COMPONENTS

A disc brake has three major components: a caliper, rotor and pair

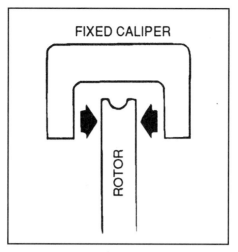

A fixed caliper does not move so it has two or four opposing pistons that force each pad against the rotor simultaneously when hydraulic pressure is applied.

of brake pads. When you step on the brake pedal, pressure from the master cylinder goes to the caliper forcing one or more pistons to squeeze the inner and outer brake pads against the rotor. This creates friction, which slows the vehicle and produces heat. When the brake pedal is released, the caliper loosens its grip, allowing the square cut seals around the pistons to retract the pads slightly. The rotor also helps kick the pads back slightly, too.

This eliminates the need for return springs that are necessary in drum brakes to pull the shoes back away from the drum.

Calipers

Disc brake calipers come in two basic varieties: floating and fixed. Floating calipers are mounted on slides or bushings that allow the caliper to move sideways when the brakes are applied and released.

Floating Calipers—Floating calipers typically have a single piston located on the inboard side of the caliper. Single piston floating calipers are used on most vehicles because they are simpler and less expensive to manufacture than fixed calipers or ones with multiple-pistons.

When the brakes are applied on a vehicle with a single piston, floating caliper, the piston moves outward and pushes the inner pad against the rotor. This forces the caliper to slide inward slightly and pull the outer pad up against the rotor. When the pedal is released, the caliper slides out slightly as the pads are kicked away and

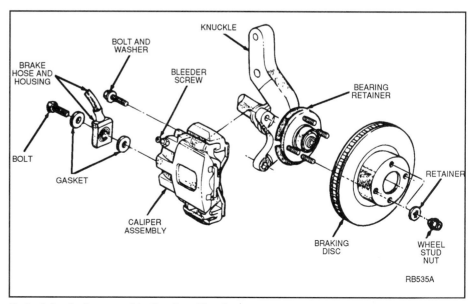

Typical disc brake assembly. Courtesy Chrysler.

Caliper problems can often be caused by corroded mounting pins, bushings or slides. These parts should also be replaced when you're doing a brake job.

The calipers should be carefully inspected for fluid leaks, cracked dust seals or other damage. Most experts recommend rebuilding calipers even if they are not leaking.

retract from the rotor. Thus, the caliper is constantly moving in and out as the brakes are applied and released.

It should be obvious that a floating caliper must be free to move if it is going to do its job properly. If the caliper slides or bushings are rusty, worn or damaged, the caliper can hang up on its mountings causing the pads to wear unevenly. If you find more wear on the inner pad than the outer one, it means the caliper isn't sliding. A sticky or frozen caliper may also cause the brakes to drag if the caliper does not slide so the outer pad can kick away from the rotor. This

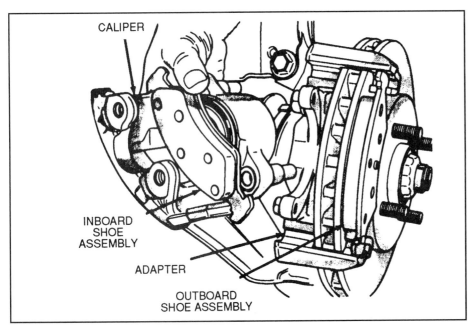

If a floating caliper hangs up due to rust, corrosion or dirt, it can cause uneven pad wear. The inner pad usually wears more than the outer pad because it does all the work. Courtesy Chrysler.

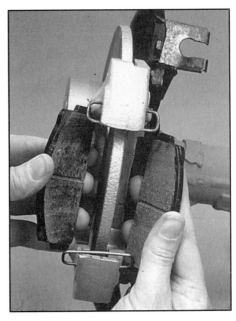

Inspecting pads on a disc brake with a solid (unvented) rotor. Courtesy Wagner.

24

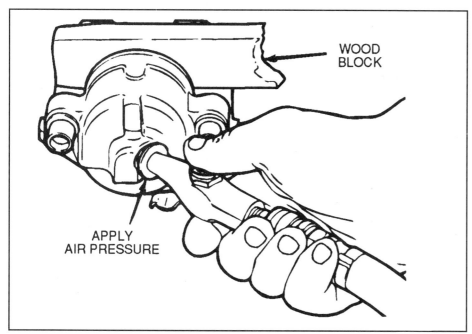

WOOD BLOCK

APPLY AIR PRESSURE

To replace the seal inside a caliper, you have to pull or force the piston out of its bore. CAUTION: Be careful if you're using compressed air because the piston can pop free with considerable force! Place a piece of wood or a rag in front of the piston to stop it. Courtesy Brake Parts, Inc.

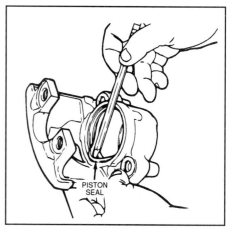

PISTON SEAL

Once the piston has been removed, the seal can be removed from the caliper bore. Light sanding can be used to clean up the caliper bore, but if the bore is badly corroded or deeply pitted you'll have to replace the caliper. Courtesy Brake Parts, Inc.

may cause increased wear on the outer pad as well as a steering pull to one side because of the constant drag. So anytime you see uneven pad wear with a floating caliper, it means the caliper is hanging up.

Fixed Calipers—Fixed calipers don't suffer from such problems because the position of the caliper is rigidly fixed over the rotor. A fixed caliper is not free to slide from side to side, so it needs pistons on both sides of the rotor to squeeze the pads against the rotor. There may be one, two or even three pistons on each side of the caliper.

When the brake pedal is depressed, hydraulic pressure from the master cylinder goes to both sides of a fixed caliper. This forces both sets of pistons to simultaneously push the inner and outer pads against the rotor. When the pedal is released, both sets of pistons retract as the pads kick out and retract from the rotor.

Caliper Problems—Both floating and fixed calipers can sometimes "freeze up" or lock if a piston becomes jammed or stuck in its bore due to corrosion or swelling. Steel and aluminum pistons can corrode while phenolic (plastic) pistons can sometimes swell from overexposure to moisture (flooding, wet weather or even too much moisture in the brake fluid).

When a caliper piston sticks, one of two things can happen: the brake won't apply or won't release. If a caliper piston hangs up and fails to move when the brakes are applied, you'll feel a sharp pull towards the side with the "good" caliper because of the uneven braking action side-to-side between the two front wheels. This creates a potentially dangerous situation because it makes your vehicle more difficult to control when braking and cuts your braking power nearly in half (which increases the stopping distance). If the brakes apply but a caliper piston sticks and fails to

release, it creates an even worse situation because the caliper may lock up the rotor tight and prevent the wheel from turning at all! You may then have to tow your vehicle home or to a garage so repairs can be made.

Caliper Servicing—If you're replacing disc brake pads on a vehicle with relatively low mileage (say under 40,000 miles), you can probably leave the calipers alone unless they are leaking or sticking (uneven pad wear would tell you the calipers need attention). Even so, most professionals say it's still a good idea to rebuild or replace the calipers when the pads are replaced to restore the brakes to "like new" condition—especially if your vehicle has accumulated a lot of miles (more than 40,000) since the last brake job. Here's why:

Accumulated dirt and corrosion on the caliper pistons can act like an abrasive against the piston seals. So even if the pistons are not sticking, the constant rubbing against the piston seals will eventually cause the seals to wear and leak. It's also important to note that caliper pistons gradually

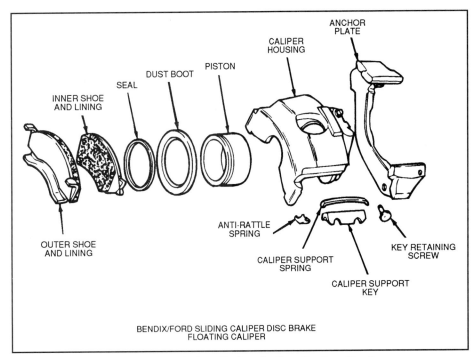

Typical Bendix style caliper assembly for a Ford application. Courtesy Bendix.

move further and further out in their bores as the pads wear. When the pistons are shoved back in to accommodate new, thicker pads, any dirt or corrosion that's on the pistons will be forced back under the seal. What's more, rubber piston seals harden with age. The loss of elasticity makes them less able to retract the pistons which can increase pad drag and wear.

If you neglect the calipers when replacing pads, therefore, you're taking a risk. You may get by for awhile, but sooner or later the seals will leak. When they do, they'll probably contaminate and ruin the new pads you installed. So why do the job twice? Bite the bullet and do the calipers when you replace the pads.

It's also important to pay close attention to the condition of the caliper slides, pins and bushings on floating calipers. They need to be inspected closely for wear, rust, cracks or other damage. Mounting surfaces, bushings, pins and slides need to be cleaned and lubricated with high temperature brake grease so the calipers can move freely.

Rebuilding Calipers—When a caliper is removed, inspect the mounting hardware closely for wear, corrosion or damage, and replace any parts that are not in perfect condition. The caliper itself needs to be inspected for broken ears, elongated or worn guide pin or mounting holes, cracks in the casting, porosity leaks or worn mounting surfaces—any of which would be grounds for replacement.

If the caliper casting is okay, it can be disassembled for further inspection. Removing the piston(s) can be difficult because of the pressure exerted by the seal and accumulated rust and corrosion. Be careful not to scratch or damage the piston (or caliber bore) if it will be reused. In other words, don't try to pry it out with a screwdriver or grab it with a pair of Vise-Grips.

There are special pullers that can be used to extract pistons that have a recessed cup in their face. A technique that works well on most applications is to remove the bleeder screw from the caliper and use compressed air to blow the piston out. **Caution:** The piston can exit with considerable force so keep your fingers out of the way and cushion the piston with a shop rag or piece of foam.

Most caliper bores will show signs of corrosion and pitting. As long as the bore isn't too bad, it can be cleaned up by lightly sanding with fine grade (#600 grit or finer) crocus cloth. The bore should be lubricated

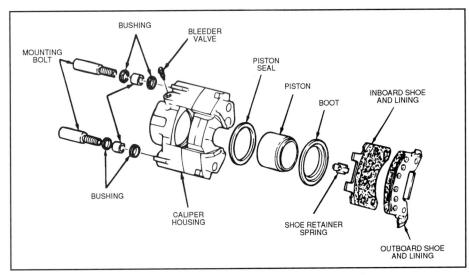

Typical Delco Moraine floating caliper assembly on a GM front-wheel drive car. Courtesy Delco Moraine.

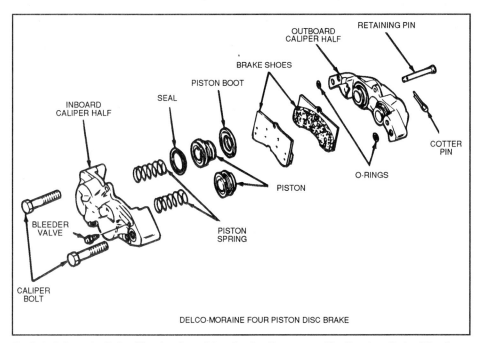

Exploded view of a Delco Moraine four-piston fixed caliper assembly. Courtesy Delco Moraine.

with brake fluid and polished with a circular motion to smooth out minor imperfections. Honing with a drill-powered brake hone may be necessary to restore a more badly worn or corroded caliper. But if you have to increase the inside diameter of the bore by more than about .002 inches, the caliper is too far gone to be rebuilt. You'll have to replace it.

Note: These guidelines apply to cast iron and steel calipers only. You should not attempt to rebuild an aluminum caliper because the bore in an aluminum caliper has an anodized surface to protect against corrosion. Sanding the bore would destroy the thin anodized coating leaving the caliper vulnerable to corrosion, leakage and piston sticking. So if the bore is rough or pitted, replace the caliper with a new one or a remanufactured caliper that has been sleeved with stainless steel.

Under no circumstances should anything other than brake cleaner or brake fluid be used to clean caliper bores or pistons. Petroleum and mineral-based solvents can leave a residue that will attack and damage rubber piston seals.

As for the caliper pistons, a close inspection is necessary before you can decide whether or not they're in good enough condition to risk reusing. Corrosion is not a problem with phenolic pistons but it is with steel and aluminum pistons. Some discoloration on a steel piston is normal, but if the piston is rusted, pitted or damaged in any way it must be replaced. The same goes for aluminum pistons. Phenolic pistons need to be checked for cracks, nicks or chips. Replace a phenolic piston if it has any damage on the sealing surface. Cosmetic damage on the front of the piston won't hurt anything as long as it doesn't cause a problem with the brake pad.

Sandpaper or any other abrasive should never be used on a steel piston in an attempt to smooth it. Most steel pistons are nickel- or chrome-plated to inhibit corrosion. Sanding the piston would destroy this protective coating and leave the piston vulnerable to rust and corrosion.

If a piston has to be replaced, the best advice is to use the same type of replacement piston (steel, aluminum or phenolic) as the original. Dimensional variations between different types of materials may cause sticking problems if one type of piston is substituted for another in some applications.

Some people like steel pistons better than phenolics because steel is a stronger material. Others prefer phenolic pistons because they don't rust and don't conduct heat to the brake fluid in the caliper like a steel piston can. Keeping heat away from the brake fluid can be a real challenge in some front-wheel drive (FWD) applications, so if the vehicle manufacturer uses phenolic pistons in their calipers, they should not be changed to steel.

If you're replacing a caliper with a new or remanufactured caliper, make sure the piston in the replacement caliper is the same (steel, aluminum or phenolic) as the one in the old caliper. Using different types of pistons on opposite sides of a vehicle can sometimes upset brake balance causing a pull to one side. Both calipers, therefore, should have the same type of pistons.

In rear-wheel drive applications, it isn't usually isn't as important to use the same type of piston as what was originally used on the vehicle. So some replacement calipers may have steel rather than phenolic pistons, or vice versa.

Rear Calipers

Vehicles that have four-wheel disc brakes have either locking or conventional (floating or fixed) rear

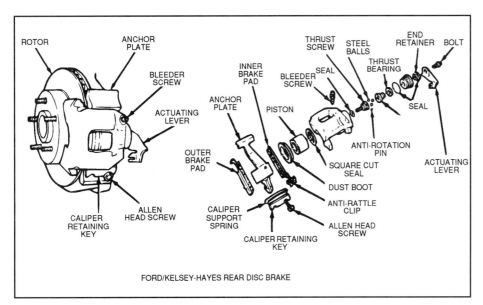

FORD/KELSEY-HAYES REAR DISC BRAKE

Typical Ford rear locking caliper assembly. Courtesy Kelsey-Hayes.

calipers. Locking calipers are used if the caliper serves as the parking brake. Locking calipers have a cam or screw mechanism inside the caliper piston that pushes the piston out and holds it there to apply the parking brake. A conventional non-locking caliper is used if the parking brake is provided by a "mini-drum" brake inside the rear rotors.

Locking calipers are easy to identify because the caliper has an arm or lever attached to it.

GM Locking Calipers—General Motors has used a Delco Moraine locking caliper on many of its four-wheel disc brake applications since the late 1970s. With this design, the parking brake cable pulls a lever on the back of the caliper which rotates a screw inside the caliper. The screw turns against a nut and cone adjuster mechanism inside the piston assembly and shoves the piston out to lock the brake. Releasing the brake cable allows the piston to retract. The cone acts like a one-way clutch to take up slack as the pads wear, so the parking brake is self-adjusting.

The piston has a small vent hole to equalize internal pressure, which unfortunately also allows moisture to get inside the piston assembly. When this happens, rust forms in the self-adjuster mechanism and piston bore which can lead to binding and a frozen caliper—especially when the parking brake has not been used for some time.

When the pads are changed on one of these applications, or when the caliper itself is replaced, the D-shaped locking tab on the back of the inboard pad must fit into the indentation in the caliper piston. The locking tab prevents the piston from rotating, which is necessary for the self-adjusting mechanism to function correctly.

You also have to be careful not to mix up the left and right side piston assemblies which are not interchangeable on these calipers. Both pistons and calipers are marked L or R to avoid such mix-ups.

Ford Locking Calipers—Ford has used a Kelsey-Hayes caliper design since 1975 that locks via a somewhat different principle. When the parking brake cable pulls on the lever on the

back of this caliper, the lever shaft turns a little plate that has three balls in three indentations. Rotating the plate causes the balls to ride up out of the indentations and to push against a thrust screw that forces the piston out. Like the GM caliper, the Ford unit has an automatic self-adjuster mechanism inside the piston assembly to compensate for wear. The Kelsey-Hayes calipers don't use a vented piston which makes them somewhat less prone to internal corrosion and binding. As with GM, there are right and left calipers which are not interchangeable.

Import Locking Calipers—On many import applications, you find an Akebono single piston locking caliper on the rear brakes. The same caliper design is also used on Subaru front brakes, with similar designs on other import applications by Sumitomo and Girling. The Akebono caliper uses a cam and wedge-shaped pawl to apply the parking brake. Pulling the cable rotates the cam against the pawl, which pushes a threaded self-adjuster screw in the back of the piston out to force the pads against the rotor. The self-adjuster screw rotates slightly as the parking brake is applied and takes up slack to compensate for normal pad wear.

Rebuilding Locking Calipers

Overhauling a locking caliper with a parking brake mechanism is not an easy job because the self-adjusting mechanism inside the piston is difficult to disassemble, clean, lubricate and reassemble correctly. In many instances, the parts are too badly corroded to be reused anyway, so replacing the caliper with a new or remanufactured unit is probably your best option.

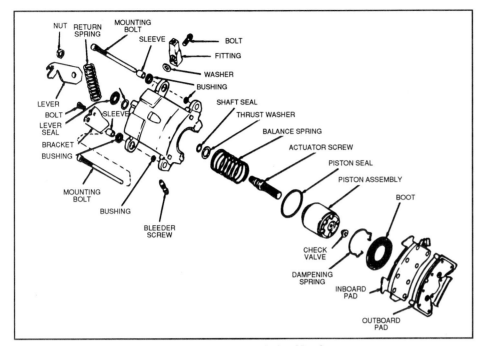

Typical GM rear locking caliper assembly. Courtesy Delco Moraine.

If you do attempt to rebuild a locking caliper, be sure to lubricate the self-adjusting mechanism prior to reassembly with high temperature brake grease (never ordinary chassis grease!). This will keep the adjuster working freely and help protect it against further corrosion.

As a rule, vehicles with four-wheel disc brakes tend to have a slightly lower brake pedal than those with a conventional front disc/rear drum arrangement because the rear pads have to travel a further distance when the brakes are applied. This condition can be aggravated if the rear caliper pistons are out of adjustment or the self-adjusters are frozen and leave too much space between pad and rotor. This can also happen if you replace a caliper and forget to adjust the piston to eliminate the excess play between pads and rotor (which should be less than 1/16 inch).

Working the parking brake level will usually take the play out of an adjuster. If the brakes don't adjust, the self-adjusting mechanism is frozen

and the caliper needs to be overhauled or replaced.

The reverse can also happen, that is, a rear caliper can drag if you install a new set of pads and there isn't sufficient play in the self-adjuster for the pads to clear the rotor. To back off the self-adjuster on GM and Ford brakes, the piston must be screwed back into its bore—which usually requires a special tool. If the self-adjuster fails to back off, then the caliper will need to be overhauled or replaced.

Parking Cable Adjustment—The adjustment of the parking brake cable is also important for the locking caliper to function correctly. Too tight and there may not be sufficient travel to work the self-adjusters and/or the brakes may drag. Too loose and the parking brake may not hold the vehicle.

You should get into the habit of using your parking brake regularly even if your vehicle has an automatic transmission because doing so will help maintain the proper adjustment

of the caliper piston self-adjuster mechanism.

The procedure for adjusting the parking brake cable on a locking caliper generally goes as follows:

With the parking brake released, loosen the cable turnbuckle. Then pump the brake pedal several times to make sure there is normal clearance between pads and rotor. Tighten the cable turnbuckle until the levers on the calipers just begin to move (zero slack in the cable). Rotate the wheel to make sure the pads are not dragging. Then push either caliper lever as far away from the cable as it will go while watching the lever on the opposite side. If it moves, the cable is too tight and should be backed off slightly. Repeat this procedure for both sides. The final adjustment position should lock the brakes within four to seven clicks of the parking brake pedal or handle.

NonLocking Rear Calipers w/Mini-Drums

Rear disc brakes with mini-drum parking brakes inside the rear rotors can be found on Corvettes, Camaros and numerous import applications. The mini-drum parking brake works like a conventional duo-servo drum brake. The brake cable rotates an expander that pushes both shoes outward against the inside of the rotor drum. But unlike a full-sized drum brake, there's no self-adjuster mechanism for the star wheel to compensate for shoe wear. This is because one isn't needed. The only time the parking brake is applied is when the vehicle is at rest so shoe wear is nil. The shoes normally last the life of the vehicle. Nor does the thickness of the shoe linings matter as long as there is enough lining left to

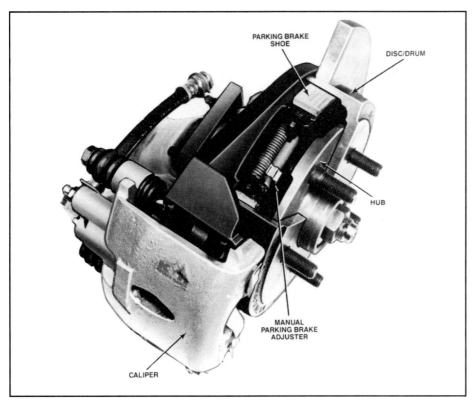

Non-locking rear caliper with a "mini-drum" style parking brake inside the rear rotor. Courtesy Chrysler.

hold the car on an incline with normal cable travel.

Mini-drum parking brakes within a rear rotor are not as vulnerable to sticking as locking calipers because the drums lack a self-adjuster mechanism and the shoes have return springs. If the parking brake fails to release, it's usually due to corrosion inside the parking brake cable sheath—which is a more common problem than one might think because most people use "Park" to lock the wheels rather than the parking brake.

When the rotors are reinstalled, the parking brake shoes can be adjusted by turning the rotor to line up an access hole with the star adjuster wheel inside and then spreading the shoes until a slight drag is felt by turning the adjuster wheel. The adjuster should then be backed off slightly and all the slack taken out of the brake cable.

Rotors

The rotor's job in a disc brake is to provide a surface against which the pads can be squeezed by the calipers to create friction. The rotors must be smooth and flat for proper braking, and capable of absorbing and dissipating a considerable amount of heat.

Rotors come in two basic types: "vented," which have cooling fins between the rotor faces, and "nonvented" or "solid" rotors, which have no cooling fins. Vented rotors cool better and can handle higher brake loads, so they are typically used in heavier vehicles and performance applications. The two types of rotors are not interchangeable because vented rotors are much thicker than nonvented rotors. So if you want to upgrade from solid to vented rotors, you also have to change calipers.

Rotors are made of cast iron and are generally a one-piece or solid casting. But the rotors on some late model cars have a stamped steel center section with a cast iron disc. These are called "composite" rotors, and can be a real source of trouble.

Composite Rotors—Composite rotors were introduced in the early

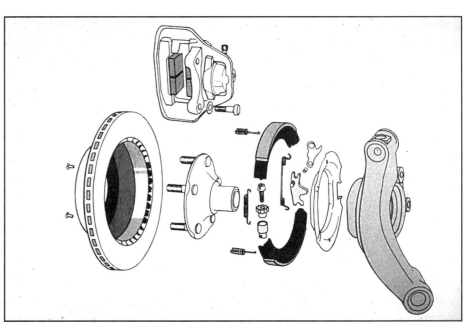

Here's an exploded view of the mini-drum style parking brake inside the rear rotor. Courtesy Wagner.

The condition of the rotors is extremely important for safe braking, so they should be carefully inspected anytime you suspect a brake problem or are replacing the pads.

1980s as a way to reduce weight. A typical composite rotor is about 20% lighter than a comparable cast iron rotor. Some composite rotors also use gray cast iron in the disc because it dampens noise better than ordinary cast iron. Many composite rotors are also "directional," which means the cooling fins between the rotor faces are curved rather than straight to draw air through the rotor for better cooling. These rotors are usually marked "left" and "right" and must be installed on the appropriate side for proper air flow.

The trouble with composite rotors is that they are not as rigid as one-piece cast rotors. Consequently, they tend to warp as they accumulate miles and wear. They are also more difficult to resurface, and must be supported with special adapters or large bellcaps when turned in a lathe. And they're more expensive than ordinary rotors. So many aftermarket suppliers are now offering conventional one-piece cast iron rotors for vehicles originally equipped with composite rotors.

Rotor Servicing—Rotors must be smooth and flat, so it's sometimes necessary to have them resurfaced. This may be necessary if the rotors are worn unevenly or have hard spots that are causing a pedal pulsation when you apply the brakes. Resurfacing may also be necessary if you're replacing pads and find the rotors are rough or badly scored.

If a rotor is cracked or damaged, replacement would be required. Hard spots can be ground off by resurfacing, but usually extend below the surface and return within a few thousand miles. That's why some vehicle manufacturers recommend replacing rather than resurfacing rotors with hard spots. As for warpage or distortion, resurfacing is okay as long as the rotor can be restored without exceeding safe limits.

But what if the rotors look okay? Should you have them resurfaced anyway? There are two schools of thought on this subject. As long as the rotors are in reasonably good condition (light scoring only that does

not exceed 0.015" in depth, warpage that generally does not exceed 0.0005", no hard spots or heat cracks), there's no reason to resurface them unless you've been experiencing a noise problem—in which case resurfacing will help restore an optimum surface for quiet operation. Not turning the rotors also helps extend their useful service life. The trouble is, if you don't replace your pads until they're worn to the point where metal is scraping against metal, you'll chew up or destroy your rotors. Then you'll have no choice but to resurface or replace them. New rotors aren't cheap, so don't put off replacing the pads if you know they're getting thin.

Rotor Thickness—Another important item that should always be checked when inspecting the brakes or replacing pads is rotor thickness. The rotors should be measured with a micrometer to make sure they are not worn beyond the minimum "safe" specifications—even if they appear to be in good condition. The minimum discard thickness is usually marked on the rotor itself. But if you can't find it, look it up in a shop manual. If the rotors are too thin (worn to or beyond the minimum discard thickness, or cannot be resurfaced without exceeding the vehicle manufacturer's minimum refinish specification), they must be replaced.

The difference between the discard and minimum refinish thickness is the margin the vehicle manufacturer believes is necessary to allow for normal wear between brake jobs. It varies considerably from one vehicle manufacturer to the next and according to the vehicle size and the type of brakes used. The margin specified on most domestic passenger

Rotor Thickness

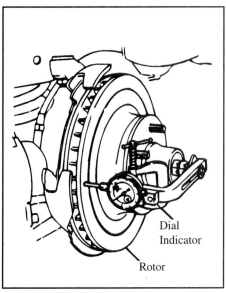

Dial
Indicator

Rotor

You need a dial indicator setup like this to measure lateral runout on a rotor. Courtesy Brake Parts, Inc.

Measure rotor thickness with a micrometer. If a rotor is worn down to the minimum service or discard specification, or cannot be resurfaced without exceeding either limit, it must be replaced. Rotor parallelism should also be checked by measuring the rotor's thickness at six evenly spaced points around the rotor. More than about .0005 in. of variation in thickness between the thickest and thinnest points can cause an annoying pedal vibration when the brakes are applied. Courtesy Wagner.

cars is around .015" compared to a range of .020" to .030" for most imports.

A rotor that's worn or turned too thin may not be able to absorb and dissipate heat quickly. This can make the brakes run hot, accelerate pad wear and reduce braking effectiveness possibly to the point of brake fade. Overheating can also cause rotor warpage and a pulsating brake pedal. Excessive wear may even lead to failure of the rotor itself!

Thickness should be measured at six evenly spaced points around the rotor. The smallest measurement should be used since this will tell you how far the rotor will have to be machined to restore the surface.

Measuring at various points around the rotor will also reveal any variations in rotor thickness or "parallelism." Both surfaces of the rotor must be within the manufacturer's specified tolerances for parallelism otherwise the rotor can cause excessive pedal travel (by kicking the pads too far out as it

turns), front end vibration, pedal pulsation and chatter. The parallelism specs recommended by the various vehicle manufacturers range from as low as .0001" to as high as .0008" because some vehicles are much more sensitive to this type of problem than others. So it's a good idea to refer to a shop manual for the exact specs for your vehicle.

Rotor Runout—Another dimension that needs to be checked is rotor runout. Lateral runout is the movement of the rotor from side to side as it turns. Excessive runout will kick the pads out as the rotor turns, creating excessive clearance that requires increased pedal travel when the brakes are applied. Runout specifications vary from as low as .002" to as high as .006", with .0035 being a ballpark figure for a majority of applications. To be safe, always refer to the specs listed by the vehicle manufacturer.

Runout is checked while the rotor is still on the car with a dial indicator. If runout exceeds the recommended

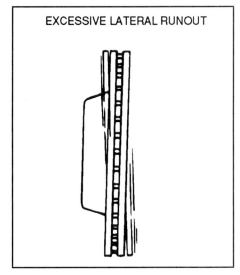

EXCESSIVE LATERAL RUNOUT

Too much runout makes the rotor wobble as it rotates. More than about .0035 in. of runout may cause a pedal pulsation. Runout problems may be due to improper machining of the rotor and/or hub, the presence of rust or dirt between the rotor and hub, or warpage in the rotor itself. Courtesy Brake Parts, Inc.

limit, the rotor must be resurfaced or replaced. On-car rotor resurfacing is recommended by some vehicle manufacturers (Honda, GM and Ford) for certain applications to minimize runout problems, which means you may have to take your vehicle to a dealer or shop if you find a runout problem.

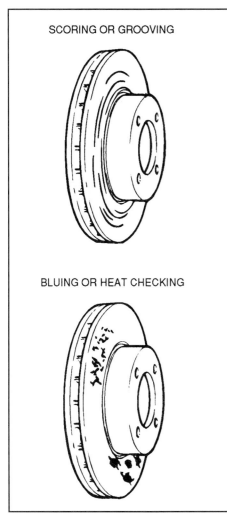

SCORING OR GROOVING

BLUING OR HEAT CHECKING

Light scoring of a rotor is normal and can usually be removed by resurfacing. But bluing or heat checking indicates severe overheating and the need for rotor replacement. Courtesy Brake Parts, Inc.

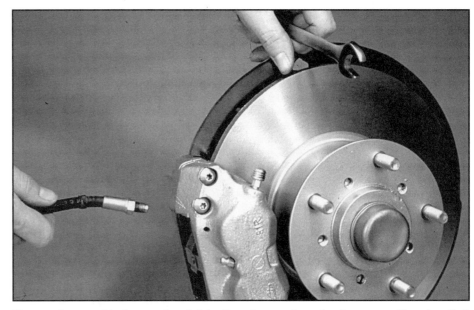

If your rotors need to be resurfaced, take them to an auto parts store or machine shop that offers this service. The cost is usually minimal. After resurfacing rotors should have a nice finish like the one shown above. Courtesy Wagner.

Rotor Resurfacing—Resurfacing rotors isn't something you can do yourself, but many auto parts stores and machine shops have brake lathes and will do the job for a reasonable fee. All you have to do is pull the rotors off your vehicle and take them to the shop. A pair of rotors can usually be cut in less than 45 minutes, so you should be able to get same day service.

The shop doing the resurfacing should take care to remove the least amount of metal as possible from your rotors. Deep cuts shorten the life of the rotor and tend to leave a rougher finish which may accelerate pad wear and contribute to noisy operation. Cutting a rotor at too fast a crossfeed rate to save time can also leave a rough finish on the surface. What works best is a shallow cut at a slow feed rate.

Most experts today recommend a rotor finish of 40 to 60 micro-inches or smoother for quiet disc brake operation. This is achievable with most bench lathes or on-car rotor refinishing equipment provided the operator follows the proper procedures and keeps his tools sharp.

One way to tell if a rotor is smooth enough after it's been resurfaced is to give it the "ballpoint pen" test. Draw a line on the rotor with an ordinary ballpoint pen. If it leaves an unbroken line, the rotor should be smooth enough. But if the line is broken into a series of tiny dots, the rotor is too rough. Take it back and have the shop redo the job.

Though it isn't absolutely necessary, applying a non-directional swirl or crosshatch finish by lightly sanding the rotors with #120 or #150 grit sandpaper after they've been turned is a good way to guarantee quiet operation.

Another step that's often overlooked but can affect the operation of your brakes is cleaning the rotors after they've been resurfaced. The microscopic debris that's left on the surface of the rotors can become embedded in new pads causing them to squeal. The best way to remove this debris is to scrub the rotors with soapy water and a stiff brush. Brake cleaner and other solvents don't do as thorough a job, so use soap and water for best results. Then dry the rotors before they're installed.

Disc Brake Pads

A disc brake has two pads: an inner pad and an outer pad. A "set" of replacement pads for a vehicle with disc/drum brakes, therefore, would contain four (4) pads total (one pair for each side). If the vehicle has four-wheel disc brakes, then you'd need a set of pads for the front brakes and a second set for the rear brakes.

The inner and outer pads may or

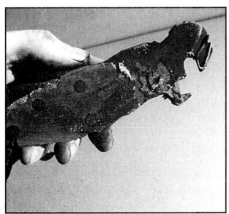

This is what can happen if you put off replacing a worn set of pads too long. The pads will self-destruct and chew up the rotors.

Comparing the amount of wear on the inner and outer pads will tell you if the caliper is working properly.

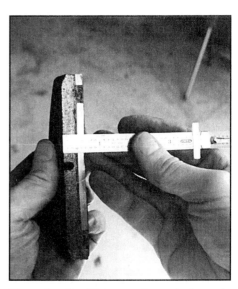

Measuring the thickness of your brake pads will tell you whether or not it's time to replace them. If the pads are worn down to the minimum thickness specified by the vehicle manufacturer, it's time for new ones.

may not be physically interchangeable on a given vehicle, so if you're doing a brake job pay close attention to what each pad looks like so you don't get the inner and outer pads mixed up. Most replacement pads are not marked as to which is which.

In front-wheel drive (FWD) cars and minivans, brake temperatures tend to be much higher than those in rear-wheel drive (RWD) vehicles because the front brakes handle a higher percentage of the total brake load. Consequently, most of FWD cars have "semimetallic" brake pads that can handle higher temperatures than asbestos or nonasbestos organic (NAO) pads. Friction materials are covered in Chapter 6.

The friction linings on the pads may be bonded (glued) or molded to the steel backing plate, or they may be held in place with rivets. Bonded or molded pads are generally stronger than riveted pads, and can wear more than riveted pads before they have to be replaced.

Pad Replacement—Given enough time and miles, brake pads eventually have to be replaced because they wear. There is no rule as to how long a given set of pads or a "brake job" should last. The same set of pads that

go 60,000 miles on vehicle A may only last 25,000 miles on vehicle B. It all depends on the type of driving that's done (stop-and-go city driving is a lot harder on the brakes than highway driving), the driving and braking habits of the person behind the wheel, the weight of the vehicle, the type of pads used, and the design of the brake system itself.

It's safe to say that the more the brakes are used, the faster they're going to wear out. It's also obvious that the hotter the brakes run, the quicker the more wear they're going to suffer. "Riding the brakes" is a bad habit that will wear out a set of pads in record time.

The only general rule that does apply is that disc brake pads should be replaced when there's less than about 30% of the original lining thickness left. Most new pads are about 1/2" thick, so when they're worn down to about 1/8" it's time for new ones. Pads with riveted linings may have less margin for wear. The pads should be replaced when the linings are worn to within 1/16" of the rivet heads.

New pads are also a must if the original pads have been fouled by brake fluid from a leaky caliper, or contaminated by grease from a failed wheel bearing grease seal. It doesn't make any difference how much meat

is left on the linings because there's no way to clean them once they've been contaminated. If reused, contaminated linings can grab, chatter and cause the brakes to pull.

Another reason for replacing pads is to get rid of a squeal. Noisy brakes are common on many FWD cars and minivans these days because of semimetallic pads which tend to be much harder than asbestos or NAO pads. The noise is actually caused by vibration. No rotor is perfectly true (zero lateral runout) so the pads tend to vibrate and chatter when they're squeezed against the rotor, a problem which has been further aggravated by hard pads such as semimetallics.

Noise can also be caused by vibration between the backs of the pads and the calipers if the pads do not fit tightly. Loose or missing antirattle clips, shims or insulators on the back of the pads can contribute to the problem. In fact, anything that increases the vibration amplifies the noise that's generated. This includes excessive runout or roughness on the face of the rotor, glazed linings, loose pad rivets or bonding, or rusted, worn or loose caliper mountings.

When buying replacement pads, always follow the part number listings in the supplier's catalog. Generally speaking, most say to use the same type of lining material as the original linings. Semimetallic linings must always be used on vehicles originally equipped with such. Never substitute cheaper asbestos/organic linings for semimetallics because doing so could literally put you or a loved one's life on the line. Asbestos doesn't have the temperature or wear resistance of semimetallic linings, so there's the potential for overheating and brake fade as well as accelerated pad wear. Nor should NAO linings be substituted for semimetallics unless the supplier says it's okay to do so.

Pad Upgrades—In many instances, you can upgrade to a superior material (like a semimetallic or a premium grade NAO). But follow the supplier's recommendations. Differences in the friction characteristics (aggressiveness) between different types of linings may create brake balance problems in some applications if you try to cross index part numbers on your own.

Also avoid the temptation to buy the cheapest pads you can find. The cheap fix may save you a few bucks in the short run, but the performance of "economy" grade linings may be disappointing and life may be far less than what you'd get with standard or premium grade linings. Some premium linings will give double or even triple the life of less expensive linings, which will save you money in the long run.

Installing Pads—When the new pads are installed, they must be held

When new disc brake pads are installed, make sure any mounting tabs or ears are properly positioned and tight to prevent rattles or noise.

securely by their positioning ears and/or antirattle springs, clips or insulator shims, otherwise they can vibrate and chatter creating a noise problem. The application of a dampening shim, noise control compound or adhesive to the back of the pads is recommended to help keep the brakes quiet. The backings dampen vibrations and prevent metal-to-metal contact between the pads and caliper. The caliper mounts should also be cleaned and greased with high temperature brake grease, and the plastic insulators on the mounting pins or bolts replaced and lubricated as needed.

Using the correct break-in procedure can also help you get the most out of your new pads and prevent them from becoming squealers. Many aftermarket replacement pads are not "postcured" when they're manufactured (a process which requires an additional eight hours of oven baking). This lowers manufacturing costs but also requires a special break-in procedure for proper pad performance and life. If a new set of pads that have not been

postcured are subjected to a series of rapid panic stops before they've had a chance to break in, overheating can cause them to glaze and become noisy.

Break-In Procedure—The recommended break-in procedure for pads that have not been postcured is to make 20 normal stops from about 30 mph, or 20 "slow downs" from about 50 mph to 20 mph using light pedal pressure. Allow at least 30 seconds between stops for the brakes to cool. You should also avoid hard stops for the first 150 miles of driving. If you're installing pads that have been postcured, no special break-in procedure is required.

Some replacement pads are coated with a special "transfer film" that eases break-in and reduces noise. Similar results can also be achieved by using various aerosol products that are designed for this purpose (never use any type of spray lubricant or grease as doing so will ruin the pads!). Spraying on a transfer film "softens" the break-in process which helps extend the life of the pads and reduces noise.

Drum brakes also come in a wide variety of configurations. Courtesy Wagner Brakes.

Up until the early 1970s, drum brakes were used both front and rear on almost all passenger cars and light trucks. But for the past three decades, most vehicles have only used drums on the rear. The automakers still cling to the old drum brake technology because drums are less expensive to manufacture than disc brakes, and they work well enough on the rear wheels for many applications.

The typical drum brake assembly consists of the drum itself, a wheel cylinder, a pair of shoes, return springs and hold down springs for the shoes, a backing plate and one or two anchor pins to support the shoes, a self-adjuster mechanism to maintain lining clearances, and a parking brake mechanism.

The forward shoe, which is referred to as either the "primary" or "leading" shoe is the one closest to the front of the vehicle. The rear shoe, which is called the "secondary" or "trailing" shoe, is the one closest to the rear of the vehicle.

It's important to know the difference between these two shoes because on some vehicles the shoes are not interchangeable because of differences in size, design or lining materials. To help you identify which is which, new shoes may be marked.

HOW THEY WORK

The leading and trailing shoes work somewhat differently depending on the type of drum configuration that's used. One of the advantages of a drum brake is that the shoes experience a "self-energizing" effect when the brakes are applied, which means a drum brake requires much less pedal effort than a disc brake to maintain friction.

When hydraulic pressure from the master cylinder reaches the wheel cylinder, it pushes the pistons in the wheel cylinder out. The pistons, in turn, push against the shoes and force them outward against the drum. As the linings on the shoes make contact with the rotating drum, friction between the linings and drum tries to drag the shoes along with the drum.

If the leading shoe is connected at the bottom to the trailing shoe rather

Drum brakes may not have the stopping power of disc brakes, but they're usually adequate for the rear wheels on most vehicles.

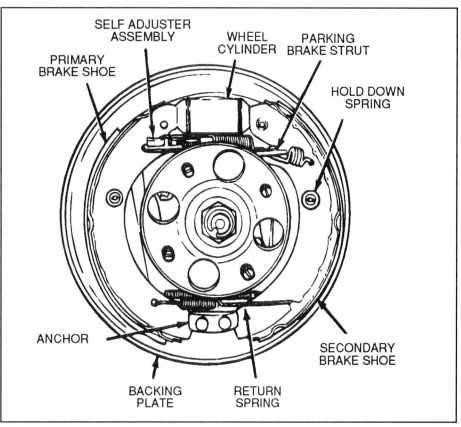

SELF ADJUSTER ASSEMBLY

PRIMARY BRAKE SHOE

WHEEL CYLINDER

PARKING BRAKE STRUT

HOLD DOWN SPRING

ANCHOR

BACKING PLATE

RETURN SPRING

SECONDARY BRAKE SHOE

Major components of a typical drum brake. Courtesy Ford.

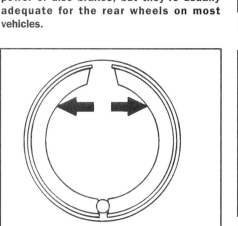

When hydraulic pressure is applied to the pistons in the wheel cylinder, the pistons move out and force the shoes against the drums to apply the brakes.

than an anchor pin, the wedging action of the leading shoe will continue right around the circle and transfer to the trailing shoe, causing it to wedge tighter against the drum.

DUO-SERVO BRAKES

Duo-servo brakes have one anchor

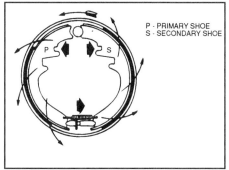

P - PRIMARY SHOE
S - SECONDARY SHOE

When the shoes contact the drum, a "wedging effect" takes place that attempts to rotate the shoes with the drum. But the anchor pin at the top prevents the shoes from rotating. This creates a self-energizing effect that pulls the shoes tighter against the drum and reduces the amount of pedal pressure that's needed to apply the brakes. Courtesy Brake Parts, Inc.

pin at the top of the backing plate. This configuration allows the drum's rotational force to push the leading shoe against the trailing shoe to increase braking friction. When backing up, just the reverse happens. The trailing shoe pushes against the

leading shoe to push the leading shoe tighter against the drum. The advantage of this design is that it increases the aggressiveness of the brake while reducing pedal effort.

With duo-servo brakes, the trailing shoe does more of the brake work than the primary shoe when driving forward. As a result, the linings on the trailing shoe tend to wear more rapidly than those on the leading shoe. On many duo-servo brakes, the lining on the trailing shoe is longer than the one on the primary shoe to compensate for the increased wear. The leading and trailing linings may also be of different composition to further compensate for differences in loading and friction.

If the position of the shoes are accidentally reversed during installation, the shorter lining in the rearward position will experience

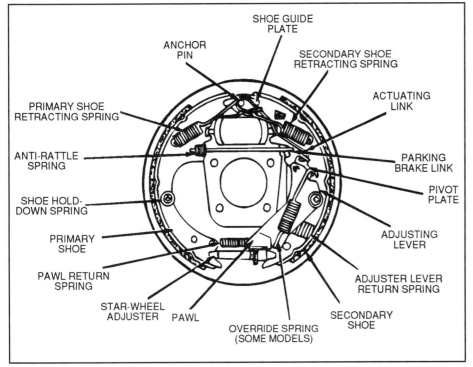

PRIMARY SHOE RETRACTING SPRING

ANCHOR PIN

SHOE GUIDE PLATE

SECONDARY SHOE RETRACTING SPRING

ACTUATING LINK

PARKING BRAKE LINK

PIVOT PLATE

ANTI-RATTLE SPRING

SHOE HOLD-DOWN SPRING

PRIMARY SHOE

PAWL RETURN SPRING

STAR-WHEEL ADJUSTER

PAWL

OVERRIDE SPRING (SOME MODELS)

SECONDARY SHOE

ADJUSTER LEVER RETURN SPRING

ADJUSTING LEVER

A typical duo-servo drum brake with a self-lever adjuster. The primary shoe pushes against the secondary shoe via the star-adjuster when the brakes are applied. This style of brake is used on most rear-wheel drive vehicles.

rapid wear. Braking ability may also be adversely affected.

The duo-servo drum brake is most commonly used on rear-wheel drive applications where added stopping power is needed at the back brakes to overcome engine torque to the drive wheels. Duo-servo brakes are not commonly used, however, on front-wheel drive cars because the duo-servo action is too aggressive. The front brakes do most of the work in FWD applications, so less braking ability is needed at the rear. If the rear brakes are too aggressive they may lock up and skid during hard braking or a panic stop.

NON-DUO-SERVO BRAKES

Non-duo-servo brakes have an anchor pin at the bottom of the brake backing plate between the leading and trailing shoes. The anchor plate at the bottom prevents any transfer of torque

from the leading to the trailing shoe when traveling ahead. The non-duo-servo brake is not as aggressive as the

duo-servo, which makes it better suited to rear drum brakes on front-wheel drive cars.

With non-duo-servo brakes, the linings on the leading shoe tend to wear more rapidly than the linings on the trailing shoe. This is because the leading shoe does most of the work when traveling forward. When backing up, the trailing shoe handles most of the braking.

DRUMS

The drum is usually made of cast iron but some are aluminum with a cast iron liner. The drum provides the friction surface against which the linings rub when the shoes are pushed outward by hydraulic pressure in the wheel cylinder. As the linings rub against the drum, they generate friction to slow the wheel and bring the vehicle to a halt. This generates a lot of heat, which the drum absorbs

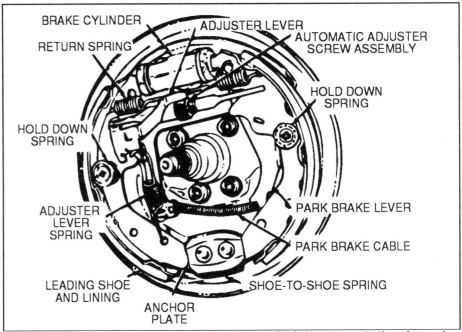

BRAKE CYLINDER

RETURN SPRING

ADJUSTER LEVER

AUTOMATIC ADJUSTER SCREW ASSEMBLY

HOLD DOWN SPRING

HOLD DOWN SPRING

ADJUSTER LEVER SPRING

LEADING SHOE AND LINING

ANCHOR PLATE

PARK BRAKE LEVER

PARK BRAKE CABLE

SHOE-TO-SHOE SPRING

Typical non-duo-servo drum brake. The anchor plate at the bottom prevents the primary shoe from pushing against the secondary shoe, so there's no self-energizing effect as the brakes are applied. This type of brake requires more pedal pressure and is less aggressive than a duo-servo design, so it is used on the rear brakes of many front-wheel drive passenger cars. Courtesy Chrysler.

On most vehicles, the drum should pull right off once the wheel has been removed and the brake adjuster backed off. But rust, corrosion and age can hold a drum fast. So you may have to use a puller like this to pop it loose. Never beat on the side or lip of a drum with a steel hammer in an attempt to loosen it because you'll probably damage or break the drum.

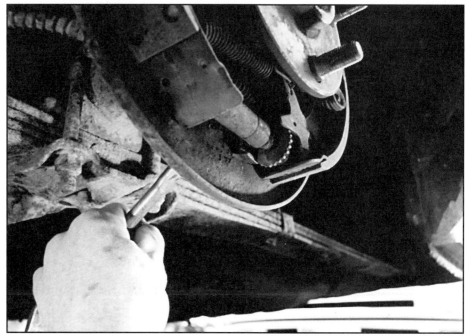

Inserting a brake adjusting tool or standard screwdriver through the opening on the backing plate will allow you to back off the star wheel adjuster. This is necessary so the shoes will clear the drum, allowing the drum to be removed. The drum has already been removed in this photo to show the adjuster inside.

and dissipates so the linings don't get too hot and begin to fade. Some drums have cooling fins that increase their cooling capacity. The drum also shields the internal brake components from road splash and dirt. There may also be a spring wrapped around the outside of the drum to help dampen vibrations and noise.

Front drums on older rear-wheel drive cars and trucks are mounted on a spindle and supported by a pair of wheel bearings. The rear drums on rear-wheel drive cars and trucks are mounted on the axle hub, while those on front-wheel drive cars and minivans are either mounted on a spindle or hub. Most of these will have sealed wheel bearings, but some may have bearings that require

periodic service.

Drum Removal

The drums should be removed anytime you suspect a brake problem or need to inspect the brakes. Even if you're only replacing a set of pads on the front disc brakes, you should still remove one or both drums and take a peek inside. Why? Because you can't tell a thing about the rear brakes without looking inside the drums. The drums, linings and hardware must all be in good condition to provide safe braking. So don't take chances. Always inspect all four brakes even if you're only doing a pad replacement up front.

The first step in removing any drum is to back off the shoes so the linings will clear the drum. This is necessary because as the drums wear, they often develop a ridge that will hang up on the shoes when you attempt to pull the drum off.

On most drum brakes that have a

star adjuster mechanism, access to the star wheel is usually possible through a small slit or hole in the backing plate. A rubber plug is usually located in the hole or slit to keep out road splash and dirt. The plug will have to be pried out before you can insert a screwdriver or brake spoon tool through the opening to turn the star adjuster (be sure to replace the plug afterwards—or install a new one if the original is missing).

On most applications, the adjuster can be turned to loosen or tighten the brakes by working the end of your screwdriver or brake spoon tool up or down against the star wheel. To loosen the brakes on some applications, it may be necessary to insert a second screwdriver through the opening to hold the lever away from the star wheel so it can be turned in the opposite direction.

You usually turn the star wheel one way on one side of the vehicle to loosen the brakes, and the opposite

Drums usually develop a ridge as they wear. This ridge can hang up on the shoes when you try to remove the drum, so it's important to make sure you've backed off the adjuster enough so the shoes will clear the drum.

way on the other side. To tighten the brakes, you turn both adjusters in the opposite direction as before.

As you turn the star wheel, rotate the wheel by hand while feeling for brake drag. This will tell you if the brakes are getting looser or tighter. If the wheel turns freely, the brakes are getting looser. If you hear scraping noises or the wheel starts to drag, the brakes are getting tighter.

Once the shoes have been backed off, you can remove the front drums on older rear-wheel drive cars and trucks by (1) pulling or prying the dust cap off the hub, (2) removing the cotter pin and lock ring, and (3) backing off the spindle nut that holds the outer wheel bearings in place. The drum will then slide right off the spindle.

On front-wheel drive cars and minivans that have sealed wheel bearings, the rear drums usually pull off the hub once the rear wheels have been removed and the brake adjusters backed off. But some drums may be attached to the hub by one or two

small screws or snap washers on the lugs.

On rear-wheel drive vehicles, the rear drums are supposed to pull off the axle hubs once the rear wheels have been removed. But time and corrosion have a way of cementing old drums in place, making them difficult to remove.

Removing Stuck Drums—If a drum is stuck and won't come off (and isn't hanging up on the shoes because you forgot to back off the adjuster), use care because cast iron is brittle and can be easily cracked if you try to beat the drum loose with a steel hammer. To remove a stubborn drum, use a propane torch (never anything hotter!) to apply heat to the face of the drum in the area between the lug nuts and center hole. Also, squirt some penetrating oil around the lugs and center opening. Then pound on the face of the drum between the lugs with a soft (rubber or brass) hammer to help loosen it. Some professional brake technicians use an air hammer with a blunt tip in the same way to

vibrate a drum loose.

If the drum still refuses to budge, you'll have to rent or buy a drum puller or large gear puller that has long enough legs to grasp the back edge of the drum. Center the puller on the drum and make sure the legs have a good grip on the edge of the drum. Then position the puller's thrust screw against the axle hub. As you begin tightening the puller screw, tap on the face of the drum with a soft hammer to help pop it loose. You can also apply heat and more penetrating oil. Proceed cautiously because a puller can generate a lot of pull on the drum.

Caution: Drums will sometimes pop free with considerable force when removed with a puller. Also, don't let the drum and puller fall onto a hard concrete floor because the resulting impact may damage the drum you've worked so hard to remove. (Hint: position an old rug, blanket or rags under the drum to cushion it in case you drop it when it pops loose.)

Drum Inspection

Once the drums are off, check them carefully for wear. Stamped or cast on the face or outside of most drums is a "maximum diameter" or "machine to" specification, which refers to the maximum allowable inside diameter of the drum that is permitted *after* the drum has been resurfaced. The drum may also have a "discard" specification. If the drum is already worn to discard spec, or can't be remachined without exceeding the maximum diameter limit, discard it.

Measuring the inside diameter of a drum requires a special drum gauge. Most machine shops and auto parts stores that resurface drums and rotors will have a drum gauge and can measure your drums for you to

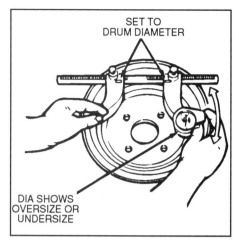

Drums should always be measured with a gauge to determine if the drum is worn out or cannot be resurfaced. If the inside diameter of a drum exceeds the vehicle manufacturer's maximum service or discard specification, the drum must be replaced. Courtesy Brake Parts, Inc.

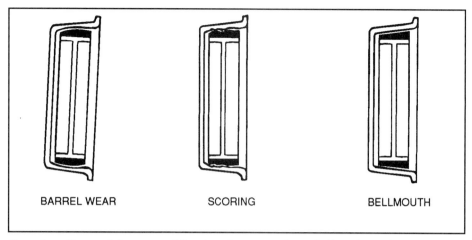

Examples of types of drum wear. Minor barrel wear, scoring or bellmouth can be corrected by resurfacing. But if the wear is too deep, you'll have to replace the drum. Courtesy Brake Parts, Inc.

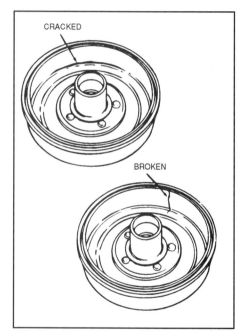

Defects such as these cannot be corrected, so a new drum is your only option. Courtesy Brake Parts, Inc.

determine their condition.

Warning: If a drum is worn to the maximum diameter or discard thickness, or cannot be resurfaced without exceeding the maximum specs, it must be replaced.

Replacing Drums—There are five good reasons why worn drums must be replaced:

1. Thin drums are dangerous drums. If not replaced, the drum can wear to the point where it may literally disintegrate. And if the drum fails, so do your brakes!

2. The increased inside diameter of a badly worn drum won't match up with a new set of linings unless the linings are arced (and who does that these days?). Consequently, the linings only make contact in the middle which reduces their effective braking ability.

3. Drum wear increases shoe travel. If worn excessively, the self-adjuster mechanisms may not be able to take up all the slack resulting in a low pedal. There's also the chance that the wheel cylinder may overextend to the point where it leaks or comes apart, causing brake failure.

4. Thin drums can't absorb and dissipate as much heat as thick ones. There's less mass in a worn drum so the brakes may overheat and fade much sooner.

5. Thin drums can contribute to noise by failing to dampen vibrations.

So always measure the drum's inside diameter with a drum gauge. If the drum's diameter is less than .030" of the maximum diameter spec, there isn't enough metal left in it for resurfacing and it must be replaced. Most passenger car and light truck drums are designed with enough metal to allow about .060" of wear (or resurfacing) before replacement is necessary.

Drums also need to be inspected for the following conditions:

• Minor pitting and scoring are acceptable as long as the grooves are not too deep and can be removed by resurfacing. Grease or oil contamination must be removed before the drum is reused.

• Cracks of any kind are dangerous and mean the drum needs to be replaced. Cracks can result from thermal stress or mechanical stress. Either way, they weaken the metal.

• Out-of-round or an egg-shaped drum can result from applying the parking brake when the drum is hot. The

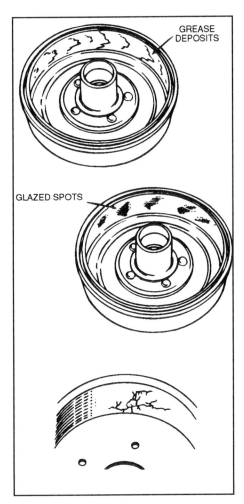

GREASE DEPOSITS

GLAZED SPOTS

Grease spots are nothing to worry about in a drum, and can be removed with brake cleaner or alcohol. Do not use a petroleum-based solvent or anything that leaves a film. Glazed spots (hard spots) can sometimes be removed by resurfacing, but they usually come back so replacement would be recommended. Cracks are bad news and require drum replacement. Courtesy Brake Parts, Inc.

locked position of the shoes prevents the drum from contracting normally as it cools resulting in permanent distortion. This can cause a pedal pulsation when the brakes are applied. Drum runout should not exceed .005" If the runout cannot be removed by resurfacing, replace the drum.

• A "bellmouth" condition can occur in wide drums if the inner edge of the drum distorts outward. The result is uneven shoe-to-drum contact, uneven

lining wear and reduced braking efficiency. To check for this condition, measure the inside diameter of the drum close to the inside and outside edges of the drum. If there's a difference of more than .005", the drum needs to be resurfaced or replaced.

• Barrel wear on the drum where the center portion is worn more than the edges. If the distortion can't be removed by resurfacing, it will have to be replaced.

• Hard spots or glazed spots in the drum. These are caused by excessive heat that brings about metallurgical changes in the metal. Hard spots can be identified by raised or discolored patches on the drum friction surface. Hard spots can cause chatter, pedal pulsation and grabbing when the brakes are applied. Resurfacing will shave the tops off any hard spots, but they usually come back once the drum is returned to service and starts to wear again. The only permanent cure for hard spots is a new drum.

Drum Resurfacing

If the drums are rough, they need to be resurfaced to restore the friction surface to like-new condition. Rough drums will eat up a new set of shoes very quickly, so don't skip this important step.

Drums should always be resurfaced in pairs. Never do one drum and not the other because differences in diameter can affect side-to-side brake balance. The inside diameters of both drums should be within .010" of each other. A greater difference may cause undesirable variations in brake force side-to-side.

If you're installing new drums, most

come from the factory in a finished condition and are ready to install. Resurfacing a brand-new drum is unnecessary and needlessly shortens the drum's life. Even so, some professional brake technicians will still take a light cut on a new drum just to make sure the drum is true (concentric). Experience has taught them that new drums aren't always as round as they're supposed to be.

When you take your drums to a machine shop or parts store to have them resurfaced, the first thing they should do is measure the inside diameter of each drum to see if the drums can still be safely turned. If the metal is too thin, there's no point in turning them. You'll need new drums.

If the drums can be resurfaced, the next step is to mount them on a lathe. A silencer band may be wrapped around the outside of the drum to dampen vibrations and reduce the possibility of creating chatter marks as the drum is resurfaced. The person who's resurfacing your drum should then remove the least amount of metal that's necessary to restore the drum surface, and no more. This will prolong the life of your drums.

As a rule, the best drum finish is achieved with a slow, shallow cut. The smoother the finish, the better. A lathe speed of 100 to 200 rpm with a cross feed rate of no more than .002" per minute and a depth of cut of less than .002" will usually produce an ideal surface.

If the drums are turned too quickly, the tool bit can leave tiny grooves in the surface which can chew up a new set of linings as well as make noise. How can you tell if your drums have been refinished properly? Try writing your name on the friction surface with a ballpoint pen. If you see a

These linings may not appear to be worn because the rivet heads are still well below the surface of the linings. Even so, there's no way to know if the linings meet the vehicle manufacturer's minimum thickness specifications unless you measure them.

continuous line of ink, the finish should be smooth enough to perform properly. But if the ink line is broken up into little dots, the surface is too rough. Ask them to do your drums over again—and this time to not to hurry so much.

BRAKE SHOES

While the drums are off, you can inspect the condition and thickness of the shoes or linings. The linings need to be replaced if they are worn to the minimum thickness specified by the vehicle manufacturer. Generally speaking, it's time for new linings when riveted friction material is worn down to within 1/32" (.030") of the rivet heads, or when bonded linings are worn to within 1/16" (.060") of the shoe itself. Always look up the vehicle manufacturer's specifications in a shop manual or brake reference book because some vehicles cannot handle as much wear as others due to

differences in brake design.

Caution: Though you might postpone some repair expense by waiting until the brake linings are worn to the limit to replace them, you might wait too long. If the linings wear too far (either to the rivet heads or all the way down to bare steel), it can chew up the drums, possibly damaging them to the point where they can no longer be resurfaced and have to be replaced. Then where are your savings? There's also a danger of brake failure if what's left of the linings separate from the shoes. It should also be obvious that badly worn linings may not be able to stop your vehicle safely. So don't wait if the linings are getting thin. Replace them now while you have the drums off.

Removing Shoes

Shoes are removed by first undoing the return springs, then releasing the hold-down springs. The hold-down springs are held in place by steel pins that pass through the shoes from the backside of the backing plate. A cup

shaped clip locks the pin to keep the hold-down springs in place. Twisting the cup 90 degrees will release the pin.

New linings come on new or recycled (rebuilt) shoes. In the old days, brake mechanics would drill out the rivets, remove the old linings from the shoes and rivet new ones in their place. They'd also arc grind the shoes so the contour of the new linings would match the inside diameter of the drum. Grinding reduced break-in and noise while providing better initial braking action. But both practices have long since been abandoned because (1) rebuilding brake shoes is too time consuming, (2) many brake linings are bonded today which makes removal nearly impossible, and (3) grinding brake linings generates dust which may still be hazardous even if it contains no asbestos.

BRAKE HARDWARE

Something else that needs to be carefully inspected while the drums

Measure the linings at their thinnest point where wear is greatest. This is usually in the middle of the shoe. If the lining is at or below the minimum acceptable thickness, it's time to replace them.

Weak return springs can allow the shoes to drag. So always inspect the hardware anytime you work on the brakes. Replacing the springs will assure proper brake operation.

are off are the springs and other hardware that hold the drum brake together and allow it to work.

The hardware includes the return springs, shoe hold-down springs, and other clips and cables that are part of the assembly. Brake hardware is subjected to high temperatures when the brakes get hot. This can weaken springs over time. As the springs age, they may lose tension, stretch or even break. Weak return springs are bad news because they can allow the linings to drag against the drum, which accelerates lining wear, reduces fuel economy and makes the brakes run hot. A dragging brake can also make a vehicle pull to one side. So don't ignore the condition of the hardware when you're inspecting or replacing the linings.

Inspection & Replacement

Springs that have stretched, show signs of heat discoloration or other damage should be replaced. The same goes for any other parts that are broken, distorted, badly rusted, damaged or missing. But even if the hardware looks okay, it's hard to tell if the springs are as strong as they once

were. If your vehicle has a lot of miles on it or has been driven hard (by you or a former owner), chances are the springs may be weak and need to be replaced. New hardware isn't that expensive, and will give you peace of mind that your brakes have been restored to like-new condition.

Caution: Be careful when removing or changing hardware because the "wrong" tool or technique may damage parts. Yanking or

twisting off springs with ordinary pliers may bend or stretch the springs.

Also, note the relative position of all the springs and other parts so you can reassemble them the same as before. Doing one brake at a time may be a good idea so if you can't remember where something goes, all you have to do is look at the opposite brake to figure it out (which is always easier than trying to decipher an illustration or picture in a manual).

When you're reinstalling springs, make sure you use the correct springs in the correct locations. Some are of different length and/or configuration. Others may be of different strength and won't work properly if installed in the wrong location. To help avoid confusion, springs are often color coded.

SELF-ADJUSTERS

The self-adjusters on drum brakes also deserve close attention. Rust and corrosion are the main culprits here, but wear can be a factor, too. If an

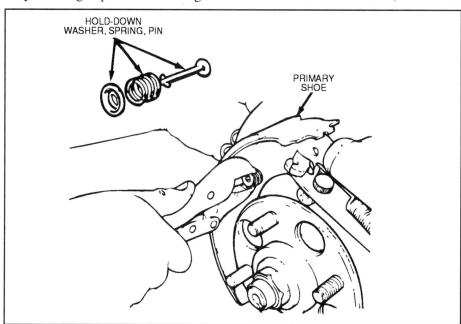

The shoe hold-down springs can be removed by twisting the washer 90 degrees to release the pin, or by twisting the pin to release the washer. Courtesy Ford.

This old self-adjuster looks pretty cruddy. But as long as it works okay, it can be reused. Penetrating oil can help loosen up rust and corrosion, and a coating of brake grease will assure smooth operation.

adjuster doesn't turn freely, it can't maintain the proper lining to drum clearance. As the linings wear, the clearance between the linings and drum will gradually open up and increase pedal travel. Eventually the point may be reached where there isn't enough pedal travel left to apply the brakes.

The most common type of automatic adjuster uses a "star wheel." It works like a ratchet. A spring-loaded lever that's pressed up against the wheel only allows the wheel to turn one way. As the linings wear, the movement of the brake shoes works the lever up and down (which usually only occurs when backing up). As the lever catches on the notched star wheel, it rotates the wheel slightly— but only if the linings have worn enough to allow it. This one-way action backs out the threaded adjuster screw and forces the shoes further apart to take up the slack between the linings and drum to maintain brake adjustment automatically. The spacing between the notches on the star wheel prevent the lever from overtightening the brakes to the point where they'd drag against the drum.

So make sure the self-adjusters turn freely. If rusted or frozen, lubrication probably won't help. Replace them. It's also important to check the edge of the lever that works the star adjuster for wear. If the lever's edge has become rounded, it can slip and fail to keep the brakes adjusted. Replace the lever if it is worn.

Caution: Adjusters are directional and are not interchange-able left to right on most vehicles. If you accidentally mix them up and install the adjusters on the wrong sides, the brakes will become progressively looser rather than maintain proper adjustment!

Adjusters should be lightly lubricated with high temperature brake grease to keep them turning free and to help inhibit corrosion.

Other Types of Adjusters

A different type of adjuster is used on some non-duo-servo drum brakes that uses a spring-loaded strut between the shoes to maintain proper shoe spacing and brake adjustment. The strut has no star wheel or threaded screw mechanism, but uses a sliding latch type of arrangement to adjust shoe spacing. Application of the parking brake expands the adjuster.

On brakes that use a strut adjuster rather than a star wheel, a plug usually has to be knocked out of the drum to release the adjuster. A punch tool is needed to push in on the protruding part of the strut rod assembly. This releases the latch allowing the return springs to retract the shoes for easier drum removal. If the strut assembly has not been damaged, it can be reused.

On some vehicles (Ford Escort, for example, with 7-inch drums), a

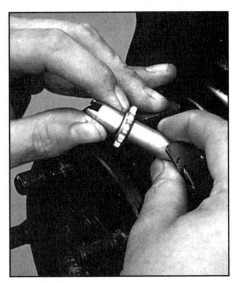

Drum brake self-adjusters that do not turn easily must be replaced with new ones.

spring-loaded "quadrant" adjuster is used to maintain shoe adjustment. Notches on the adjuster increase shoe spacing as wear permits. The adjuster is tightened by working the parking brake. Others use a ratchet-like mechanism that works two notched pawls against one another to regulate shoe spacing.

BACKING PLATES

The backing plates that support the shoes need to be inspected for wear, cracks or other damage. Raised pads on the backing plate allow the shoes to slide back and forth as the brakes are applied and released. Over time, these pads can become worn causing noise and/or interfering with the smooth operation of the brakes. If the pads have developed a ridge, therefore, the ridge should be filed down or ground smooth to restore the pad. If the pad is worn through or cracked, you'll have to replace the backing plates (which are bolted to the axle housing or steering knuckle).

The raised pads should be lightly lubricated with high temperature brake grease (never ordinary chassis

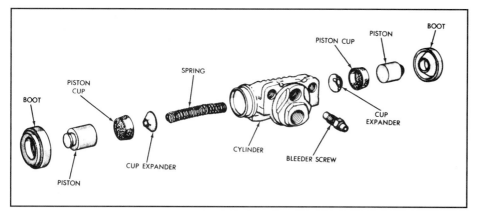

Typical rear wheel cylinder assembly. The wheel cylinder should be rebuilt or replaced if you see any sign of leakage around the boots.

grease!) to assure smooth operation of the shoes.

The anchor pins or bolts on the backing plate should also be inspected to make sure they're secure. Also, check the mounting of the wheel cylinder. On some General Motors applications, the wheel cylinder is mounted in such a way that it may become loose and twist, causing the brakes to fail. If the wheel cylinder is loose, the backing plate should be replaced. There are also aftermarket

kits available that include reinforcing brackets to prevent the wheel cylinder from turning.

WHEEL CYLINDERS

The wheel cylinder in a drum brake provides the hydraulic muscle that forces the shoes outward against the drum, so it must be leak-free and work smoothly for the brakes to work properly. Inside the wheel cylinder are a pair of steel, phenolic or aluminum

pistons separated by a small spring. On the inside face of each piston is a cup shaped rubber seal that opens inward. This allows hydraulic pressure to push the seal tightly against the inside bore of the wheel cylinder housing as the pistons are pushed outward. Rubber dust seals on both ends of the wheel cylinder keep dirt and debris out of the piston bore.

The most common type of problem you'll find here is fluid leaking past worn seals. Corrosion causes pitting in the bores, which over time can wear the seals and cause them to leak. Rubber also hardens and deteriorates with age, which can cause leakage, too. So if you see any fluid or wet spots around the wheel cylinders, they'll have to be rebuilt or replaced.

Rebuilding is the least expensive way to go because the only things you replace are the seals and dust boots (some kits may also include new pistons). But to rebuild the wheel cylinder successfully, you usually have to hone the piston bore to smooth out the roughness and pitting that caused it to fail in the first place. If the bore is too badly worn, grooved, scratched, cracked or otherwise damaged, though, you're wasting your time trying to rebuild it. What you need is a new or remanufactured wheel cylinder. Attempting to rebuild a questionable wheel cylinder is asking for trouble because there's a risk it will leak. And if there's one thing you don't want in a hydraulic brake system, it's a leak. Loss of fluid can lead to loss of pedal and brake failure. Fluid can also contaminate and ruin the brake linings. So don't take unnecessary chances. If a wheel cylinder is leaking, replacing it is a lot less risky than attempting to rebuild it. What's more, if one cylinder is

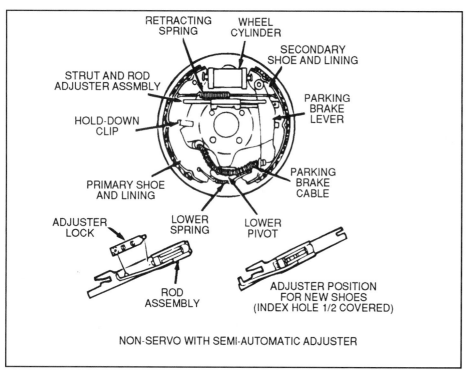

Drum brake with a strut type of adjuster.

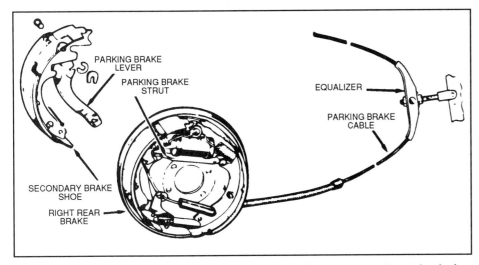

PARKING BRAKE LEVER

PARKING BRAKE STRUT

EQUALIZER

PARKING BRAKE CABLE

SECONDARY BRAKE SHOE

RIGHT REAR BRAKE

Typical parking brake. Most problems here are caused by infrequent use and rusted or broken cables.

leaking, chances are the other may soon be leaking if it isn't already.

If your wheel cylinders are not leaking, on the other hand, and you're redoing the brakes, you would probably be well advised to rebuild the wheel cylinders if your vehicle has a lot of miles on it. Don't fool yourself into thinking, "If it ain't broke, why fix it?" because the seals are probably nearing the end of their service life. They may not be leaking yet, but who's to say how much longer they'll last? To avoid unnecessary risks, therefore, you should always rebuild or replace high mileage wheel cylinders when relining your brakes.

DRUM REINSTALLATION

One of the most common mistakes do-it-yourselfers make when they've had a set of drums turned is not cleaning them before they go back on their vehicle. Resurfacing leaves a lot of debris as well as torn and folded metal on the inside surface of the drums. Much of this debris will be knocked off by the brake linings when the brakes are first applied, but some of it will become embedded in the

linings and may contribute to a noise problem. So for best results, scrub the inside of the drums with soapy water and a stiff brush. And if you're really picky, lightly sand the inside of the drum with #120 or #150 grit sandpaper before you wash them.

Once the drums have been resurfaced and cleaned, keep your greasy fingers off of the inside surface. Handle the drums with care and do not store them on end or drop them otherwise you may knock your drums out of round.

If your drums are the type that have integral wheel bearings, inspect the bearings and races carefully. Replace the bearings if they're not in perfect condition. Clean and repack the bearings with a high temperature wheel bearing grease. And don't be tempted to reuse the old grease seals. They'll probably leak. Throw the old grease seals away and install new ones, making sure you drive them in squarely without damaging them (use a seal driver, or the poor man's alternative: a flat block of wood and a rubber hammer).

Also, check the condition of the wheel studs, and replace any that are broken or damaged. Old studs can be

driven out from the front with a punch and hammer. To install a new stud, push it as far as it will go through the opening from the backside, then use a lug nut installed backwards (flat side towards the hub) to pull the stud the rest of the way in.

Adjusting Shoes

When you're ready to reinstall the drums, you can use a special "drum/shoe gauge" to preadjust the shoes to the inside diameter of the drums. But since it's unlikely that you'll have one of these in your tool box, just make sure the shoes are backed off enough so the drums will slip easily into place. If the shoes are out too far, the drum will jam as you try to push it over the shoes. Don't try to force it into place because doing so may damage the linings. Pull the drum off, turn the adjuster to retract the shoes and try again.

Once the drums are in place, the shoes should be adjusted until they just clear the drum (little or no drag felt when the drum is rotated by hand).

Warning: If you forget to adjust the shoes, you may end up with too much pedal travel and no brakes! Reducing the clearance between the shoes and drum is necessary to minimize the distance the brake pedal has to travel to apply the brakes.

Caution: If you've adjusted the brakes and don't have normal pedal travel, there is probably air in the lines. You'll have to remove the air by bleeding the brakes.

PARKING BRAKE

The parking brake is another part of the drum brake that may need some attention, too. It's often overlooked

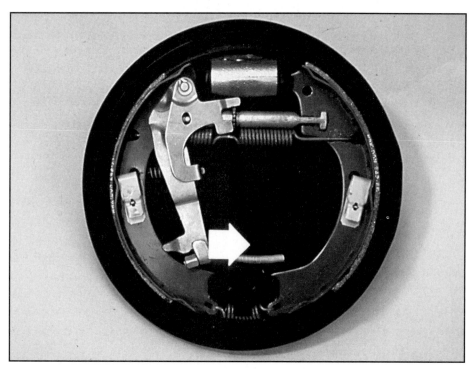

Applying the parking brake moves the linkage as shown to force the shoes out against the drum.

when doing a brake job because it isn't directly involved with normal braking. But it serves two very important purposes: it prevents your vehicle from rolling when parked, and it can also serve as an emergency brake should your hydraulic brakes completely fail.

Because so many vehicles today have automatic transmissions, many people use their parking brake only rarely—if at all. They simply shift the transmission into "Park" to keep the vehicle from rolling. But this practice can lead to trouble because if the parking brake isn't used often enough, it can corrode and stick. On some vehicles, using the parking brake regularly is also necessary to maintain proper adjustment of the rear brakes. So using your parking brake regularly is a good idea.

The parking brake system is pretty simple. On vehicles with drum brakes in the rear, applying the parking brake pulls a pair of cables that are attached to arms on the secondary brake shoes. This forces both pairs of shoes outward against the drums to lock the brakes.

On most vehicles, the left and right parking brake cables come together and are attached to a lever linkage called an "equalizer" yoke under the vehicle. The equalizer yoke balances or equalizes the amount of force that's applied to both cables when the parking brake is applied. The equalizer linkage, in turn, is connected to a single cable that runs to the parking brake lever or pedal. An adjustment screw may be located on the front cable where it connects to the equalizer, or where the cable

attaches to the parking brake lever.

Rust is the main concern with the brake cables and linkage. Rust can cause the cables to bind in their sheaths, preventing the brakes from being applied or released. If one cable freezes up, the equalizer can't do its job so only one wheel will lock. Though this may not create a problem when the parking brake is used for parking, it could create a serious handling problem should the system ever be called upon in an emergency situation. The imbalance would likely cause the one wheel to lock up and skid, possibly throwing your vehicle into a spin.

The equalizer linkage can also rust up, interfering with proper application and release. Or its hinge pivot can sometimes rust or break loose rendering the parking brake useless.

When you're redoing your brakes, therefore, always check the operation of both parking brake cables and the equalizer linkage. Apply the parking brake to see if the linkage is working properly and that the brakes will hold the vehicle. Then check to see that the brakes release fully. If there's any binding and/or corrosion, clean and lubricate the cables (if possible) or replace them. Also lubricate the pivot point on the equalizer linkage. Use a moisture-resistant general purpose grease or brake grease to lubricate the parts—never oil (because it attracts dirt and will soon run off) or a lightweight aerosol lubricant (which is fine for penetrating and loosening things up but doesn't have the staying power of grease).

Semimetallic linings can withstand much higher temperatures than NAO or asbestos linings, hence their widespread use on front wheel drive vehicles. Courtesy Wagner.

When you purchase a set of brake pads or shoes for your car or truck, the person at the parts counter will ask you the year, make and model of your vehicle so he or she can look up the appropriate linings in a catalog. You may then be asked if you want a particular brand or grade (economy, standard or premium) of linings. If you're wise, you'll choose a premium grade lining that gives you the best braking performance. The old saying "You get what you pay for" is especially true with brake linings because cheap linings seldom last or perform as well as premium linings.

CHOOSING A REPLACEMENT LINING

One of the main differences in brake linings today is cost. Because the retail market is so price sensitive, most brake manufacturers offer several different grades of linings in their product mix. The economy, standard and premium grades of linings might be ranked "good, better and best."

Economy grade linings are the lowest priced linings and contain the least expensive ingredients. Consequently, they do not perform or last as long as standard or premium grade linings. Economy grade brake linings are designed for the budget conscious do-it-yourselfer who only wants a "cheap fix" and isn't interested in how long the linings will last or how well they'll perform. Most professional brake technicians would not even consider installing them on a customer's vehicle because they know the customer would not be satisfied with them. The brake manufacturers say all grades of linings, including the economy grades, are safe and meet government regulations. But government regulations only establish "minimum" performance standards. Why settle for less when for a few bucks more you could install a really good set of linings on your vehicle?

Standard grade linings are roughly the equivalent of original equipment linings. They should last and perform about the same as the original brake linings that came on your vehicle—which may or may not be what you're

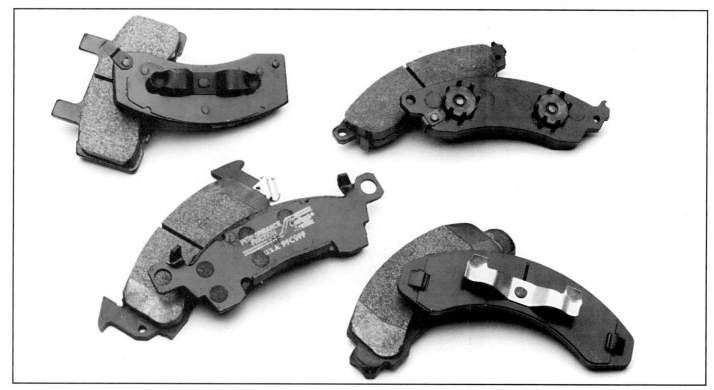

Brake linings come in a variety of materials and in various grades (economy, standard and premium). Buy the best replacement linings you can afford if you're serious about brake safety, performance and longevity.

looking for depending on how they performed. Most OEM brake linings are good quality and have been subjected to extensive testing. Even so, the OEM linings on some vehicles tend to wear quickly and/or be noisy.

Premium grade linings are the most expensive but also contain the best ingredients. These linings are designed to give you the longest life, the quietest operation and the best all-round stopping power. The difference in cost between the premium and standard grades isn't that much, so it usually makes sense to upgrade to the best linings.

Brand Preference

As for the subject of brands, all we can say is that some brand name friction products perform better than others—but not necessarily in all applications. Brand A may have the best set of pads for a late-model 5.0-liter Mustang, but Brand B may have

pads that perform best on a Camaro or Corvette. Friction materials are undergoing constant change, so it's impossible to say any particular brand of lining is better than another all around or even for a specific vehicle application.

The best advice here is to buy brake linings from a brand name supplier you recognize. Many auto parts stores sell private label or "no name" friction products. The linings may be supplied by one or more brand name manufacturers, or they may come from God knows where. The private label or no name linings may be just as good as the more expensive brand name products, or they may not be as good. Considering the fact that your brakes are probably the most important safety item on your vehicle, why takes chances on a white box product when for a few bucks more you can buy quality linings backed by a well-known supplier's reputation?

THE EVOLUTION OF FRICTION MATERIALS

Friction materials have been evolving at an ever-quickening pace in recent years. Up until the 1980s, virtually all brake linings contained asbestos (typically 40 to 60% of the total ingredients in the lining material). As a friction material, asbestos is pretty good stuff. It is relatively cheap compared to other fibers, provides reasonable service life, doesn't chew up rotors or drums, and is fairly quiet. The fibers have a tensile strength equal to that of high grade steel, and can withstand temperatures of up to several hundred degrees. Asbestos comes from the minerals chysotile and amphibole, which is mostly mined in Canada.

The arrival of front-wheel drive in the 1980s and increasing health concerns over exposure to asbestos dust, however, meant new friction materials had to be developed. Front-wheel drive and downsized brake systems required higher temperature linings that could withstand temperatures several times higher than asbestos. Thus, "semimetallic" disc brake pads with their high steel content and ability to absorb and dissipate heat rapidly came into widespread use. Semimetallic linings had been around for some time, but were used primarily in performance applications because they required a lot of pedal effort until they heated up. But today, much improved semimetallic pads are used on almost all front-wheel drive cars and minivans as well as many performance applications.

Asbestos Hazard

Another factor that played a major role in the demise of asbestos was the Environmental Protection Agency's efforts to ban it. Back in 1986, the agency said it wanted to phase out all products (including brake linings) that contained asbestos. The EPA wanted to ban the stuff because asbestos fibers were thought to be a carcinogenic (cancer-causing) material.

Asbestos poses no danger as long as the fibers are encapsulated within the fillers and binders in the brake linings. But as the linings wear, the fibers are exposed, flake loose and become part of the dust that coats brake components. If this dust then gets into the air while you are working on the brakes, the asbestos fibers may pose a potential health risk. The needle-like fibers lodge in the lungs where they remain forever and become an ongoing source of irritation. This leads to scarring of delicate lung tissue, and eventually the development of cancer in many cases.

You can't tell much about what's in a set of linings by their appearance alone. Most linings that contain asbestos are brown to light gray in color, while those that contain non-asbestos organic (NAO) fibers are black. But regardless of what's in the linings, use care when cleaning the brakes to avoid inhaling the dust.

The destructive process can take 15 to 30 years before the damage starts to cause noticeable symptoms.

The Occupational Safety and Health Administration (OSHA) has established exposure limits for professional technicians in the workplace. OSHA also says brakes should be carefully washed with liquid solvent or wetted down with an aerosol cleaner and wiped clean before you work on them because you have no way of knowing if the dust contains asbestos. Washing or wiping off the dust will minimize your exposure to the fibers and hopefully reduce the risk of any long term ill-effects from breathing asbestos fibers.

Warning: Never use an air hose to blow brake dust out of brake drums or off of brake parts. Doing so can blow zillions of microscopic asbestos fibers into the air where they will remain airborne for hours. With just one breath, you can inhale millions of fibers! Eventually the dust will settle throughout your garage, but that doesn't mean the danger has passed because the dust will cling to clothing and form a nearly invisible coating on the floor and exposed surfaces. Every time the dust gets stirred around (by sweeping or vacuuming the floor, using air tools, etc.), the fibers will get airborne again posing an ongoing threat to anyone who might be exposed to them. The only way to get rid of the dust is to wash it away.

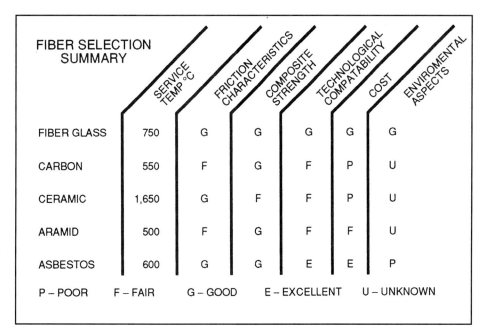

FIBER SELECTION SUMMARY	SERVICE TEMP °C	FRICTION CHARACTERISTICS	COMPOSITE STRENGTH	TECHNOLOGICAL COMPATABILITY	COST	ENVIROMENTAL ASPECTS
FIBER GLASS	750	G	G	G	G	G
CARBON	550	F	G	F	P	U
CERAMIC	1,650	G	F	F	P	U
ARAMID	500	F	G	F	F	U
ASBESTOS	600	G	G	E	E	P
P – POOR   F – FAIR   G – GOOD   E – EXCELLENT   U – UNKNOWN

Comparison of various fibers used in brake linings.

Asbestos Still A Danger—The EPA's proposed ban on asbestos never came to pass because it was overturned in federal court—but not before it set in motion a large scale shift away from asbestos by most friction material suppliers and vehicle manufacturers. New "nonasbestos organic" (NAO) friction materials were introduced to replace asbestos, and were quickly adopted by the vehicle manufacturers. By 1992, asbestos brake linings were no longer being installed on new cars or trucks by the vehicle manufacturers (except for a couple of applications which have since been discontinued).

The status of asbestos today is this: You won't find it on any new vehicles, but it is still available in the aftermarket. Asbestos is found primarily in some economy grade linings, which may or may not be labeled as to their fiber content (which is another good reason why you should avoid "questionable" linings from unknown suppliers). The asbestos linings are marketed as a more economical (cheaper) alternative

to higher priced nonasbestos (NAO) shoes and pads. The linings are primarily for low temperature brake applications such as the rear shoes and front pads on older rear-wheel drive cars and trucks that came originally equipped with asbestos or NAO linings (not semimetallic linings).

Warning: Asbestos should NOT be used to replace semimetallic linings on front-wheel drive applications because asbestos can't take the heat. Rapid lining wear and possible brake fade may occur if asbestos is used in an application that requires semimetallic linings.

The reason why asbestos can't take the heat is because asbestos is an insulator. It inhibits the transfer of heat. Consequently, it does nothing to help cool a disc brake rotor. As the temperature goes up, the coefficient of friction drops and wear accelerates, especially above 350 degrees F. As the linings get hotter, their ability to generate friction begins to drop off and it takes more and more pedal pressure to produce the same amount of stopping power. Eventually the

point is reached where the linings can't take any more heat and the brakes begin to fade. This can be a very unnerving experience if you've ever had it happen because you may not be able to stop your vehicle. Brake fade may occur after a series of rapid stops or as a result of prolonged braking as when driving down a mountain (a good reason not to "ride" the brakes!).

SemiMetallic Linings

Semimetallic friction materials, by comparison, are good conductors of heat and help draw heat away from the rotor. Semimetallic linings can withstand much higher temperatures that would fry asbestos linings. On front-wheel drive vehicles with small solid rotors, front brake temperatures over 400 to 500 degrees are not uncommon—which is beyond the safe working temperature for asbestos or even many NAO linings. So semimetallic linings are typically required and recommended for high heat and high performance applications.

Semimetallic (semi-met) linings use chopped steel wool as their reinforcing fiber and primary ingredient. They can be easily distinguished from asbestos and NAO pads by their appearance (tiny metal fibers and particles) and the fact that a magnet will stick to the linings.

Steel wool makes an excellent reinforcing fiber because it's strong and carries heat. But the high steel content of semimetallic linings also gives them different braking characteristics than asbestos or NAO. For one thing, semimetallic linings are harder, which means more wear on the rotors. Harder pads also tend to be noisier pads, though the use of special surface transfer coatings and integral

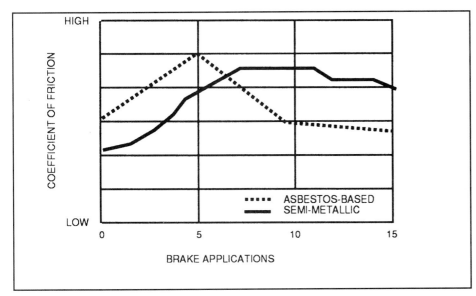

This chart shows how asbestos linings begin to heat fade with repeated brake applications, while semimetallic linings do not.

insulator shims in some pads have all but eliminated this problem. Semimetallic pads may also require more pedal pressure to achieve the same degree of braking friction, especially when cold.

Nonasbestos Organic (NAO) Linings

Nonasbestos organic linings use glass fiber, aramid fiber (such as Kevlar) or other fibers (carbon, ceramic, etc.) for reinforcement. The properties of the NAO lining depend on the type of fiber used as well as the other ingredients. If they contain brass or copper to improve heat management, they may be referred to as "low metallic" linings rather than NAO.

NAO linings are designed primarily as replacements for asbestos lined drum brake shoes. But they are also being used to replace the linings on front disc brake pads that do not use semimetallic linings as original equipment.

Performance-wise, NAO linings are more like asbestos linings than semimetallics. They tend to be poor conductors of heat rather than good conductors like semimetallics. Consequently, they can't handle as high a brake temperature as semimetallics.

The development of NAO brake linings has progressed through many generations of materials. Today's NAO brake lining materials generally outperform asbestos in virtually every aspect, including wear and noise. Many NAO formulas also are easy on drums and rotors causing very little wear.

REPLACEMENT RECOMMENDATIONS

The safest recommendation is to always replace same with same when relining your brakes (except for asbestos). Replace semimetallic pads with semimetallic pads, and NAO shoes or pads with NAO. If you have an older vehicle that has asbestos linings, upgrade to NAO shoes or pads to eliminate the health risks associated with asbestos dust.

Some older rear-wheel drive vehicles (notably '80 and up Chevrolet Chevettes and Citations, and '76 to '79 GM A-bodies such as the Monte Carlo, Grand Prix, Cutlass, etc.), use a "hybrid" combination of semimetallic and asbestos disc brake pads. The inner pads were one type of lining while the outer pads were the other. The recommendation here would be to stick with the original combination.

As for "upgrading" to semimetallic linings from asbestos or NAO, follow the recommendations of the friction material supplier. Semimetallics work best in applications where the brakes run hot, which may include any vehicle used for towing a trailer as well as race cars and off-road applications.

New Application Specific Friction Materials

The aftermarket always follows the original equipment market. Whatever changes the vehicle manufacturers make in friction materials the aftermarket will sooner or later have to match. The latest trend at the OEM level is a proliferation of new "application specific" friction compounds, some of which are semimetallic compounds, some are NAO compounds, and some are "low-metallic" compounds that contain copper and brass instead of chopped steel wool or iron powder to dissipate heat.

New friction materials are being developed and introduced at a much faster pace these days than in the past because the auto makers want to more closely "tune" the performance characteristics of their brake linings to individual vehicles rather than using the same compound for a whole family of vehicles. This has taken on added importance with the arrival of

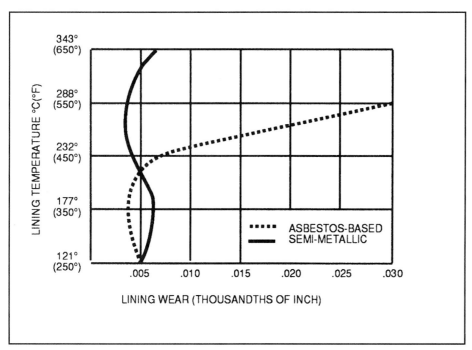

The rate at which a set of brake linings wear depends on temperature. This chart shows how asbestos lining wear goes up sharply above 450 degrees while semimetallics show little change all the way to 650 degrees.

antilock brake systems (ABS), which require very precise and predictable friction characteristics. Consequently, engineers have been tweaking formulas to develop a much broader spectrum of friction products that optimize brake performance, wear and noise.

Aftermarket suppliers who are also OEM friction material suppliers have the upper hand in this game because they've already done their homework for the car makers. So it's easier for them to introduce a new friction material that is "application specific" for a certain vehicle than a supplier who has no OEM experience.

Unfortunately, some aftermarket suppliers don't stay in lock step with every change that takes place at the OEM level. Others could care less because they only cater to the low end of the market where price is all that counts. As a result, the replacement shoes and pads you buy may or may not be the best ones for your vehicle.

This goes back to what we said earlier about buying premium grade linings from a reputable brand name supplier. Cheap linings may not provide the same degree of stopping power, fade resistance or recover as quickly as an application specific friction material.

The use of more and more application specific friction materials has generated a proliferation of new friction formulas. Aftermarket suppliers who used to make only a couple of different semimetallic and NAO friction formulas for all their brake linings now include several dozen different formulas in their product mix, with new ones being added all the time. Engineers are constantly juggling such variables as wear, noise, stopping power and fade resistance to optimize their products. As a result, hundreds of different proprietary friction compounds have been developed—so there's no such thing as a "universal" or "generic" semimetallic or NAO friction

compound. Each is different and each has its own unique properties and advantages.

The ingredients used to make brake linings are a concoction of various binders and fillers with various mineral and synthetic fibers (such as fiberglass, aramid fiber, etc.) added for strength and reinforcement. Brake manufacturers are very secretive when it comes to divulging information about the exact formulations they use, but such ingredients as talc, silica, graphite, shredded rubber (in some bonded shoes) and even crushed walnut shells may be added as fillers and "friction modifiers". Metallic particles (steel, copper or brass) may be added to improve thermal conductivity. Various types of phenolic resins are used like glue to hold the ingredients together, and the resulting friction characteristics, wear resistance, temperature resistance and overall performance of the lining compound will depend on the relative proportions of these ingredients.

Why Matching Is So Important

The friction characteristics of the original equipment brake linings on your vehicle affect the aggressiveness of your brakes, which in turn plays a role in how easily the brakes lock up when braking hard on various kinds of road surfaces. If you install a set of front pads that are more aggressive than the original pads, it could upset the front-to-rear brake balance that was designed into your brake system increasing the danger of the front wheels locking up and skidding in a panic stop situation or when braking on a wet or slick road. Even if your vehicle has ABS, a change in the friction characteristics of the linings may have an adverse effect on the operation of your ABS system. Replacement pads that are less aggressive or have less fade resistance than the original pads, on the other hand, may increase pedal effort as well as stopping distance. Either way, you may be dissatisfied with the results.

That's why aftermarket friction suppliers have been adding all these new compounds to their product lines. By making linings that are more closely the feel and performance of your original linings, most such problems can be avoided.

Unfortunately, most brake pads and shoes look pretty much the same when you open the box. So you can't really tell if the friction material will be a good match for your vehicle or not. You have to assume the friction supplier did their homework and put a material that best suits your needs in the box.

EDGE CODES

One the side of most brake linings is an alphanumeric "edge code" that reveals something about the hot and cold friction characteristics of the friction material. But the markings may or may not be the same as the ones on your old linings. Chances are you can't read the edge codes on your old linings anyway because the linings are too badly worn. It doesn't make much difference, though, because edge codes are relatively meaningless when it comes to comparing friction characteristics. The markings are based on a simple "Chase" test performed with a one-inch square sample of material using a special laboratory procedure. Edge codes alone don't give the whole

picture because the actual performance characteristics of two different friction materials with identical edge code ratings may perform quite differently when installed on your vehicle.

Brake suppliers have been struggling with this issue for a long time, and have tried to come up with a better system for comparing friction materials. The Society of Automotive Engineers (SAE) has developed a new dyno test procedure (J1652) that correlates friction performance for front disc brake pads, and a similar test (J1653) for rear brake shoes. But the new rating system has yet to be adopted for various reasons (namely lack of acceptance among certain brake suppliers whose products may not compare favorably!).

The National Highway Traffic Safety Administration (NHTSA) has tested aftermarket brake linings and found that most friction materials are

acceptable regardless of how they are marked. Brake linings on all new vehicles must pass a federal performance test (FMVSS135) that requires burnished brakes to bring a vehicle to a halt within 204 feet from 60 mph. But there are no comparable standards for aftermarket linings, nor are there any government requirements that aftermarket linings must be equivalent to the OEM linings they replace—which is yet another reason why you should avoid buying cheap linings for your vehicle.

If your vehicle has ABS, which is particularly sensitive to any changes in friction characteristics, you should try to find linings from a supplier who offers application specific replacement linings.

How do you know if you're getting an application specific friction material in a set of brake pads or shoes? Read the box or the supplier's literature. If the supplier says the

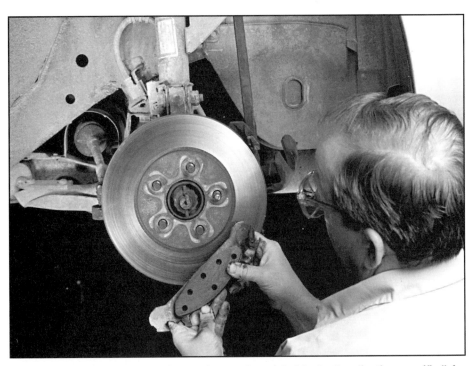

Most premium grade brake linings today are formulated to be "application specific," for optimum brake performance. This is done by "tweaking" the ingredients in the lining formula to more closely match the braking requirements of the vehicle. Courtesy Wagner.

linings are application specific, then you must assume they're telling the truth. However, if there's no mention of being application specific, the linings may or may not be a close match.

BREAKING IN NEW LININGS

When brake linings are manufactured, some friction materials receive more "curing" than others, which affects how quickly they break-in once they're installed on your vehicle. The more time they spend in the curing oven at the factory, the less amount of postcure that's needed to break them in.

Always follow the suppliers directions for breaking in a new set of pads or shoes. As a rule, you should avoid heavy braking or panic stops for the first 150 to 200 miles of driving. In other words, take it easy until the linings are fully postcured. If you don't you may end up with problems such as glazing, squealing and a hard pedal.

Hard braking right after installation should be avoided because it may glaze new pads. This is because semimetallics are relatively high in resin content and the resin tends to flow out of the material if the pads are overheated. Average semimetallic brake temperatures are in the neighborhood of 350 degrees, and heavy braking can heat the brakes to 500 degrees or higher.

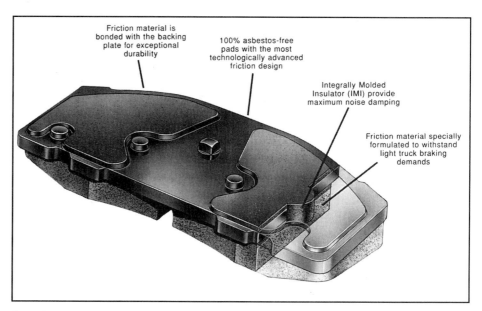

Friction material is bonded with the backing plate for exceptional durability

100% asbestos-free pads with the most technologically advanced friction design

Integrally Molded Insulator (IMI) provide maximum noise damping

Friction material specially formulated to withstand light truck braking demands

Some brake pads now have integrally molded insulators inside to dampen noise. Courtesy Wagner.

Semimetallic Pads

Semimetallic pads can ordinarily handle such temperatures with no difficulty once they're fully seated. But right after installation the pads will be riding on the high spots, which can cause localized overheating and glazing.

The best way to break in new semimetallic pads is to make 15 to 20 gradual stops from about 30 mph using light to moderate brake pedal pressure. About 30 seconds should be allowed between stops for brake recovery.

If you experience increased brake effort after replacing semimetallic pads on a car originally equipped with the same, it may mean the rotors were not refinished properly (or not at all!), or you didn't give the pads enough

time to break in. Either way, you get to do the job over again—so make sure you do it right the first time.

If the brakes are noisy (and weren't before), it means one of two things: either the rotors were not finished smoothly enough and/or the pads are loose. Noise problems can be minimized by lightly sanding the rotors with #120 or #150 grit sandpaper after they've been turned to create a non-directional swirl finish, and/or using insulating shims, a noise control compound or brake grease on the backs of the pads to dampen vibrations. It's also very important than any clips or anti-rattle springs that go on the pads be properly installed to eliminate play that could contribute to vibration and noise.

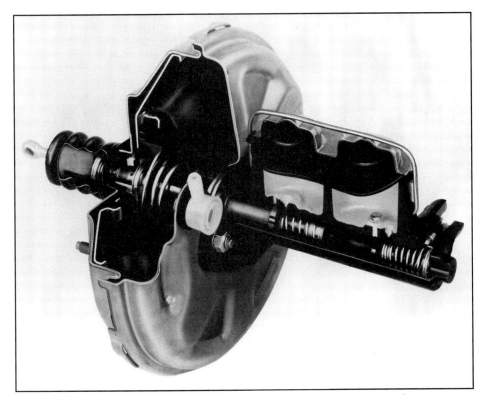

Power brakes have become standard on most vehicles today because disc brakes require more pedal effort than drum brakes.

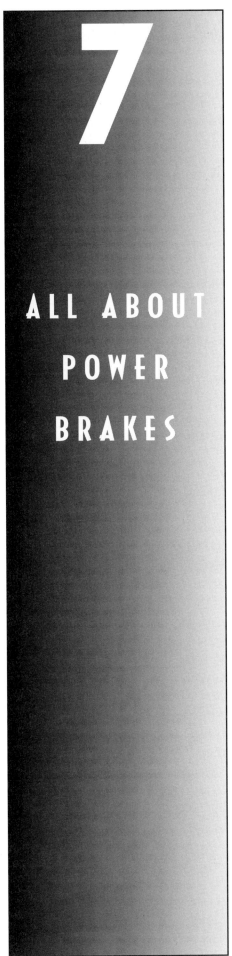

Power brakes assist normal braking by boosting or multiplying the effort applied to the brake pedal by the driver's foot. The amount of force multiplication depends on the application, but can be double or even triple the force applied at the brake pedal. The net result is reduced pedal effort for easier braking.

As mentioned in the introduction of this book, power brakes have become standard equipment on most vehicles today partly because of disc brakes (which require more pedal effort than drum brakes because they lack a self-servo effect), and because the motoring public has come to expect "feather-touch" braking. Power brakes do not decrease a vehicle's stopping distance nor do they have anything to do with antilock braking. Their sole function is to reduce pedal effort.

There are essentially three types of power brakes: vacuum assist, Hydro-Boost and electrohydraulic.

VACUUM ASSIST

Vacuum is good for a lot of things, like sucking gas through a carburetor, opening and closing airflow doors in your climate control system, and for providing extra muscle for braking. But to assist braking, it takes a lot of vacuum.

How can something take a lot of nothing? After all, vacuum is the absence of atmospheric pressure. The answer is the higher the vacuum, the greater the atmospheric push to fill the void. As some famous scientist once said, "Nature abhors a vacuum." What he meant was as soon as you punch a hole in the air (create a vacuum), the surrounding air tries to rush right in to fill it back up. So the push that a vacuum brake booster gives to the master cylinder is actually atmospheric air pressure.

At sea level, air pressure is 14.7 lb. per square inch, which equals about 30 inches of vacuum on a gauge. The average engine can't pull that much

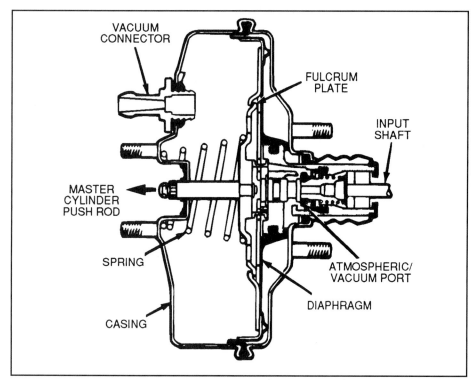

Typical vacuum booster assembly. Courtesy Ford.

vacuum, so the most intake vacuum you're going to read is about 20 to 22 inches. Most engines pull a steady 16 to 20 inches of vacuum at idle. One exception is a diesel, which has no throttle to create a restriction and thus no intake vacuum. So diesels have to use an auxiliary vacuum pump if they have a vacuum brake booster.

How the brake booster uses vacuum to provide power assist is amazingly simple. The original "Master-Vac" power brake booster that became the predecessor to virtually all vacuum boosters today was patented back in the 1950s by Bendix. The booster housing is divided into two chambers by a flexible diaphragm. A vacuum hose from the intake manifold on the engine pulls air from both sides of the diaphragm when the engine is running. When the driver steps on the brake pedal, the input rod assembly in the booster moves forward. This blocks off the vacuum port to the backside of the diaphragm and opens

an atmospheric port that allows air to enter the back chamber. Suddenly, the diaphragm has vacuum pulling against one side and air pressure

pushing on the other. The result is a forward push that helps shove the push rod into the master cylinder for power assist.

The amount of power assist that's actually provided by the booster depends on two things: the size of the diaphragm and the amount of intake manifold vacuum produced by the engine. The larger the diaphragm, the greater the boost. An 8-inch booster with 20 inches of engine vacuum will provide about 240 lb. of brake assist—which is roughly double the input force. A 10-inch booster can triple the applied brake force.

Vacuum Booster Troubleshooting

From this, it should be obvious that the vacuum booster needs two things to do its job: a good vacuum supply from the engine, and a good diaphragm. A vacuum supply hose that's loose, leaky, collapsed or

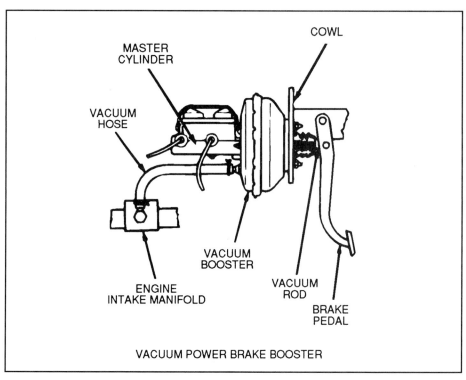

VACUUM POWER BRAKE BOOSTER

Vacuum is supplied to the power brake booster by a hose that connects to the intake manifold on the engine. Courtesy Brake Parts, Inc.

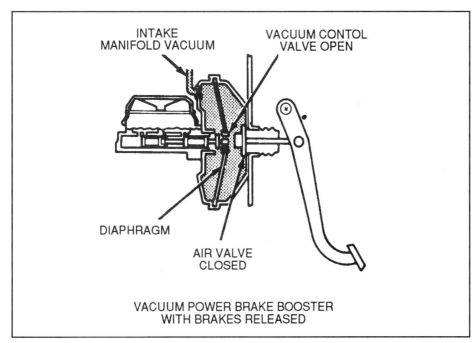

When the brakes are not being applied, the vacuum control valve inside the booster is open and the air valve is closed. Courtesy Brake Parts, Inc.

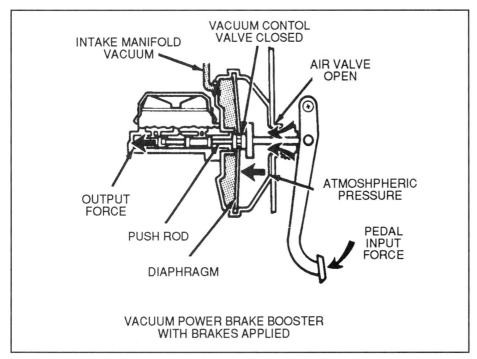

When the brake pedal is depressed, the vacuum control valve is closed and the air valve opens so atmospheric pressure can push against the diaphragm to boost pedal effort. Courtesy Brake Parts, Inc.

restricted may not allow the booster to receive enough vacuum to provide the usual amount of power assist. Consequently, it takes more pedal effort to get the same braking as before.

A restricted vacuum hose will cause boost to drop off when the brakes are applied in rapid succession. This happens because the blockage slows the return of vacuum in the booster.

To check engine vacuum, connect a vacuum gauge to the supply hose that runs from the intake manifold to the booster. A low reading (below 16 inches) may indicate a hose leak or obstruction, a blockage in the exhaust system (plugged catalytic converter, crushed pipe, bad muffler, etc.), or a problem in the engine itself (manifold vacuum leak, bad valve, head gasket, etc.).

The condition of the diaphragm inside the booster is also important. If cracked, ruptured or leaking, it won't hold vacuum and can't provide much power assist. Leaks in the master cylinder can allow brake fluid to be siphoned into the booster, accelerating the demise of the diaphragm. So if you find brake fluid inside the vacuum hose, it's a good indication your master cylinder is leaking and needs to be rebuilt or replaced. Wetness around the back of the master cylinder would be another clue to this kind of problem.

To check the vacuum booster, pump the brake pedal with the engine off until you've bled off all the vacuum from the unit. Then hold the pedal down and start the engine. You should feel the pedal depress slightly as engine vacuum enters the booster and pulls on the diaphragm. No change? Then check the vacuum hose connection and engine vacuum. If okay, the problem is in the booster and the booster needs to be replaced.

Vacuum boosters also have an external one-way check valve at the hose inlet or in the inlet hose itself that closes when the engine is either shut off or stalls. This traps vacuum inside the booster so it can still provide one or two power assisted stops until the engine is restarted. The valve also helps maintain vacuum when intake vacuum is low (when the

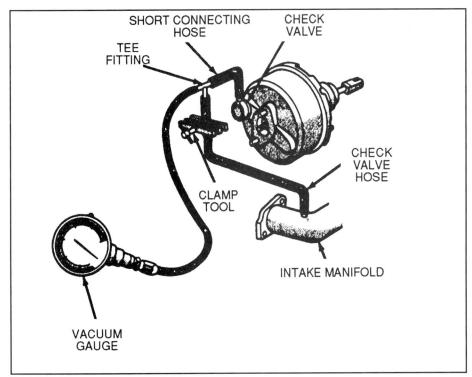

Loss of power assist can be caused by vacuum leaks inside or outside the booster. So one of the first things that needs to be checked if you suspect a booster problem is the booster's vacuum supply. Connecting a vacuum gauge to the booster supply hose will tell if there's sufficient vacuum to operate the booster. Courtesy Chrysler.

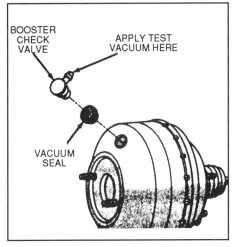

The booster check valve is supposed to hold vacuum in the booster. The valve is replaceable on most boosters. Courtesy Chrysler.

If you have to replace a bad vacuum booster, a remanufactured unit will save you money compared to a new one. Courtesy Raybestos.

engine is under load or is running at wide open throttle). You can check the valve by removing it and trying to blow through it from both sides. It should pass air from the rear but not from the front.

Replacing a vacuum booster is a fairly straightforward job, though not necessarily easy depending on how buried the booster is in your engine compartment. All you have to do is disconnect it from the brake pedal on the inside and unbolt the master cylinder. The pushrod that runs from the booster into the back of the master cylinder must have the specified amount of play, so check a service manual for the particulars. Most require a small amount of play so the master cylinder will release fully preventing brake drag, but some late model GM and Bendix applications have zero play.

HYDRO-BOOST

Though not as common as vacuum booster power brake systems, the Bendix "Hydro-Boost" system dates back to 1973. The system uses hydraulic pressure generated by the power steering pump rather than engine vacuum to provide power assist.

Inside the Hydro-Boost unit, which fits between the master cylinder and brake pedal the same as a vacuum

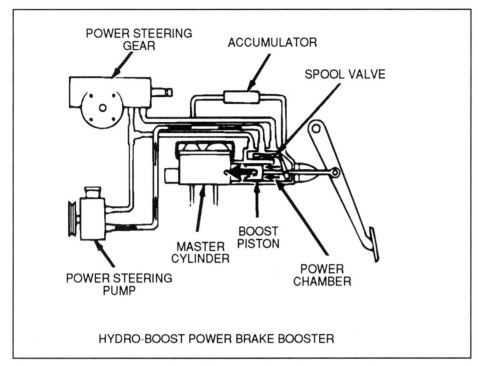

POWER STEERING GEAR

ACCUMULATOR

SPOOL VALVE

POWER STEERING PUMP

MASTER CYLINDER

BOOST PISTON

POWER CHAMBER

HYDRO-BOOST POWER BRAKE BOOSTER

Hydro-Boost power brakes use hydraulic pressure from the power steering pump to assist braking, and can generate more force than vacuum-assisted systems. Courtesy Bendix.

booster, is a spool valve and piston assembly. When the driver steps on the brake pedal, the pushrod slides forward and changes the position of the spool valve. This opens a valve port that routes power steering fluid into the cavity behind the piston to push it forward and apply the brakes.

Another component in the Hydro-Boost system is a pressure "accumulator." Some are nitrogen pressurized while others are spring loaded depending on the application. The accumulator's job is to store pressure as an emergency backup in case pressure is lost (engine stalls or

power steering pump drive belt breaks). There's usually enough reserve pressure in the accumulator for 1 to 3 power assisted stops (which is 1 to 3 more power assisted stops than you'd get with a vacuum booster if the engine stalled).

Troubleshooting Hydro-Boost

Problems with a Hydro-Boost system can be caused by spool valve or piston wear inside the Hydro-Boost unit, fluid leaks or loss of pressure (worn pump, slipping pump belt, etc.).

A simple way to test the Hydro-Boost system is to pump the brakes five or six times with the engine off to discharge the accumulator. Then press down hard on the pedal (about 40 lb. of force) and start the engine. Like a vacuum booster, you should feel the pedal fall slightly when the engine starts, then rise.

The leak down of the accumulator can be checked by pumping the brakes several times while the engine is running, then shutting it off. Let your vehicle sit for about an hour, then try the brakes without starting the engine. You should get 2 or 3 soft brake applications before it takes more effort to push the pedal.

Slow brake pedal return may be caused by excessive seal friction in the booster, faulty spool action or a restriction in the return line to the pump. Grabby brakes are probably the result of contamination in the system or a broken spool return spring. If the brakes tend to goon by themselves, you've probably got a case of restricted return flow or a defunct dump valve. Excessive pedal effort can usually be attributed to internal leakage or the seeping of fluid past the accumulator/booster seal.

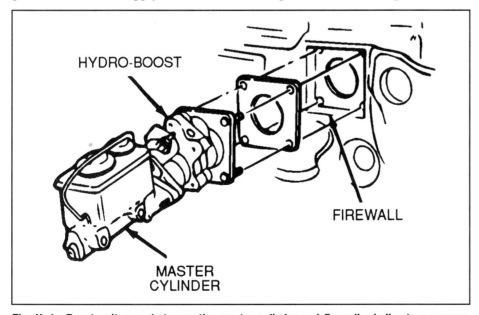

HYDRO-BOOST

MASTER CYLINDER

FIREWALL

The Hydro-Boost unit goes between the master cylinder and firewall, similar to a vacuum booster. Courtesy Bendix.

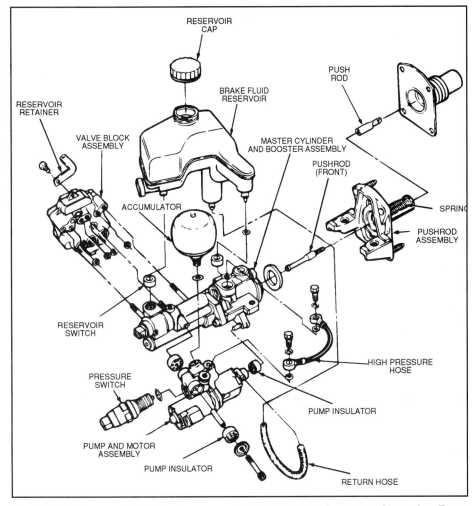

RESERVOIR CAP

BRAKE FLUID RESERVOIR

RESERVOIR RETAINER

VALVE BLOCK ASSEMBLY

MASTER CYLINDER AND BOOSTER ASSEMBLY

ACCUMULATOR

PUSH ROD

PUSHROD (FRONT)

SPRING

PUSHROD ASSEMBLY

RESERVOIR SWITCH

HIGH PRESSURE HOSE

PRESSURE SWITCH

PUMP INSULATOR

PUMP AND MOTOR ASSEMBLY

PUMP INSULATOR

RETURN HOSE

Electrohydraulic power brake boosters are used with integral ABS systems. Shown is a Teves Mark 2 system. Boost pressure is created by a pump motor and stored in a high pressure accumulator. When the brake pedal is depressed, pressure from the accumulator assists braking. Courtesy Teves.

If a problem turns out to be in the booster itself, you'll have to replace it.

Caution: Depressurize the accumulator by pumping the brake pedal half a dozen times before you open up any plumbing connections, or else you might get blasted by high pressure brake fluid.

ELECTROHYDRAULIC POWER ASSIST

On vehicles with integral antilock brake systems where the master cylinder is part of the hydraulic control assembly (Teves Mark 2 ABS, Bosch III ABS, Delco Powermaster 3 ABS, Bendix 10 and Jeep ABS), an electric pump with a nitrogen pressurized accumulator is used to provide power assist.

With these systems, power assist is provided by pressure stored in the accumulator. We're talking LOTS of pressure here, from 675 up to 2600 psi depending on the system and application. When the driver steps on the brake pedal and the pushrod moves forward, it opens a valve inside the master cylinder that allows stored pressure from the accumulator to enter a cavity behind the piston assembly. This pushes the piston forward and applies the brakes.

A pressure switch on the master cylinder monitors the stored pressure in the accumulator, and closes a switch to turn on the electric pump when pressure drops below a preset minimum. It then turns the pump off when pressure is back up to where it should be.

Troubleshooting

Problems with an electrohydraulic power assist system will usually be due to a bad pump motor, a leaky accumulator, or internal problems in the master cylinder assembly. Because it's all part of the ABS system, electrical problems with the pump motor or pressure switch as well as low fluid level or low pressure will usually trigger a fault code and activate the ABS warning light. To find out what's wrong, you'll have to hook up a scan tool or use the appropriate diagnostic procedure to pull out the trouble codes. Accurate diagnosis here requires referral to the applicable shop manual.

The electric pump and accumulator can usually be replaced separately if there's a problem, but the master cylinder and hydraulic control unit are replaced as an assembly (which is very expensive!).

Caution: As with Hydro-Boost systems, you must always depressurize the accumulator before working on any part of the brake system or opening up any plumbing. On these applications, the pedal needs to be pumped 30 to 40 times with the engine off (or until an increase in pedal effort is clearly felt) to bleed off all the pressure from the accumulator. Once the accumulator has been fully depressurized, it's safe to open up the hydraulic lines for repairs.

Troubleshooting common brake problems almost always requires inspecting the brakes.

There comes a time in the life of every vehicle when the brakes need attention. Brakes are a wear item so eventually the linings wear out. But sometimes other things go wrong with the brakes, which means you have to troubleshoot the system to figure out what needs fixing. So let's proceed to some common and some not-so-common problems you're apt to encounter.

Brake Warning Light

If the light is on all the time, it could mean you simply forgot to release the parking (emergency) brake. The brake warning light remains on when the brake is set as a reminder. But if the light stays on when you release the parking brake, you've got a problem.

In some cases, the brake warning light may remain on if the switch on the parking brake pedal or lever is misadjusted or sticking. Nothing is wrong with the brakes and a simple adjustment is all that's needed to solve the problem.

A light that remains on, or comes on when you apply the brakes, though, usually means low brake fluid and/or a loss of hydraulic pressure in one side of the brake system. In either case, the fluid level in the master cylinder should be checked. Adding brake fluid to the master cylinder reservoir may temporarily solve your problem. But if there's a leak in the system, the new fluid will soon be lost and the warning light will come back on.

Brake fluid leaks are serious because they may cause the brakes to fail! So don't drive your vehicle until the problem has been identified and fixed. Leaks can occur in brake hoses, brake lines, disc brake calipers, drum brake wheel cylinders or the master cylinder itself. Wet spots at hose or line connections would indicate fluid leakage and a need for repairs.

Leaking brake fluid can contaminate the brake linings, causing them to slip or grab. The uneven braking action that results may cause the vehicle to veer to one side when the brakes are applied. Brake shoes or

SYMPTOMS	LOW FLUID LEVEL	AIR IN HYDRAULIC SYSTEM	BRAKES NEED ADJUSTMENT	BRAKE FADE DUE TO OVERHEATING	GREASE OR FLUID ON LININGS	LININGS GLAZED	WET BRAKES	FAULTY VACUUM BOOSTER	LINKAGE BINDING	WEAK FLEXIBLE HOSES	LOOSE OR WORN WHEEL BEARINGS	LOOSE OR WORN FRONT END PARTS	FRONT WHEELS OUT OF ALIGNMENT	LOOSE DISC BRAKE CALIPER	WARPED BRAKE DISC	ECCENTRIC BRAKE DRUM	FAULTY WHEEL CYLINDER	FAULTY MASTER CYLINDER	WEAK OR BROKEN RETRACTING SPRINGS	SCORED BRAKE DRUMS	DIRT IN BRAKE MECHANISM	CLOGGED OR KINKED BRAKE LINES
PLAY IN PEDAL	●	●	●						●								●	●				
HARD PEDAL				●	●	●	●	●	●								●	●				●
SPONGY PEDAL	●	●							●													
PEDAL SINKS TO FLOOR	●																●	●				
PEDAL VIBRATES		●									●	●			●	●						
BRAKES GRAB					●															●		
BRAKES DRAG			●						●										●	●		●
BRAKES PULL			●		●		●				●	●	●	●		●				●		●
ERRATIC BRAKING			●		●						●	●		●	●	●				●		
SQUEAL OR CHATTER			●			●									●	●					●	

Brake troubleshooting chart.

pads that have been contaminated with brake fluid cannot be dried out and must be replaced.

ABS Warning Light

If your car or truck is equipped with antilock brakes (ABS), a second warning light is usually provided to warn you if a problem occurs in your ABS system. The ABS lamp comes on when the ignition is turned on for a bulb check, and should go out after the engine starts. If the ABS warning light remains on or comes on while driving, it indicates a fault has occurred in the ABS system.

What happens next depends on the nature of the fault. On most applications, the ABS system disables itself if the ABS warning light comes on and remains on. This should have no effect on normal braking. But it also means your ABS will NOT be available in an emergency situation or when braking on a wet or slick surface.

CAUTION: If the brake warning light also comes on and remains on while the ABS warning light is on, it signals a serious problem. Your vehicle may not be safe to drive. The brakes and ABS system should be inspected immediately to determine the nature of the problem!

If the ABS light comes on momentarily then goes out, the nature of the problem is probably minor and the ABS system will usually remain fully operational. Some vehicle manufacturers call this kind of fault a "nonlatching" fault (meaning it isn't serious enough to disable the ABS system).

Regardless of the type of fault that occurred to trigger the ABS warning lamp, a special "code" is recorded in the ABS module's memory to aid in diagnosing the problem. On some vehicles this code can be retrieved by putting the ABS system into a special diagnostic mode. The code is then flashed out through the ABS warning lamp. The code number refers to a diagnostic chart in a service manual that must be followed to pinpoint the faulty component. On other applications, a scan tool must be plugged into the vehicle's diagnostic connector to read out fault codes.

Diagnosing ABS problems requires a fair amount of knowledge and expertise (as well as special equipment in many applications), so this job may be better left to a competent professional.

Disc Brake Squeal

High pitched squeals can be very irritating but do not usually mean anything is wrong with your brakes. Even so, you should always investigate a noise problem to determine what's causing it.

Squeals are usually caused by vibrations between disc brake pads, caliper and rotor. The intensity of the squeal depends on the hardness of the brake linings (semimetallic pads in front-wheel drive cars are the worst offenders), the rigidity of the caliper mounting, rotor finish and vehicle speed. Possible causes include:

• *Glazed Brake Pads*—When pads become glazed (very smooth and glassy), they tend to squeal. Replacing the pads may temporarily eliminate

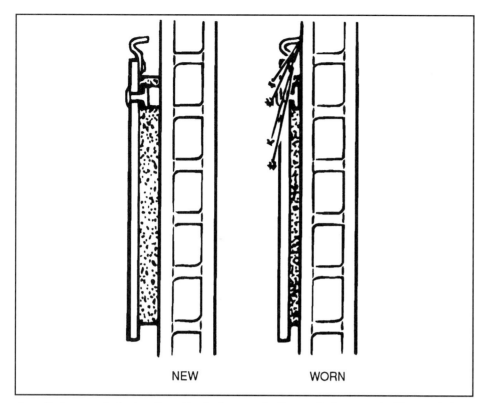

NEW   WORN

Squealing or scraping noises from disc brakes may be the result of worn pads. Many pads have wear indicators that make noise when the pads wear down and allow the indicators to make contact with the rotor. Don't ignore such a warning because worn pads (and sometimes the wear indicators themselves) can score the rotors. Courtesy Brake Parts, Inc.

the noise, but unless the underlying problem that caused the pads to glaze in the first place is diagnosed and corrected, the noise will likely return.

The most common cause of pad glazing is overheating, which may be the result of brake drag caused by a sticky caliper or a problem in the hydraulic system (such as a restriction in a brake line that prevents the brakes from releasing fully, or a misadjusted stop light switch that is creating residual pressure in the master cylinder). A sticky or frozen caliper will often cause the pads to wear unevenly depending on the design of the brake system. If the inside pad is worn more than the outside pad on a single piston floating caliper, for example, it would tell you the caliper is hanging up and needs attention. To prevent this kind of problem, make sure the caliper slides and bushings

are clean, rust-free and properly lubricated with high temperature brake grease.

• *Missing Insulator Shims*—Many disc brakes have shims on the backs of the pads to dampen vibrations. If someone else relined your brakes and forgot to install the required shims, the pads may be noisy. You can buy replacement shims if the shims are missing, or apply a noise control compound or brake grease to the backs of the pads (never the front!) to help cushion the pads and dampen vibrations between the pads and calipers.

• *Worn Disc Brake Hardware*—The mounting hardware (springs, shims, keyways, clips, pins, bushings, etc.) that align the caliper and pads with the rotor may become worn and

loose with age. This can lead to improper alignment and noise. Misalignment can also cause hot spots and glazing. The cure here is to replace the worn hardware.

• *Outboard Pad Looseness*—Many outboard disc brake pads are held in place by retaining ears built into the steel backing plate. These ears must be tight and secure to prevent the pad from moving and becoming improperly aligned. If the pad is loose and making noise, bend the ears so the pad will be held securely.

• *Wear Indicators Touching the Rotor Surface*—Many disc brake pads have small wear indicator tabs. The tabs produce a loud squealing noise when the pads wear down and the tab starts to rub against the rotor. This is your clue that it's time to replace the pads. Don't ignore the warning because if you wait too long, you may chew up your rotors.

• *Rough Rotor Finish*—If the rotors are too rough, the pads will chatter and squeal. Resurfacing the rotors to restore a like-new finish may be all that's needed to eliminate the noise. But if your vehicle has semimetallic disc brake pads, sanding the rotors with #120 or #150 grit sandpaper after they've been turned to produce a smooth nondirectional swirl finish is a good idea to assure quiet braking.

Scraping Noises From the Brakes

Metallic scraping noises usually mean repairs are needed. Possible causes of this kind of noise include:

• *Worn Pads or Shoes*—If riveted pads or shoes are worn down to the

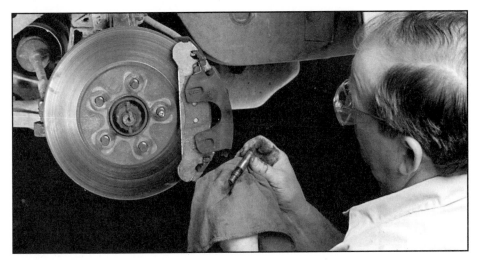

Uneven pad wear can be caused by rusted or corroded caliper bushings, pins or slides. These parts need to be carefully inspected, cleaned and lubricated with brake grease to assure proper operation.

rivet heads, or if bonded pads or shoes are worn down to the backing plates, the metal-to-metal contact that results with the rotor or drum will produce a metallic scraping or grinding noise when the brakes are applied. Not only does this create an unsafe braking condition, but it can be very damaging to rotors and drums. In addition to replacing the worn linings, it will probably be necessary to resurface or replace the rotors and/or drums.

• *Improper Caliper Alignment*—If the caliper is misaligned with respect to the rotor and spindle, you may hear metallic scraping sounds. The cure is to realign the caliper by installing new disc brake hardware. Anything that is damaged or worn should be replaced. If the caliper itself has broken mounting ears or badly corroded or worn guides, then it will have to be replaced.

• *Rust or Mud on Caliper Housing or Rotor Edge*—Inspect the brake components and remove any debris or buildup of rust that's found. The caliper and/or rotor may have to be replaced if rusted to the point where it

interferes with proper operation.

• *Loose or Broken Drum Hardware, or Debris Inside the Drum*—Loose "junk" inside the drum will rattle and scrape as the drum turns, and may even wedge itself between the shoes and drum causing the brake to bind. If you hear noise from the vicinity of the drum, therefore, you'll have to pull the drum to investigate.

• *Loose or Worn Wheel Bearings*—This may also be accompanied by steering looseness or wander. **Warning:** Do not ignore noisy wheel bearings. Noise indicates roughness or damage that may cause sudden failure of the bearings and loss of a wheel!

Raise the wheel off the ground and feel for roughness as you turn it by hand. Also, try to wobble the wheel back and forth to feel for looseness. The only way to be absolutely sure, though, is to remove and inspect the wheel bearings, then replace or clean and repack them as needed. You can't do this with sealed wheel bearings, so if there's any play or roughness, the bearing assembly or hub needs to be

replaced.

Disc Brake Rattle

A rattle that's heard at low to moderate speed, usually when encountering bumps, may be caused by the following:

• *Antirattle Springs or Clips Missing or Installed Improperly*—Replace the antirattle springs or hardware and make sure the pads are positioned properly.

• *Clearance Problem Between Pads and Rotor*—Pads that are not the proper thickness for the application may cause a noise problem. The cure is to replace them with ones that are right for the application.

• *Frozen Caliper*—If a floating caliper is hung up and cannot center itself over the rotor, it may produce a rattling noise when the brakes are applied. Remove the caliper, clean and lubricate all moving surfaces, and replace the slides or bushings.

• *Improper Rotor Finish*—Disc brake chatter can be caused by rotors that have been improperly finished. A brake lathe cuts grooves in a rotor that resemble the grooves in a phonograph record. If the ridges are too pronounced, they'll grab the pads and make them chatter up and down whenever the brakes are applied. The cure here is to have the rotors refinished.

Pedal Vibrates

A pulsating brake pedal, which may be accompanied by a shuddering or jerky stop usually means you have warped rotors or out-of-round drums. But the same symptom can sometimes be caused by loose wheel bearings, a bent axle shaft or loose brake parts.

The faces of a rotor must be parallel (within .0005 inch on most vehicles) and flat (no more than about .002 to .005 inches of runout) otherwise you may feel a pulsation in the brake pedal when you step on the brakes.

You can usually spot a warped rotor by the telltale glazed or discolored patches on its faces. Resurfacing the rotor to restore the faces will usually eliminate the pulsation, but hard spots often return so you may have to replace the rotors to get rid of the problem permanently. If a rotor is bent, replacement is your only option.

Warped rotors can be caused by dragging brakes, overheating and/or unevenly tightening the lug nuts—which is why you should always use a torque wrench, not a four-way lug or an impact wrench to final tighten the lug nuts.

A drum can sometimes be warped out-of-round by applying the parking brake when the brakes are hot. As the drum cools, the force of the shoes causes it to distort out of shape.

Erratic Braking

A catchall phrase that covers a lot of territory, erratic (not "erotic") braking generally means uneven brake action. It can also encompass grabbing, pulsating and pulling. Contaminated brake linings (brake fluid or grease), misadjusted drum brakes, loose or binding calipers, a faulty metering or proportioning valve, mismatched brake linings (a higher friction lining or different material on one wheel or one side), restricted brake lines, loose front end parts or wheel bearings, or even mismatched tire inflation pressures may make your brakes behave strangely.

Pulling

Pulling to one side when the brakes are applied signals uneven braking action. This happens when the brakes on one side are not working as well as those on the opposite side. The vehicle pulls towards the side that creates the most friction. Oil or grease contaminated linings on one side, misadjusted brakes, a bad wheel cylinder or caliper, a dragging brake, even loose wheel bearings, front end parts or underinflated tires can cause a brake pull.

Grabbing

Oil, grease or brake fluid contaminated linings are the most frequent cause of brake grab followed by scored drums or rotors. A loose caliper can also interfere with smooth braking.

Oil can come from a leaky rear axle seal and grease from a leaky wheel bearing seal. Never reuse an old seal when repacking or replacing wheel bearings.

Dragging

A hot wheel, a sudden appetite for brake linings and/or a drop in fuel economy are all symptoms of brake dragging. Age and corrosion are two factors that can bring about dragging so check for things like weak or broken retracting springs on drum brakes, a frozen or corroded caliper piston, a floating caliper that has ceased to float because the mounting pins or bushings are corroded tight (uneven wear between the inner and outer pads is a dead giveaway to this problem), overextended drum brake self-adjusters, an emergency brake cable that fails to fully release, or a defective quick take-up valve in the master cylinder on a late model GM product.

An over adjusted stop light switch can sometimes prevent the brake pedal from coming all the way out which leaves a residual pressure in the system and causes the brakes to drag. On a diagonally split hydraulic system, the right front caliper is frequently the one that drags. The left rear drum brake has retracting springs to resist the residual pressure but there's nothing to prevent the caliper piston from pushing out.

Glazed brake linings can increase pedal effort and stopping distance. Glazing is usually the result of improper break-in of new linings or overheating.

Erratic or uneven braking can be caused by fluid or grease on the linings. The wheel cylinder on this drum brake was leaking badly (the dust boot was completely gone!), allowing fluid to drip onto the linings.

Low Pedal

A low brake pedal that has to be pumped repeatedly to bring a vehicle to a stop may be due to a low fluid level, drum brakes that need adjustment or air in the lines.

The first thing you should check is the fluid level in the master cylinder reservoir. If the level is low, there's a leak somewhere in the brake hydraulics that must be found and repaired. Adding fluid will only cure the symptom, not the cause, and sooner or later the level will be low again creating a dangerous situation. So check for leaks around the master cylinder, wheel cylinders, brake calipers, rubber brake hoses and steel brake lines.

If the fluid level is okay, check the adjustment of the rear brakes (assuming the car is a late model with discs up front and drums in the rear—if it has drums all the way around, check the front ones first). The shoes should be close enough to the drums to produce just a hint of drag when the wheels are rotated by hand. An excess of slack probably means the self-adjusters are either frozen or fully extended. Refer to a shop manual for the brake adjustment procedure on your vehicle. If adjusting the drum brakes fails to eliminate the low pedal, you'll have to pull the wheel and drum to free-up or replace the adjusters and/or replace the worn brake shoes.

If the fluid reservoir is full and the brakes are properly adjusted but the pedal is low (or feels spongy), there is probably air in the brake lines. Air is compressible, so every time you step on the pedal, the bubbles collapse instead of transferring pressure to the brakes. The cure here is to "bleed" the brake lines.

Bleeding the brakes involves flushing the lines with fresh hydraulic fluid (see Chapter 3). The basic procedure for bleeding brakes is to start at the wheel furthest from the master cylinder. You'll need a piece of clear plastic tubing about 18 inches long. One end of the tubing should fit tightly over the small bleeder screw on the back of the wheel cylinder or brake caliper. The other end should be inserted into a clear glass or plastic container. Loosen the bleeder valve on the wheel to be bled, then slowly push the brake pedal all the way to the floor to force fluid through the line. Release the pedal slowly, wait a few seconds, then repeat until clean, clear fluid and no bubbles are visible in the clear plastic tubing. Retighten the bleeder screw, remove the plastic tubing and proceed to the next wheel. Make sure you add fresh fluid to the master cylinder while bleeding the brakes so the fluid reservoir doesn't get too low and allow air to be pumped into the lines.

Normally you bleed the rear brakes first and then the front—except on front-wheel drive cars with diagonally split hydraulic systems. On these vehicles, you bleed opposing wheel pairs doing the right rear and left front pair first followed by the left rear and right front brakes. On late model GM cars, the quick take-up valve in the master cylinder takes about 15 seconds to reseat between pumps. Pump it too quickly while bleeding the system and you won't get any pedal. If pressure bleeding, remember to open the metering valve otherwise you won't get all the air out of the front brake lines. Refer to a shop manual for the specific brake bleeding procedure for your vehicle.

Spongy Pedal

A brake pedal should be firm with a predictable amount of resistance. But when it feels squishy you can bet there's probably air in the lines and a leak somewhere. Fixing the leaks and bleeding the system should eliminate the soft pedal. Sometimes, however, the cause is something like a ballooning brake hose, a worn out drum, warped brake shoes or new shoes that have not yet seated.

Pedal Sinks To Floor

There's nothing more assuring than a nice firm brake pedal—and nothing more unnerving than a pedal that slowly sinks to the floor while you're pressing on it. This condition is most noticeable when sitting at a stop light. By the time the light turns green, the pedal may have dropped several inches or may require pumping to keep your vehicle from creeping ahead. This is usually caused by one of two things: a worn master cylinder or a leak in the hydraulic system. If a leak's responsible for the fading pedal, the system will soon lose all its fluid and the brakes will cease to work at all.

The first thing to check is the fluid level. If low look for a leaky brake hose, brake line, wheel cylinder or caliper. A full fluid reservoir and no visible leaks means the master cylinder is worn out and needs to be rebuilt or replaced.

Hard Pedal

Excessive pedal effort may be due to a faulty power booster if you have power brakes. The booster may be defective or the loss of assist may be because of insufficient vacuum due to a leaky hose, vacuum reservoir or a vacuum leak elsewhere.

To check the vacuum booster, pump the brake pedal several times with the engine off to bleed off any vacuum that may still be in the unit. Then hold your foot on the pedal and start the engine. If the booster is working, you should feel the amount of effort required to hold the pedal drop and the pedal itself may depress slightly. If nothing happens, check the vacuum connections with the booster unit and run a vacuum check on the engine (a minimum of 17 inches is needed). No

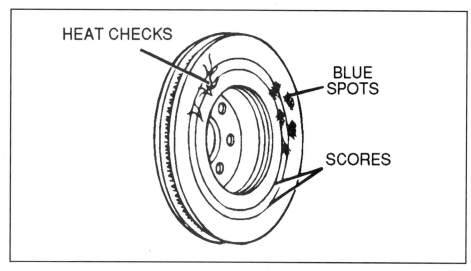

Rotor defects such as these are common, but can usually be cleaned up by resurfacing. If the rotor is cracked, though, it must be replaced. Blue spots indicate warpage and hard spots on the rotor surface. The spots result from overheating, which in turn is caused by lack of parallelism (which may be the result of distortion caused by uneven torquing of the lug nuts). Courtesy Brake Parts, Inc.

vacuum leaks but still no power assist means you need a new booster.

Sometimes a faulty check valve will allow vacuum to bleed out of the booster causing a hard pedal when the brakes are applied. This can be checked by starting the engine (to build vacuum) then shutting it off and waiting four or five minutes. Then try the brake pedal to see if there is any power assist. You should get at least a couple of assists if the check valve is holding. If not, replace the check valve.

With Hydro-Boost—If your vehicle has Hydro-Boost, a hard pedal can be caused by a loose power steering pump belt, a low fluid level, leaks in the power hoses, or leaks or faulty valves in the Hydro-Boost unit itself—which require replacing the booster.

A hard pedal on a vehicle without power brakes can be caused by glazed or worn linings, grease or oil on the brake linings, wet brakes, seized or frozen wheel cylinders and/or brake caliper pistons, a defective master cylinder or, on rear-wheel drive

applications, the use of semimetallic linings which typically require more pedal effort than asbestos or NAO linings (especially when cold).

No Parking Brake

If you pull the parking brake lever or step on the pedal and the brake fails to hold your vehicle on a hill, maybe all you need is a simple adjustment. As a rule, most hand levers and pedals should travel only about 4 or 5 "clicks" when properly adjusted. If the handle or pedal travels too far, it may not pull the linkage and cables tight enough to set the brake.

If you feel little or no resistance when applying the parking brake, the equalizer yoke or cables may be broken.

If the parking brake handle or pedal is frozen, rusted cables are the most likely cause. If you can't free them up with penetrating oil, you'll have to replace them.

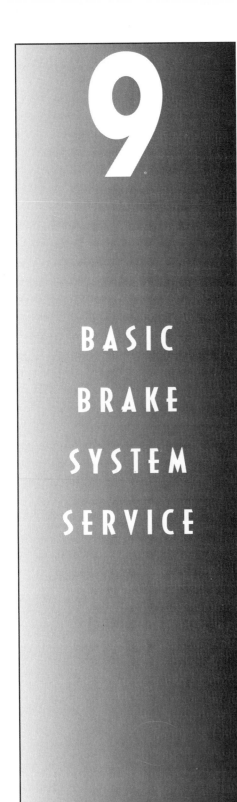

Before you start any work on the brakes, make sure the vehicle isn't going anyplace by chocking the wheels, placing the transmission in Park (or gear if it's a manual). Don't set the parking brake, though, if you have to pull one or both brake drums.

Any time your vehicle needs brake work, you should ask yourself, "Is this something I really want to do myself?" If you don't feel competent enough to tackle a do-it-yourself brake repair, don't! Brakes are a critical safety item that must be serviced correctly. Don't take chances if you have doubts about your own capabilities. Pay a professional to fix your brakes.

But hey, this is a brake book for do-it-yourselfers, so you probably won't even be reading this chapter unless you were ready to do the work yourself. So let's proceed and get through the preliminaries before we tell you how to do first class brake repairs.

SAFETY PRECAUTIONS

Brake work is not difficult to do, but there are some safety precautions you must keep in mind before you proceed. Brake work requires you to raise your vehicle so the wheels can be removed to provide access to the brakes. This sounds simple enough but can create a potentially dangerous situation if not done correctly:

• First, work on a level surface to minimize the risk of your vehicle rolling or moving when the wheels are raised off the ground.

• Second, place the transmission in Park (automatic) or in gear (manual) to prevent your vehicle from rolling before you jack it up. If you're not going to work on the rear brakes or raise the rear wheels off the ground, set the parking brake, too. But if you need to work on the rear brakes, use chocks to block front the wheels.

• Loosen the lug nuts before you raise the wheels off the ground. This makes the job much easier and eliminates the danger of pushing or rocking the vehicle off the jack.

• Place a pair of sturdy safety stands under the chassis as soon as the vehicle is raised. The stands should be positioned under a structural component such as the frame rails,

Loosen the lug nuts before you raise the wheels off the ground, and always use a torque wrench to tighten them.

engine cradle or some other solid point that isn't going to move. Do this before you remove the wheels and before you start to work on the brakes. Never, repeat never, crawl under a vehicle that is supported only by a jack. Relying on a bumper jack or floor jack alone to hold a vehicle up is gambling with your life!

• Avoid exposure to brake dust. Your brakes will be dirty and coated with dust from the worn linings. The dust may contain asbestos, and even if it doesn't, brake dust isn't something you want to breathe. When the wheels are removed, wash off or clean the brakes with brake cleaner. Some aerosol brake cleaners contain toxic or carcinogenic chemicals, so note any precautions on the product's label before using (like warnings to use only in a well ventilated area). Also, never blow off the brakes with an air hose because this will force the dust into the air.

• Heed all the warnings and cautions throughout this book. Where various procedures or repairs might get you into trouble, we've tried to alert you to the potential dangers.

• If your vehicle has Hydro-Boost or integral ABS with electrohydraulic power assist (Teves Mark 2 ABS, Bosch III ABS, Delco Powermaster 3 ABS, Bendix 10 and Jeep ABS), you must fully depressurize the high pressure accumulator before starting any brake work. On Hydro-Boost applications, this is done by depressing the brake pedal 4 to 6 times with the engine off. On the integral ABS applications, you have to depress the brake pedal 30 to 40 times with the ignition off.

• Be careful not to splash brake fluid on your vehicle's finish. Brake fluid can cause paint to streak.

• Wear eye protection if you do any pounding or chiseling.

A COMPLETE BRAKE JOB

Now that we've covered the safety precautions, let's move on to what's involved in doing brake work. More specifically, let's talk about the importance of doing a "complete" brake job.

A complete brake job is the opposite of an "incomplete" brake job that overlooks things or leaves some things undone. We're talking about ignoring a leaky caliper or wheel cylinder that needs to be rebuilt or replaced, reusing old drum hardware that's badly rusted or weakened with age, forgetting to lubricate shoe pads and caliper mounts so these parts can move freely, reusing old grease seals to save a few bucks, not changing the brake fluid or bleeding the lines because it's takes too much effort, not even checking the condition of the rear brakes because you're only replacing the pads up front. Things like these can get you intro trouble — if not now, then at some point down the road.

So anytime your vehicle needs brake work, think in terms of doing a complete brake job. That doesn't mean you have to overhaul the entire brake system if it only needs a new set of linings. But it does mean doing a thorough inspection of your entire brake system so you can identify any additional items that might need adjustment, repair or replacement, and also doing those things that are necessary for preventative maintenance (like lubricating the caliper slides, shoe pads, changing the fluid and bleeding the lines). This may sound like a lot of unnecessary extra work, but it will usually save you money and trouble in the long run because it helps to prolong the life of your brake system while assuring optimum brake performance and safety.

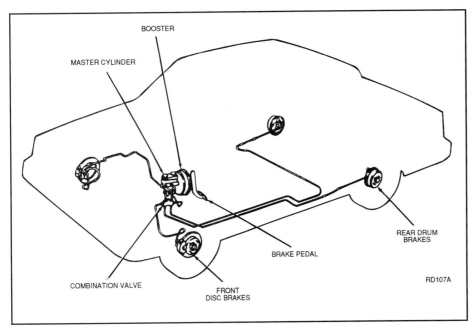

Any time you do brake work on your vehicle, you should inspect the entire system (not just the component that needs immediate attention) and repair anything else that may also need fixing. Preventative maintenance will actually save you money in the long run, and make your vehicle safer to drive. Courtesy Chrysler.

Let's say your vehicle needs new pads up front. There's no need to replace the rear shoes as long as the rear linings are in good condition. But if the shoes are marginal or have been contaminated by fluid leaks or grease, they also need to be replaced — along with any other drum components that are not in good condition. Even if the shoes are still within service limits, you should ask yourself if they'll last as long as the pads you're replacing up front. If not, then now might be a good time to replace them.

Whether or not the calipers and wheel cylinders need attention will depend on their condition. Any sign of leakage or sticking calls for immediate repair or replacement. And even if they're not leaking, sticking or frozen, you should consider rebuilding or replacing them for preventative maintenance.

What's Necessary and What Isn't

One of the pitfalls of do-it-yourself

brake work is that you don't have anyone looking over your shoulder to hold you accountable for what you do or don't do. A professional brake technician has his employer and customer to worry about as well as his own reputation. In some states, there may also be a regulatory agency that

serves as an auto repair watchdog. In any event, a professional has to guarantee his work. If a problem occurs during the warranty period, he has to fix it for free. So there are numerous incentives to do the job right the first time.

As a do-it-yourselfer, on the other hand, you are your own boss. Except maybe for your spouse or a nagging mother-in-law, you're accountable only to yourself and your own conscience. Even so, it's important to remember what's at stake. You don't want to take chances with your brakes because the consequences of doing a halfhearted job could be deadly. So the responsibility is yours for deciding what needs to be fixed and what ought to be fixed for preventative maintenance.

Repairs that should always be made include any brake parts that are worn out, broken or damaged. Brake linings worn down to minimum specifications, for example, would need to be replaced because they might not be able to create enough

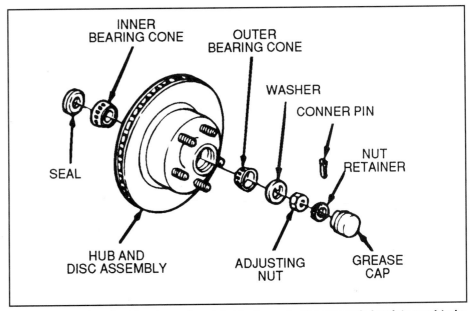

Don't overlook the wheel bearings when doing brake work. The non-sealed variety need to be cleaned, inspected and repacked with fresh wheel bearing grease periodically. Courtesy Brake Parts, Inc.

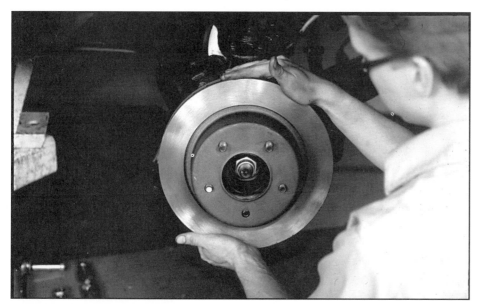

Rotors should always be resurfaced in pairs, and sanded to produce a random crosshatch finish for maximum noise suppression. Rotors should also be cleaned before they're reinstalled on your vehicle. Courtesy Wagner.

indicate a leaky booster diaphragm or vacuum connection. Power brakes are discussed in Chapter 7.

• How does the brake pedal feel? Is it firm? A soft or mushy-feeling pedal usually indicates air in the lines or leaks. A pedal that slowly sinks is a classic symptom of a worn master cylinder. Is the amount of pedal travel normal? A low pedal may indicate worn linings, the need for adjustment, defective or frozen drum brake adjusters or a low fluid level. See Chapter 8 for specifics.

• Check your stop lights (taillights & center high mounted stop light. Do all the lights come on when you press on the brake pedal? No lights may indicate a defective or misadjusted stop light pedal switch, a wiring problem or burned out bulbs in the taillights.

• Apply the parking brake. Does the pedal or handle work smoothly? Is it adjusted properly? Does the brake

friction to safely stop your vehicle. They may also damage your rotors or drums, which will end up costing you even more money. It's the same story if you find a leaky caliper, wheel cylinder, master cylinder, brake valve, hose or steel line. Leaky components must be repaired or replaced because fluid loss could lead to brake failure.

Where To Begin

Every do-it-yourself brake job should start with a thorough inspection of the entire brake system, including the antilock brake system if your vehicle is so equipped.

• First, start with a warning light check. Turn on the ignition to verify that the brake warning light (and ABS warning light if your vehicle has ABS) comes on. The light(s) should come on momentarily for a bulb check, then go out if no problems are present. No light? Then you've found a bulb that needs replacing or a wiring problem. If the light comes on and remains on (does not go out), then further diagnosis will be required to find out

what's wrong. Warning lights are covered in the previous chapter (Chapter 8) and ABS troubleshooting is covered in the next chapter (Chapter 10).

• Apply the brakes and start the engine. Does the pedal drop slightly? That's good because it indicates a good vacuum booster. No boost may

Brake lines should always be bled to remove trapped air if any hydraulic component in the system has been replaced. A fluid change is also recommended every two years or any time the brakes are relined to get rid of moisture contamination. Courtesy Wagner.

BASIC BRAKE OVERHAUL

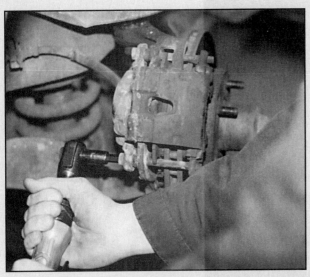

1. A disc brake overhaul begins by removing the calipers. This one is held by two bolts. Remove one...

2. ...then the other (the order doesn't matter). Be ready to catch the caliper when the last bolt comes out.

light come on? No brake warning light may indicate a bad bulb or defective or misadjusted parking brake switch. Does the parking brake hold the vehicle? Put the transmission into gear while the parking brake is applied. It should hold the vehicle with the engine idling. If it fails to hold the vehicle, it may need adjustment or repair. Now release the parking brake. Failure to release fully means the linkage or cables need attention.

• Turn the engine off, place the transmission in park (or gear if you have a manual), open the hood and check the fluid level in the master cylinder. A low level may indicate a leak or worn linings. Also, note the fluid's appearance. Dark discoloration indicates moisture contamination and the need for a fluid change.

• If you're working on somebody else's vehicle or one that you haven't driven for some time, take it for a short drive to test the brakes.

Warning: Do not test drive any vehicle that does not have a full pedal, adequate brake fluid or enough brakes left to safely bring it to a halt!

Try a couple of low speed gradual stops. How do the brakes feel? Do you feel any pulsation in the pedal? Pulsation usually indicates warped rotors that need to be resurfaced or replaced. Does the pedal feel soft or spongy? There could be air in the lines? Is pedal travel excessive? The brakes could be worn or need adjusting. Do the brakes pull to either side? Uneven braking could indicate fluid or grease contaminated linings, or a bad caliper or wheel cylinder. Do you hear any unusual noises? Scraping sounds could indicate badly worn linings or loose debris inside a brake drum. Squealing may indicate

worn or loose pads. Do any warning lights come on when you apply the brakes? A warning light could signal loss of pressure in one of the hydraulic circuits.

If the brakes are working normally, try a panic stop from about 35 to 40 mph.

Warning: Do not attempt this if you've already detected a brake problem or the brakes are defective.

Again, note how the brakes behave. Braking should be even, the pedal should remain firm and there should be no unusual noises or sensations. If the vehicle is equipped with ABS, you may feel pulsation in the pedal and hear clicking or buzzing noises from under the hood. This is normal for most ABS systems and does not indicate a problem. The ABS system should prevent the wheels from locking up and allow you to make a safe, controlled stop. If the vehicle

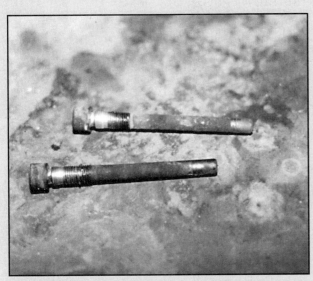

3. Note the condition of the bolts and caliper bushings. If damaged, worn or badly corroded replace them.

4. Remove the caliper from its mount and inspect the caliper and mount for wear or damage.

Continued next page

does not have ABS, the rear wheels may lock up and skid depending on how hard you brake and traction conditions. This too is normal for vehicles that do not have ABS.

• Remove a front wheel and measure the thickness of the brake pads. If worn down to minimum specifications or if wear indicators are making contact with the rotor, new linings are needed. If the pads are still above specs, you might consider replacing them anyway if they're near the end of their service life or if they're noisy.

• Note the condition of the rotors. Deep scratches or grooves indicate a need for resurfacing. Measure runout and parallelism, too. If out of specs, resurfacing or replacement is needed. Are there discolored spots, heat cracks or warpage? These may also indicate a need for rotor resurfacing or

replacement.

• Note the condition of the calipers and caliper mounts. If the pads are worn unevenly, the caliper is hanging up and is not centering itself over the rotor. This would indicate a need for disassembly, cleaning (or replacing) and lubricating the caliper slides or bushings with brake grease. If you see any signs of fluid leakage around the caliper piston seal, it would tell you the caliper needs to be rebuilt or replaced.

• Check the condition of the rubber brake hose. If cracked, frayed, worn, damaged or leaking, it needs to be replaced.

• Pull a drum and inspect the drum surface, brake shoes, hardware and wheel cylinder. If the shoe linings are at or below minimum specifications,

you need new shoes. If the linings are still above minimum specs but are getting thin, consider replacing the shoes anyway. Any wetness or leakage around the wheel cylinder means it needs to be rebuilt or replaced.

• Check everywhere for leaks: the master cylinder, proportioning valve, steel brake lines, all rubber hoses, and ABS components if your vehicle has ABS. Have a helper apply the brakes while you look underneath. Rubber hoses should not expand under pressure. Any hoses that swell under pressure need to be replaced.

GENERAL GUIDELINES ON BRAKE REPAIRS

• Always reline brakes in matched axle sets. In other words, do both front wheels, both rear wheels or all four wheels. Never do just one wheel on

BASIC BRAKE OVERHAUL, *continued*

5. If you're just replacing pads, the caliper pistons will have to be pushed back in to accept the new pads (which will be wider than the old worn pads). This can be done with a large c-clamp. You may also have to remove some fluid from the master cylinder reservoir because pushing the piston in displaces fluid back into the master cylinder.

6. The front rotors on most older rear-wheel drive cars and trucks have the wheel bearings inside the rotor hub. To remove the rotors, the dust cap has to come off.

the right or left side as this can cause the vehicle to pull towards one side when braking. Also, use the same type, grade and brand of friction material on both sides. Mismatching friction material side-to-side may also cause uneven braking and brake pull. Keep this in mind if you're buying a single "loaded" caliper assembly that comes complete with new pads. You should also replace the pads on the other caliper so both will have the same friction material.

• If you're replacing brake linings, use the same type of material as the original. Replace semimetallics with semimetallics, never asbestos or NAO. Replace NAO with NAO. Replace asbestos with asbestos or NAO. You can also upgrade from asbestos or NAO to semimetallics if the friction supplier offers such linings for your vehicle application.

• Premium quality linings will give you the best wear life, noise control and brake performance. If you can't afford the best, then go with standard grade replacement linings. Avoid economy grade linings.

• Have your rotors and/or drums resurfaced when relining the brakes unless they're in perfect condition. New linings require a smooth surface to rub against for maximum braking effectiveness. A rough or grooved rotor or drum will wear linings rapidly and reduce braking effectiveness. Warped rotors or ones with excessive runout can also cause annoying pedal pulsation.

• Rotors and drums should always be resurfaced in pairs. As a rule, there should be no more than .010 in. difference in rotor thickness or drum

diameter side-to-side.

• Rotors or drums that are worn down to minimum specifications, or cannot be resurfaced without exceeding the minimum or discard specifications must be replaced.

• New hardware is recommended for drums and calipers. Replace hardware items such as the retaining clips and return springs. Heat and age weakens these components. Self-adjusters should also be replaced if found to be corroded or frozen. Use high temperature brake grease (never ordinary chassis grease!) to lubricate the self adjusters and the raised shoe pads on the backing plates. New mounting pins and bushings will help keep disc brake calipers sliding freely. Slides and bushings should also be lubricated with high temperature brake grease.

7. Once the cap has been removed, you can get at the spindle nut.

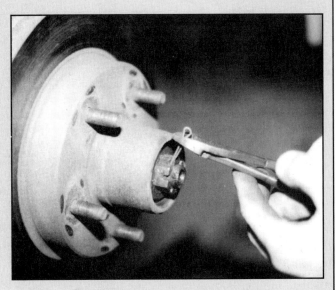

8. Most spindle nuts are held with a cotter pin, which must be removed and discarded (don't reuse the old pin, install a new one).

Continued next page

• Don't overlook the wheel bearings when relining the brakes. Check for looseness by rocking the wheel in and out. Check for roughness or noise by spinning the wheel by hand. Greasable wheel bearings should be cleaned and inspected. If worn, cracked or damaged, the bearings need to be replaced. If good, the bearings need to be repacked with high temperature wheel bearing grease. Never reuse old grease seals (they usually leak). When wheel bearings are reinstalled, they must be set with the correct amount of preload (not too tight or too loose). Wheel bearing adjustment procedures vary, so always refer to your shop manual for the specifics on your vehicle. Note: Though most front-wheel drive vehicles have sealed front wheel bearings, the rear wheel bearings on many are greasable—and often neglected.

• It is not absolutely necessary to rebuild or replace disc brake calipers or drum brake wheel cylinders when doing a brake job—as long as these components are not leaking or sticking. Even so, most experts recommend rebuilding or replacing them anyway for preventative maintenance.

• Always replace the old brake fluid with fresh fluid after relining the brakes, and bleed the brakes to remove air bubbles from the lines. Brake fluid absorbs moisture over time, which lowers its boiling temperature and promotes internal corrosion. Replacing the fluid every couple of years for preventative maintenance or when relining the brakes will prolong the life of the hydraulic components while assuring maximum brake performance

and safety.
Never reuse old brake fluid or fluid from a container that's been left open for several days or longer. The fluid will be contaminated by airborne moisture and unsuitable for further use.

• Always use a torque wrench to final tighten wheel lug nuts. This is a much more accurate method than using a four-way wrench, breaker bar, ratchet or impact wrench.

• Break in new linings gradually. Avoid sudden stops or hard braking for the first 150 to 200 miles. This will minimize the risk of glazing new pads.

Inspecting Brake Linings

How often should you check your linings? It depends on the type of driving you do. Checking the linings every six months or once a year

BASIC BRAKE OVERHAUL, *continued*

9. The spindle nut can now be removed along with the outer wheel bearing so the rotor can be pulled off the spindle.

10. When the rotor is off, remove the grease seal from he back along with the inner wheel bearing. The wheel bearings must be cleaned, inspected and regreased with fresh wheel bearing grease (never ordinary chassis grease) before the rotor goes back on the spindle. Be sure to use a new grease seal, too.

would be a general guideline. Stop and go city driving will wear the linings much more quickly than open highway driving because the brakes are used more often. So if most of your driving is done in town, you might want to check the linings more often. The same holds true if you do a lot of driving on hilly or mountainous terrain. And if you have an aggressive driving style or do any weekend racing, better plan on checking your brake linings on a much more frequent basis.

Disc brake pads can be easily inspected by removing a front wheel, but the rear drums also require pulling a drum.

It's difficult to accurately judge lining wear by appearance alone, so always measure the exact thickness of the linings at their narrowest point to determine whether or not they're still within acceptable limits. If the linings

are at or less than the minimum thickness specification (refer to a shop manual), you need new linings. Don't put off replacing the linings too long because the minimum thickness is based on the design of the brake system (how far the caliper pistons, wheel cylinder pistons and self-adjusters can safely travel) and the type of linings used (bonded, molded or riveted). Bonded and molded linings can generally tolerate more wear than riveted linings. But if you wear either type too far, you can chew up your rotors or drums.

New linings would also be needed if the wear indicators on your disc brake pads are making contact with the rotors. The indicators will make a loud high pitched squeal to warn you it's time to replace the pads.

The linings should also be replaced if they are found to be contaminated with brake fluid or grease (regardless

of wear), or if they show uneven or taper wear. Replacement would be needed if the difference in thickness from one end of the pad to the other is more than 1/16th in. (1.5 mm) on fixed calipers, or 1/8th in. (3.0 mm) on floating calipers.

ROTOR & DRUM RESURFACING

Resurfacing rotors and drums unnecessarily will obviously reduce their useful service life, but in many instances resurfacing is necessary by the time the linings are replaced. The general rule here is to resurface when necessary, and don't resurface when it isn't necessary.

As long as your rotors and drums are in relatively good condition (smooth and flat with no deep scoring, cracks, distortion or other damage), there's no need to resurface them

11. Rotor thickness must be measured to determine rotor wear and whether the rotors can be safely resurfaced. If the rotors are too thin, they're not safe and must be replaced.

12. When you take your rotors somewhere to be resurfaced on a brake lathe, the shop should remove the least amount of metal as possible to restore a smooth surface.

Continued next page

when doing a brake job. But if they're not in good condition or you've had a problem with noise, resurfacing is recommended. The factors that determine whether or not resurfacing is really necessary include:

Surface Condition—This is the most important criteria. Scoring, pitting or other minor surface imperfections should be cleaned up to restore the surface to like-new condition and to minimize noise. If a rotor or drum is cracked, however, it must be replaced.

Lateral Runout on Rotors—This must be measured with a dial indicator against the face of the rotor. If rotor wobble exceeds OEM specs, reindexing it on the hub (if possible) may help reduce runout. A better solution here is to have the rotor resurfaced in place with an "on-car" lathe. Many vehicle manufacturers

now recommend this technique, which unfortunately requires expensive equipment that only a dealer or brake shop would have. But the equipment does a fantastic job and cuts the rotor true to its axis of rotation.

Rotor Warpage—Variation in the thickness of the rotor or uneven spots on either rotor face will cause the brake pedal to pulsate or shudder when the brakes are applied. Flatness can be checked by placing a straight edge against both faces of the rotor. Thickness must be checked with a micrometer at six or more points around the rotor.

If parallelism between rotor faces exceeds OEM specs (generally about .0005 in.), or if the rotor is warped or has hard spots (which are often discolored blue or black), the rotor should be resurfaced or replaced. Hard spots that develop from

overheating or uneven tightening of lug nuts can create raised areas on the surface that often extend below the surface. The metallurgical changes in the rotor often cause the hard spots to return after a few thousand miles so replacing the rotor may be the best long term fix.

Rotor Thickness and Drum Diameter—If a rotor is close to or at the minimum thickness specification (which is stamped on the rotor or may be found in a brake service reference book), it is too thin to be resurfaced and must be replaced. The same goes for drums, except the critical dimension here is the drum's inside diameter (the maximum or discard diameter spec is stamped on the drum or listed in a reference book),

Most experts today recommend a rotor finish of 40 to 60 microinches or smoother for quiet disc brake operation. This is achievable with

BASIC BRAKE OVERHAUL, *continued*

13. Sanding the rotors after they have been turned will improve the surface finish even more and reduce brake noise.

14. Before new pads are installed, the old ones need to be inspected for uneven wear which may indicate caliper sticking. Courtesy Wagner.

most bench lathes or on-car refinishing equipment. When you have your rotors or drums resurfaced, ask that the least amount of metal be removed to maximize the remaining service life of your parts. Sanding rotors after they've been turned with #120 to #150 grit sandpaper will leave a smooth, nondirectional finish that provides an optimum surface for semimetallic pads.

Rotors should also be scrubbed with a brush and soapy water before they are reinstalled. Resurfacing leaves a lot of metallic debris on the surface which can embed itself in the new brake linings and cause noise problems. Even if the rotors or drums have not been resurfaced, cleaning is recommended to remove dirt and grease (which can contaminate new linings and cause uneven braking or grabbing).

CALIPER REBUILDING

As we've said already, it isn't absolutely necessary to rebuild or replace your calipers when relining the brakes. But not doing so may be asking for trouble later on. A caliper that's leaking brake fluid, is damaged, has a frozen piston, or is causing uneven pad wear obviously needs to be rebuilt or replaced. But what if your calipers aren't leaking? Should you rebuild them anyway for preventative maintenance?

Those who subscribe to the "don't fix it unless it's broken" philosophy of brake repair think they're saving time and money by leaving the calipers alone. Maybe so. But most brake experts say it makes sense to go ahead and do the calipers when the brakes are relined. Here's why:

Brake calipers, like any other mechanical component, wear and

corrode with age. Every time the brakes are applied, the back-and-forth motion of the caliper pistons produces a slight amount of wear. At the same time, moisture is building up in the fluid. After several years of service, the fluid may contain as much as 3% water—which is enough to produce visible corrosion in the caliper bores and on steel pistons. As the surface of the pistons become rough, they scour the seals with every application of the brakes. Eventually this will lead to fluid leaks and pad contamination.

So even if a caliper isn't leaking, it's still aging inside. Rubber piston seals and dust boots harden and become brittle over time. One of the jobs the piston seals do besides keep the fluid where it belongs is to help retract the pistons when the brakes are released. When a piston moves out, it twists the square cut seal slightly. This helps pull the piston back when the brakes

15. To overhaul a caliper, the piston(s) must be removed. Removing the bleeder screw and blowing shop air can pop the pistons out. But a rag should be positioned as shown to catch and cushion the piston. Be careful and keep your fingers out of the way because the pistons can pop free with considerable force! Courtesy Wagner.

16. Once the piston is out, it and the caliper bore can be inspected for wear and pitting. Minor surface corrosion and pitting in the bore can be cleaned up by sanding. Pitted, scored or worn pistons, however should be replaced because sanding damages the anti-corrosion coating. Courtesy Wagner.

Continued next page

are released to keep the pads from dragging against the rotors. But as a seal ages and loses elasticity, it doesn't do as good a job of pulling back the piston. Consequently, the pads start to drag resulting in reduced fuel economy, a possible brake pull and/or accelerated or uneven pad wear.

When boots get old, they often crack or split, allowing dirt and water to enter the piston bore area. The result can be accelerated seal wear, piston corrosion and sticking. What's more, if the pistons are pushed back in to accept new pads any dirt that's found its way behind the boots will be shoved back into the caliper bores. This too, can contribute to sticking, binding and wear.

So there are valid reasons for rebuilding or replacing the calipers when the brakes are relined.

WHEEL CYLINDERS

The same arguments that apply to disc brake calipers also apply to the wheel cylinders in drum brakes. As long as they're not leaking, sticking or damaged, you might be tempted to leave them alone and take your chances. But the seals inside are aging, so rebuilding them for preventative maintenance will assure trouble-free operation.

BLEEDING CONSIDERATIONS

A complete brake job also includes fresh brake fluid. Bleeding is necessary for two reasons:

1. To remove air bubbles that may have entered the system while repairs were being made, because of a leak or because the fluid level got too low. The air must be removed because it is compressible and can prevent a full, firm pedal.

2. To remove moisture contamination. Brake fluid absorbs moisture over time, which lowers its boiling point and contributes to internal corrosion. Changing the fluid periodically (every two years or when the brakes are relined) as preventative maintenance rids your brake system of unwanted moisture, restores the fluid's boiling temperature and prolongs the life of the hydraulic components by minimizing the potential for internal corrosion. This can really be a money saver if your car or truck has ABS because of the high replacement cost of the hydraulic modulator assembly.

As a general rule, the sequence or order in which the individual brakes are bled is very important to get all the air out of the system. The sequence varies from one vehicle to

BASIC BRAKE OVERHAUL, *continued*

17. When the caliper goes back on, use a torque wrench to tighten the bolts to specifications.

18. Now for the drum brakes. The hardest part of servicing drum brakes is often getting the drum loose. Pounding on the face (never the sides or edges) of the drum may help vibrate it loose without damaging it. If this doesn't work, you'll need a drum puller.

19. Once the drum comes loose, it should pull right off. If not, it may be necessary to back off the shoe adjuster so the shoes will clear the wear ridge on the inside of the drum.

another, so always refer to the bleeding sequence specified by your vehicle manufacturer. You'll find this information in a shop manual.

The most common procedure on hydraulic systems that are split front-to-rear (most rear-wheel drive cars and trucks) is to do the rear brakes first, then the fronts, starting with the wheel furthest from the master cylinder. With systems that are split diagonally (most front-wheel drive cars and minivans), the sequence is often right rear, left front, then left rear and right front.

Always use the type of brake fluid specified by the vehicle manufacturer (usually DOT 3, but DOT 4 in most European cars). DOT 5 silicone fluid is not recommended for vehicles equipped with ABS. Use clean fluid from a sealed container, and discard the old fluid.

Bleeding procedures are covered in Chapter 3.

20. Before going any further, stop and study the configuration of the brakes. Note the position of the springs and retainers and any other parts. Draw yourself a picture if you don't have a shop manual for reference so the parts can be reassembled correctly when the shoes are replaced. Another tip is to do one side at a time. That way if you get mixed up, you can always refer to the brake on the other side.

21. The brakes will be coated with dust which may contain asbestos fibers. The safest way to remove this stuff is to wash it off with brake cleaner. Aerosol cleaner can also be used to clean the brakes. But never use shop air to blow off the brakes or an ordinary household or shop vacuum cleaner to vacuum off the dust.

22. To remove the shoes, the return springs must first come off. Special tools are available to make this job easier. You can also use pliers, but be careful not to damage or bend the springs.

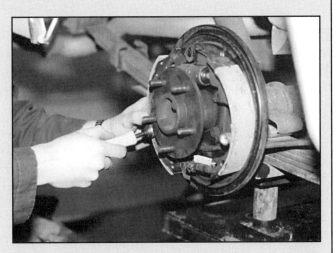

23. Next, the retaining springs and cups that hold the shoes to the backing plate have to come off. You can use a special tool as shown for this purpose or pliers.

Continued next page

BASIC BRAKE OVERHAUL, continued

24. The shoes and adjuster assembly can now be lifted off. Note the position of the parts so they can be correctly reassembled. Also, check the backplate for wear or ridges.

25. The drums will probably be rough and worn, so they'll have to be turned on a brake lathe to restore the surface.

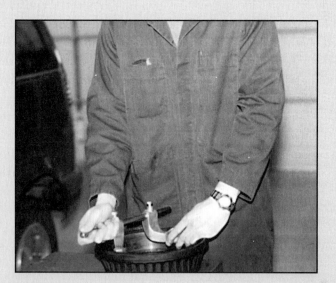

26. The drums will also have to be measured prior to turning to determine wear and whether there is enough metal left for safe turning.

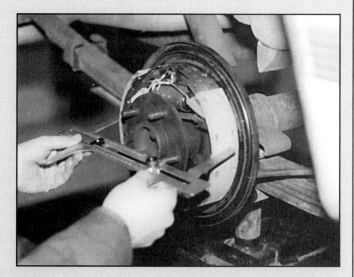

27. This tool makes adjustment easier when a freshly turned drum is installed with new shoes. The tool is adjusted to the inside diameter of the drum, and is then used to preadjust the shoes so they just clear the drum.

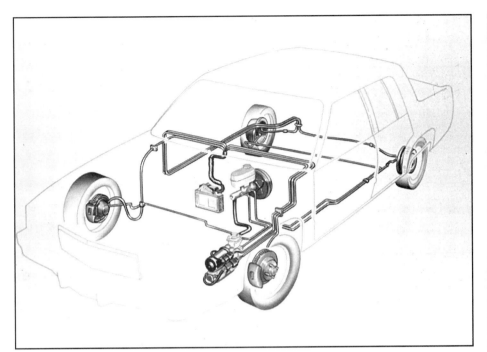

Typical ABS system components. This one is a nonintegral system for a Cadillac.

What is ABS? Think of it as an enhanced or improved version of ordinary brakes. Simply put, an ABS system is designed to prevent the brakes from locking up and skidding. This adds a significant margin of safety for everyday driving by preventing dangerous skids and allowing the driver to maintain steering control even when braking on slick or marginal road surfaces. ABS can also reduce the distance required to stop a vehicle depending on the road conditions: 10 to 15% on a dry road with good traction, and 25 to 40% on wet or slick surfaces—which may be the difference between a safe stop and an accident.

Though there are a number of different antilock brake systems in use today, one thing all share in common is the ability to control wheel lockup during hard braking. A tire that is just on the verge of slipping (10 to 20% slippage) produces more friction with respect to the road than one which is locked and skidding (100% slippage). Once traction is lost, friction is reduced and the vehicle takes longer to stop.

The only exception to this rule is when a tire is on loose snow. A locked tire allows a small wedge of snow to build up ahead of it which allows it to stop in a somewhat shorter distance than a rolling tire. That's why some vehicles have an on/off switch for deactivating the antilock system when driving on snow.

Directional stability also depends on traction. As long as a tire doesn't slip, it will roll only in the direction it turns. But once it skids, it has about as much directional stability as a hockey puck on ice. By minimizing the loss of traction, antilock braking helps maintain directional stability and steering control.

Another point to keep in mind about ABS is that it's essentially an "add-on" to the existing brake system. It only comes into play when traction conditions are marginal or during sudden "panic" stops. The rest of the time, it has no effect on normal driving or braking.

The system is also designed to be as "failsafe" as possible. Should a failure occur in the antilock control

BRAKING IN EMERGENCY OR SLIPPERY CONDITIONS

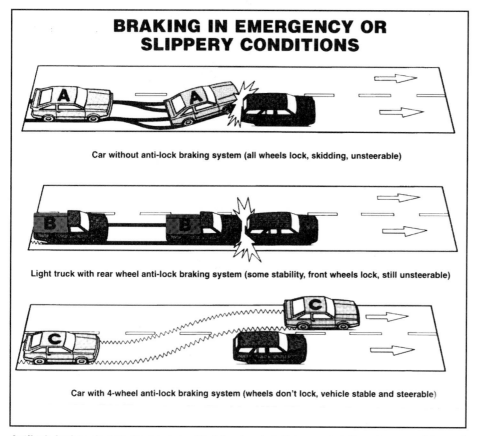

Car without anti-lock braking system (all wheels lock, skidding, unsteerable)

Light truck with rear wheel anti-lock braking system (some stability, front wheels lock, still unsteerable)

Car with 4-wheel anti-lock braking system (wheels don't lock, vehicle stable and steerable)

Antilock brakes do not decrease a vehicle's stopping distance, but they do prevent loss of control and allow you steer your way around obstacles. Four-wheel ABS is better in this respect than rear-wheel only ABS. Courtesy Bosch.

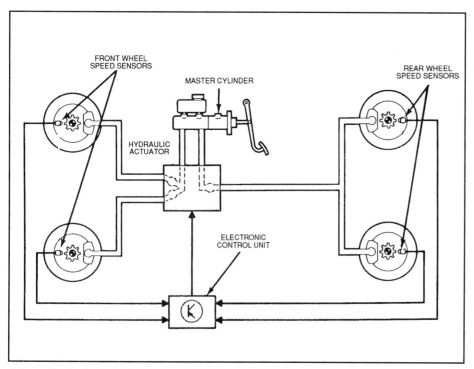

Schematic of a typical ABS system. Wheel speed is monitored by wheel speed sensors. If ABS braking is needed, the hydraulic actuator (also called a modulator) intervenes by isolating the brake circuit(s) to the wheel(s) that are starting to lock up, then rapidly cycling the brake pressure off and on so the wheel(s) can regain traction. Courtesy Brake Parts, Inc.

electronics, the system deactivates itself and the vehicle reverts to normal braking.

HOW ABS WORKS

All antilock brake systems control tire slip by monitoring the relative deceleration rates of the wheels during braking. If one wheel starts to slow at a faster rate than the others, or at a faster rate than that which is programmed into the antilock control module, it's an indication that the wheel is starting to slip and is in danger of breaking traction and locking up. The antilock system responds by momentarily reducing hydraulic pressure to the brake on the affected wheel or wheels.

Electrically operated solenoid valves are used to hold, release and reapply hydraulic pressure to the brakes. This produces a pulsating effect, which can be felt in the brake pedal during hard braking. The rapid modulation of brake pressure in a given brake circuit reduces the braking load on the affected wheel and allows it to regain traction, thus preventing lockup. It's the same as pumping the brakes, except that the ABS system does it automatically for each brake circuit, and at speeds that would be humanly impossible—up to dozens of times per second depending on the system (some are faster than others).

Once the rate of deceleration for the affected wheel comes back in line with the others, normal braking function and pressure resume, and antilock reverts to a passive mode.

SYSTEM CONFIGURATIONS

All ABS systems keep track of

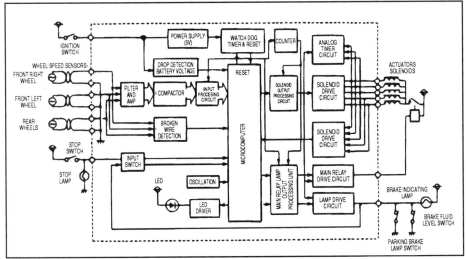

Electrical schematic for a typical ABS system. Inputs from the wheel speed sensors are monitored by the microprocessor, which decides if ABS is needed during a stop. If the microprocessor determines that one or more wheels are starting to lose their grip, it energizes and cycles the appropriate solenoids in the ABS hydraulic modulator unit to prevent lockup. The microprocessor also monitors the health of the various components in the ABS system (including itself) and illuminates the ABS warning light if a fault is detected. Courtesy Brake Parts, Inc.

On nonintegral ABS systems, the hydraulic modulator is separate from the master cylinder. This one happens to be a Kelsey-Hayes 4WAL unit on a Chevy Blazer.

wheel deceleration rates with wheel speed sensors. On some applications, each wheel is equipped with its own speed sensor. This type of arrangement would be called a "four wheel, four channel" system since each wheel speed sensor would give its input into a separate control circuit or "channel."

On other applications, fewer sensors are used. Many four-wheel ABS systems have a separate wheel speed sensor for each front wheel but use a common speed sensor for both rear wheels. These are called "three channel" systems. The rear wheel speed sensor is mounted in either the differential or the transmission. The sensor reads the combined or average speed of both rear wheels. This type of setup saves the cost of an additional sensor and reduces the complexity of the system by allowing both rear wheels to be controlled simultaneously.

Another variation is the "single channel" rear-wheel only ABS system that is used on many rear-wheel drive pickups and vans. Ford's version is called "Rear Antilock Brakes" (RABS) while GM and Chrysler call theirs "Rear Wheel Anti-Lock" (RWAL). The front wheels have no speed sensors and only a single speed sensor mounted in the differential or transmission is used for both rear wheels. Rear-wheel antilock systems are typically used on applications where vehicle loading can affect rear wheel traction, which is why it's used on pickup trucks and vans. Because the rear-wheel antilock systems have only a single channel, they're much less complex and costly than their three- and four-channel, four-wheel counterparts.

Integral & NonIntegral

Another difference in ABS systems is that some are "integral" and others are "nonintegral."

Integral systems combine the master brake cylinder and ABS hydraulic modulator, pump and accumulator into one assembly. Integral systems do not have a vacuum booster for power assist and rely instead on pressure generated by the electric pump for this purpose. The accumulators in these systems can contain over 2700 psi. The accumulator must be depressurized prior to doing any type of brake repair work by pumping the brake pedal 40 times while the key is off.

Integral ABS systems include the Bendix 10 & Bendix Jeep ABS systems, Bosch 3, Delco Moraine Powermaster III and Teves Mark 2.

Nonintegral ABS systems, which are sometimes referred to as "add-on" systems, use a conventional master brake cylinder and vacuum power booster with a separate hydraulic modulator unit. Some also have an electric pump for ABS braking (to reapply pressure during the ABS hold-release-reapply cycle), but do not use the pumps for normal power assist. Nonintegral systems do not have to be depressurized or deactivated prior to doing brake work.

Nonintegral (add-on) systems

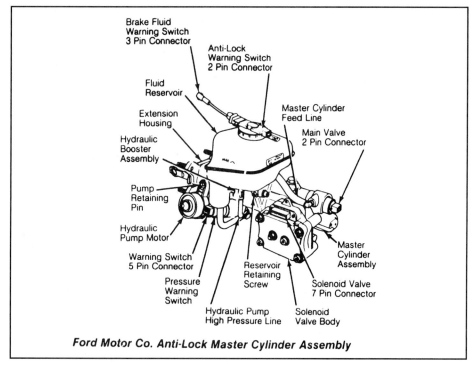

Ford Motor Co. Anti-Lock Master Cylinder Assembly

Integral ABS systems such as this Teves Mark 2 unit, combines the ABS modulator, pump, accumulator and master cylinder into one assembly. Courtesy Ford.

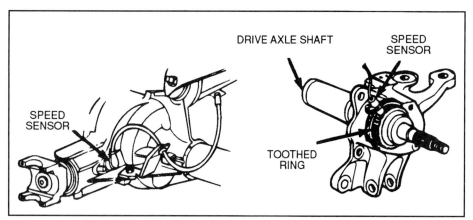

The rear wheel speed sensor on three-channel ABS systems is often mounted in the differential (left), while front sensors may be mounted in the front wheel bearing hub assembly (right). Courtesy Bosch.

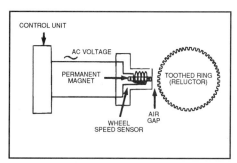

ABS wheel speed sensors use a permanent magnet to generate an alternating current (AC) signal. The sensor's output increases in frequency and amplitude as the speed of the wheel increases. A close air gap is critical for a strong signal. Some sensors have an adjustable air gap but most do not. Courtesy Brake Parts, Inc.

include Bendix 6, Bosch 2, Delco Moraine VI, Kelsey-Hayes RABS/RWAL & 4WAL, and Teves Mark 4 ABS.

BASIC ABS COMPONENTS

Basic components that are common to all antilock brake systems include: (1) wheel speed sensors, (2) an electronic control module, and (3) a hydraulic "modulator" assembly with electrically operated solenoid valves. Some systems also use an electric pump to generate hydraulic pressure for power assist as well as ABS braking.

Wheel Speed Sensors

The wheel speed sensors consist of a magnetic pickup and a toothed sensor ring (sometimes called a "tone" ring). The sensor(s) may be mounted in the steering knuckles, wheel hubs, brake backing plates, transmission tailshaft or differential housing. On some applications, the sensor is an integral part of the wheel bearing and hub assembly. The sensor ring(s) may be mounted on the axle hub behind the brake rotor, on the brake rotor itself, inside the brake drum, on the transmission tailshaft or inside the differential on the pinion shaft.

The sensor pickup has a magnetic core surrounded by coil windings. As the wheel turns, teeth on the sensor ring move through the pickup's magnetic field. This reverses the polarity of the magnetic field and induces an alternating current (AC) voltage in the pickup's windings. The number of voltage pulses per second that are induced in the pickup changes in direct proportion to wheel speed. So as speed increases, the frequency and amplitude of the wheel speed sensor goes up. The signal is sent to the ABS control module, where the AC signal is converted into a digital signal and then processed. The control module then counts pulses to monitor changes in wheel speed. On some applications (namely GM trucks with RWAL), the wheel speed sensor signal is first sent to a separate

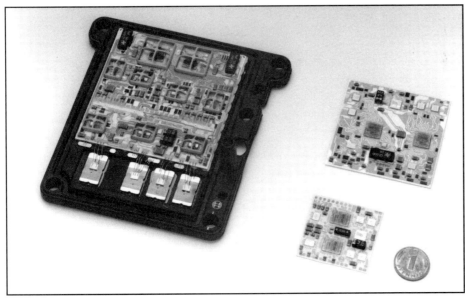

The brains of the ABS system is the microprocessor, which keeps getting smaller with each successive generation of ABS. Shown are a Bosch 2 control unit (left), a Bosch 5 unit (center), and a Bosch 5 Micro-Hybrid (right).

Tightening the set screw locks it in place.

One thing to keep in mind about wheel speed sensors is that they're affected by the size of the wheels and tires on the vehicle. A tire with a smaller overall diameter will give a slower speed reading than one with a smaller diameter. Because the ABS system is calibrated to a specific tire size, vehicle manufacturers warn against changing tire sizes. A different tire size or aspect ratio may have an adverse effect on the operation of your ABS system, so stick with the original tire and wheel specs if replacing either.

ABS Control Module

The ABS electronic control module (which may be referred to as an EBCM "Electronic Brake Control Module" or EBM "Electronic Brake Module") is a microprocessor that functions like the engine control computer. It uses input from its sensors to regulate hydraulic pressure during braking to prevent wheel

module (called a "DRAC" module) where it is converted to a DC signal. This signal is then used by both the computer and the electronic speedometer.

Air Gap—The distance or "air gap" between the end of a wheel speed sensor and its ring is critical. A close gap is necessary to produce a strong, reliable signal. You don't want metal-to-metal contact between the sensor and its ring since this would damage both. But neither do you want too much clearance. An air gap that's too wide may produce a weak or erratic signal, or worse yet, no signal at all. So if a wheel speed sensor is adjustable (many are not), refer to a shop manual for the required air gap and adjust it to specs. This is done by inserting a nonmagnetic brass or plastic feeler gauge between the end of the sensor and ring, and then tightening the set screw that locks the sensor in place. A steel feeler gauge should not be used because sliding it across the sensor tip may alter its magnetic properties and affect the accuracy of its readings. For the same

reason, never pound on a sensor or try to force it into place.

Some sensors come with a piece of paper or plastic over the end that provides just the right gap when the sensor is installed. To install this type of sensor, it is inserted until it just touches the sensor ring, then backed off just enough so the ring will turn without rubbing against the spacer.

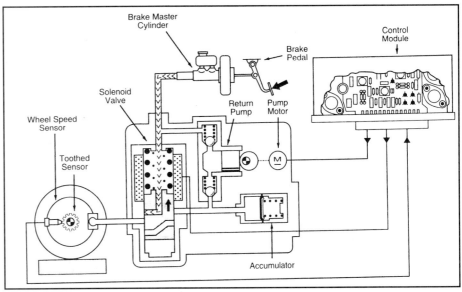

As ABS braking begins, a low amperage current is supplied to the ABS solenoid by the control module. This pulls the solenoid valve to the midway position and isolates the brake circuit to prevent any further increase in pressure that would cause the wheel to lock up. Courtesy Bosch.

ABS DO'S AND DON'TS

Antilock brake systems (ABS) are used on millions of vehicles, but many drivers still don't know the "right way" to use ABS in an emergency. So here are the "do's and don'ts" of ABS braking:

DO'S

DO keep your foot on the brake. Maintain firm and continuous pressure on the brake pedal to let four-wheel ABS work properly. Avoid pumping the brake, even if the brake pedal is pulsating. If you own a light truck with rear-wheel antilock (RWAL) brakes, apply the brake pedal with just enough force to stop your truck without locking the front wheels. This way you can maintain steering control while the rear-wheel antilock system prevents the vehicle from skidding sideways.

DO allow enough distance to stop. Follow three seconds or more behind vehicles when driving in good conditions. Allow more time if conditions are hazardous.

DO practice driving with ABS. Become accustomed to pulsations that occur in the brake pedal when ABS is activated. Empty parking lots or other open areas are excellent places to practice emergency stops.

DO consult your vehicle owner's manual for additional driving instructions regarding your ABS system.

DON'TS

DON'T drive an ABS-equipped vehicle more aggressively than a vehicle without ABS. Driving around curves faster, changing lanes abruptly or performing other aggressive steering maneuvers is risky in any vehicle.

DON'T pump the brakes. With four-wheel ABS systems, pumping the brakes turns the ABS system on and off, which decreases braking efficiency and increases your stopping distance. ABS pumps the brakes for you automatically at a much faster rate than you could do it manually, and allows better steering control. What's more, it also pumps the brakes on individual wheels as needed — which is something you can't do.

DON'T forget to steer. Four-wheel ABS can help you steer around hazardous situations, but your vehicle won't steer itself.

DON'T be alarmed by clicking noises and/or pedal pulsations when braking hard. These conditions are normal when ABS is active and lets you know the ABS system is working. There should be no ABS feedback, though, when braking normally on dry pavement. ABS should only come into play during panic stop situations or when the road is wet, icy, slick or covered with loose gravel.

ABS control module come from two sources: the wheel speed sensors and a brake pedal switch. The switch signals the control module when the brakes are being applied, which causes it to go from a "standby" mode to an active mode. At the same time, the wheel speed sensors keep it informed about what's happening while the brakes are being applied.

If the control module detects a difference in the deceleration rate between one or more wheels while braking, or if the overall rate of deceleration is too fast and exceeds the limits programmed into the control module, it triggers the ABS control module to momentarily take over. The control module cycles the solenoid valves in the modulator assembly to pulsate hydraulic pressure in the affected brake circuit (or circuits) until its sensor(s) tell it deceleration rates have returned to normal and everything's under control. At that point, normal braking action resumes under the watchful eye of the ABS system. When the brake pedal is released or when the vehicle comes to a stop, the control module returns to a standby mode until it is again needed.

Like any other electronic control module, the ABS module is vulnerable to damage caused by electrical overloads, impacts and extreme temperatures.

ABS electrical connectors should never be connected or disconnected while the key is on. Doing so can create momentary high voltage spikes in the electrical system that can damage electronic components such as the ABS control module. The ABS control module should be unplugged before any type of arc, MIG or TIG welding is done on your vehicle.

lockup. The ABS module may be located in the trunk, passenger compartment or under the hood. It may be a separate module or integrated with other electronics such as the body control or suspension computer.

Inputs—The key inputs for the

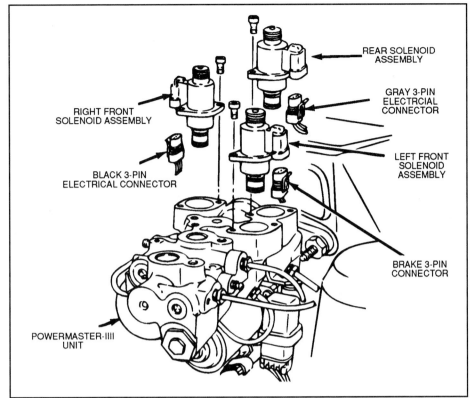

RIGHT FRONT
SOLENOID ASSEMBLY

REAR SOLENOID
ASSEMBLY

GRAY 3-PIN
ELECTRICAL
CONNECTOR

BLACK 3-PIN
ELECTRICAL CONNECTOR

LEFT FRONT
SOLENOID
ASSEMBLY

BRAKE 3-PIN
CONNECTOR

POWERMASTER-IIII
UNIT

The ABS hydraulic control unit or modulator contains electrically operated solenoid valves (one or more for each brake circuit depending on the design of the system). These solenoids are cycled on and off during an ABS stop to hold, release and reapply hydraulic pressure to the individual brake circuits. Shown is a Delco-Moraine Powermaster III ABS unit. Courtesy Delco-Moraine.

Hydraulic Modulator

The modulator valve body (which is part of the master cylinder assembly in some antilock systems but separate in others) contains ABS solenoid valves for each brake circuit. The exact number of valves per circuit depends on the ABS system and the application. Some use a pair of on-off solenoid valves for each brake circuit while others use a single valve that can operate in more than one position.

A solenoid consists of a wire coil with a movable core and a return spring. When current from the ABS control module energizes the coil, it pulls on the movable core. Depending on how the solenoid is constructed, this may open or close a valve that's attached to the movable core. When the control current is shut off, the

solenoid snaps back to its normal or rest position (which may be normally open or closed depending on what it is designed to do).

Some solenoids are designed to do more than just switch on or off to open or close a valve. Some pull a valve to an intermediate position when a certain level of current is applied to the coil, then pull the valve to a third position when additional current is provided. This design allows a single solenoid to perform the same functions as two or even three single position solenoids.

The solenoids in the hydraulic modulator assembly are used to open and close passageways between the master cylinder and the individual brake circuits. By opening or closing the modulator valves to which they're attached, brake pressure within any given circuit can be held, released and reapplied to prevent lockup during hard braking.

ABS Control Strategy

The standard ABS control strategy that's used is a three step cycle:

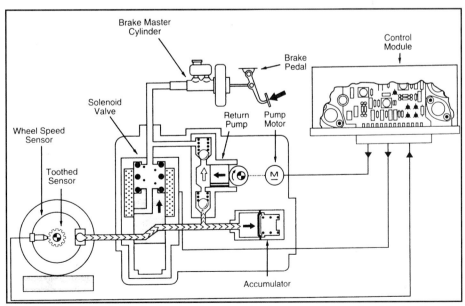

Brake Master
Cylinder

Control
Module

Brake
Pedal

Solenoid
Valve

Return
Pump

Pump
Motor

Wheel Speed
Sensor

Toothed
Sensor

M

Accumulator

To release pressure in the brake circuit so the wheel can speed up and regain traction, the current to the solenoid is increased. This pulls the solenoid to the third position, which opens a port allowing pressure to vent from the brake circuit to an accumulator. Pressure is then reapplied by cutting the current to the solenoid so it can return to its rest (normally open) position. Courtesy Bosch.

ABS is a real plus on off-road vehicles with four-wheel drive, such as this Jeep Wrangler, because it allows the driver to maintain steering control while braking on slick or muddy surfaces.

1. The first step is to hold or isolate the pressure in a given brake circuit by closing an "isolation" solenoid in the modulator assembly. This blocks off the line and prevents any further pressure from the master cylinder from reaching the brake.

2. If the wheel speed sensor continues to indicate the wheel is slowing too quickly and is starting to lock up, the same solenoid or a second "release" solenoid is energized to open a vent port that releases pressure from the brake circuit. The fluid is usually routed into a spring loaded or pressurized storage reservoir (called an "accumulator") so it can be reused as needed. Releasing pressure in the brake circuit allows the brake to loosen its grip so the wheel can speed up and regain traction.

3. The release and/or isolation solenoid(s) are then closed and/or an additional solenoid energized so pressure can be reapplied to the brake from the master cylinder or accumulator to reapply the brake. The

hold-release-reapply cycle repeats as many times as needed until the vehicle either comes to a halt or the driver takes his foot off the brake pedal. The speed at which this occurs depends on the particular ABS system that's on the vehicle, but can range from a few times per second up to 10 times per second.

The hydraulic modular is not a serviceable component, so you can't take it apart and replace internal components if it's defective. Replacement as an assembly is the only repair option.

Pump Motor & Accumulator

A high pressure electric pump is used in some ABS systems to generate power assist for normal braking as well as the reapplication of brake pressure during ABS braking. In some systems, it is used only for the reapplication of pressure during ABS braking.

The pump motor is energized via a relay that's switched on and off by the

ABS control module. The fluid pressure that's generated by the pump is stored in the "accumulator." The accumulator on ABS systems where the hydraulic modulator is part of the master cylinder assembly consists of a pressure storage chamber filled with nitrogen gas. A thick rubber diaphragm forms a barrier between the nitrogen gas and brake fluid. As fluid is pumped into the accumulator, it compresses the gas and stores pressure. When the brake pedal is depressed, pressure from the accumulator flows to the master cylinder to provide power assist. A pair of pressure switches mounted in the accumulator circuit signals the ABS control module to energize the pump when pressure falls below a preset minimum, then to shut the pump off once pressure is built back up.

Should the pump fail (a warning light comes on when reserve pressure drops too low), there is usually enough reserve pressure in the accumulator for 10 to 20 power-assisted stops. After that, there is no power assist. The brakes still work, but with increased effort.

On ABS systems that have a conventional master cylinder and vacuum booster for power assist, a small accumulator or pair of accumulators may be used as temporary holding reservoirs for brake fluid during the hold-release-reapply cycle. This type of accumulator typically uses a spring loaded diaphragm rather than a nitrogen charged chamber to store pressure.

TRACTION CONTROL

The same basic setup that allows an

ABS system to control wheel lockup during deceleration can be adapted to control wheel spin during acceleration. This is called "Traction Control," "Traction Assist" or "Acceleration Slip Reduction" (ASR).

When traction control is combined with ABS, it greatly enhances all-weather traction capabilities. Performance cars and those with low profile performance tires (which provide great dry traction but generally do poorly on wet or slick surfaces) are the ones that often benefit most from the addition of traction control.

But traction control isn't an electronic substitute for a limited slip differential or all-wheel drive. It is designed primarily to improve traction and vehicle stability on wet or slick surfaces, not for traction in deep snow or mud, or for racing.

Traction control uses the same wheel speed sensors as ABS, but requires reprogramming the ABS control module and adding additional solenoids to the hydraulic modulator. An ABS system with traction control also must have a pump and accumulator to generate and store pressure.

The traction control/ABS system monitors wheel speed during acceleration as well as deceleration (braking). If a wheel speed sensor detects wheel spin in one of the drive wheels during acceleration, the control module energizes a solenoid that allows stored fluid pressure from the accumulator to apply the brakes on the wheel that's spinning. This slows the wheel that's spinning and redirects engine torque through the differential to the opposite drive wheel to restore traction. It works just as well on front-wheel drive as it does

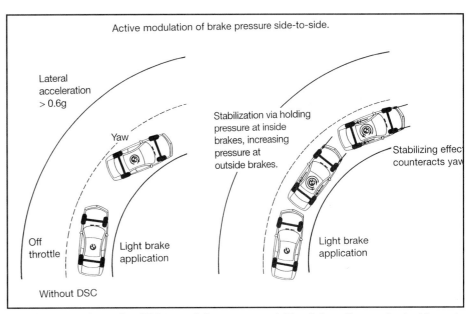

Stability control is putting ABS to work in a new way, taking it from the passive braking only mode to a full-time active mode. Stability control applies individual wheel braking as needed to maintain steering control when cornering or making sudden maneuvers.

on rear-wheel drive.

On some vehicle applications, additional control strategies may also be used to limit wheel spin. Some traction control systems add a "throttle relaxer" that pushes back against the gas pedal if the driver's foot is a little too heavy. By reducing the throttle opening, engine power is reduced to regain traction. Some applications also link the ABS/traction control computer to the engine computer electronically to retard ignition timing and/or deactivate fuel injectors to reduce power. Another strategy is to upshift the automatic transmission to a higher gear to reduce engine torque.

Many vehicles with traction control have a dash mounted switch that allows the driver to deactivate the system when desired (as when driving in deep snow). An indicator light shows you when the system is on or off, and may also tell you when the traction control system is actively engaged during acceleration. A separate warning light may be used to alert you if anything goes wrong with

the system.

Most traction control systems are only functional at speeds up to about 30 mph. At higher speeds, they are deactivated because of the adverse effects braking could have on handling and steering stability. Some traction control systems are also programmed to turn themselves off after a predetermined period of constant use to prevent excessive heat buildup in the brakes. Such might be the case if both drive wheels were buried in mud or snow and you kept on gunning the engine in a vain attempt to get free.

STABILITY CONTROL

The latest advancement in ABS technology takes antiskid and traction control to a new level. Called "stability control," it allows the ABS system to automatically brake individual wheels as needed under all driving conditions to improve or restore handling and steering control.

Stability control essentially makes ABS a full-time "expert" back seat

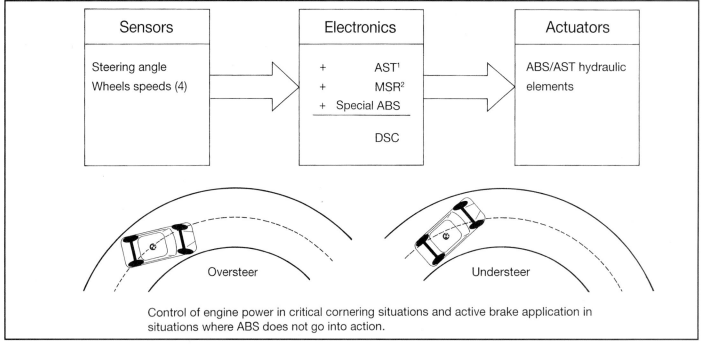

Sensors	Electronics	Actuators
Steering angle Wheels speeds (4)	+ AST[1] + MSR[2] + Special ABS DSC	ABS/AST hydraulic elements

Oversteer   Understeer

Control of engine power in critical cornering situations and active brake application in situations where ABS does not go into action.

Stability control uses inputs from the wheel speed sensors and steering to counter the effects of oversteer and understeer.

driver that's constantly monitoring how the vehicle is responding to the driver and road conditions. If a problem starts to develop, it springs into action and takes whatever measures are necessary to get things back under control. This includes reducing engine power by backing off the throttle and/or retarding spark timing, and simultaneously applying one or more brakes to counter the forces that are causing the vehicle to lose control and/or traction. The neat thing is that all this happens automatically without any driver input! Here's how it works. Additional input into the ABS system is provided by a steering angle sensor which keeps the ABS control module informed about where the driver is steering the vehicle. At the same time, the ABS control module monitors inputs from its wheel speed sensors to determine if there are any differences in the rotational speeds of the right and left front wheels. Turning a corner causes the inside wheel to rotate at a somewhat slower rate than the outside

wheel.

If a vehicle begins to oversteer in a turn and the rear end starts to come around (which would cause the car to spin out), the speed difference between the left and right front wheels increases. If the vehicle understeers (loses front traction and goes wider in a turn), the speed difference between the left and right front wheels decreases.

So anytime the ABS control module detects a difference in the "normal" rotational speeds between the left and right front wheels when turning, it immediately reduces engine power and applies braking as needed until control is regained.

The first such system to offer this capability was the 1995 BMW 750iL and 850Ci models powered by a 5.4 liter V12 engine. The system, supplied by Bosch, is called "Dynamic Stability Control" (DCS). It monitors individual wheel speeds 50 times per second (every 20 milliseconds), and is always active whether the driver is braking or not. If

the system senses an understeer or oversteer condition developing, it takes one of two courses of action depending on the amount of cornering force or lateral acceleration that's being developed.

If the vehicle's lateral acceleration is greater than about 0.6g, and the driver brakes normally (not hard enough to bring antilock braking into action), the DSC system modulates brake pressure so that the outside wheels are braked more than the inside wheels. This counteracts the oversteer or "yaw" effect that might otherwise cause the vehicle to lose control and spin out. If the driver realizes he's going too fast and hits the brakes hard enough to kick in the normal antilock braking, DSC reverts to a normal ABS braking mode allowing the system to selectively modulate rear brake pressure as needed.

A stability control system similar to one BMW uses called "Integrated Chassis Control System" (ICCS) is available on 1997 Cadillac models. The system uses corrective braking on

Components of the ESP System mounted on the Vehicle

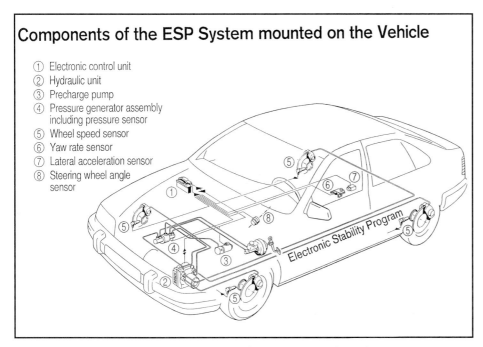

1. Electronic control unit
2. Hydraulic unit
3. Precharge pump
4. Pressure generator assembly including pressure sensor
5. Wheel speed sensor
6. Yaw rate sensor
7. Lateral acceleration sensor
8. Steering wheel angle sensor

Electronic Stability Program

This Mercedes Electronic Stability Program (ESP) system uses input from a yaw sensor to sense unwanted body motions that indicate loss of steering control. Courtesy Bosch.

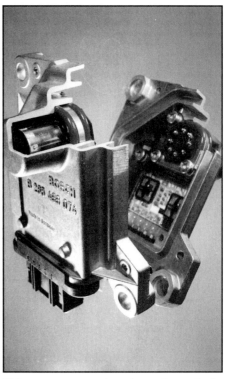

This yaw sensor uses piezo elements to detect motions that would indicate oversteer in a turn. The technology is based on missile guidance systems. Courtesy Bosch.

the front wheels only to enhance stability. Vehicle dynamics are monitored by a steering sensor, yaw sensor and lateral acceleration sensor.

An even more sophisticated "Electronic Stability Program" (ESP) was introduced in 1996 in V-12 powered Mercedes S600 models. Also made by Bosch, this system provides automatic engine torque reduction and braking if a car enters a corner too fast or makes a sudden steering maneuver. But unlike the BMW system, Mercedes adds individual front and rear braking to help the vehicle regain control.

With the Mercedes ESP system, the front brakes may be applied separately to help correct the vehicle's attitude. If the car is going into a left turn, for example, and is starting to oversteer, the ESP system will apply the right front brake to help bring it back under control. To correct an understeer condition when cornering left, the ESP system applies the left rear brake.

The Mercedes system takes inputs from two additional sensors: a lateral acceleration sensor and a "yaw velocity" sensor. The latter tells the control module if the car is turning on its axis so the computer can compare the input to the steering angle and speeds of the individual wheels.

One thing no stability control system can yet do is idiot-proof a vehicle. Stability control can certainly improve the overall handling and safety of a vehicle, but it can't overcome the basic laws of physics. If a vehicle enters a corner traveling way too fast, stability control can't magically keep it on the road. But it can help you regain control at lesser speeds (especially on slick roads).

ABS APPLICATIONS

BENDIX 3 ABS (Nonintegral)
1994 & up Chrysler Town & Country minivan
1994 & up Chrysler LeBaron Convertible & Sedan
1994 & up Dodge Caravan, Spirit & Shadow
1994 & up Plymouth Acclaim, Sundance & Voyager

BENDIX ABX-4 (Nonintegral)
1995 & up Dodge/Plymouth Neon
1996 & up Plymouth Breeze

BENDIX 6 ABS (Nonintegral)
1991 to 1993 Dodge Daytona & Spirit
1991 to 1993 Chrysler LeBaron
1991 to 1993 Plymouth Acclaim & Laser

BENDIX 9 (Jeep) ABS (Integral)
1989 to 1991 Jeep Cherokee & Wagoneer

BENDIX 10 ABS (Integral)
3/90 to 1993 Chrysler New Yorker, Imperial, Fifth Ave
3/90 to 1993 Dodge Dynasty
1991 to 1993 Dodge Caravan or Plymouth Voyager
1991 to 1992 Eagle Premier

BENDIX MECATRONIC II (Nonintegral)
1995 & up Ford Contour
1995 & up Mercury Mystique

BOSCH 2 ABS (Nonintegral)
(Japanese applications made by Nippon Ltd)
1985 & up BMW
1985 & up Audi

1985 & up Porsche
1986 to 1989 Chevrolet Corvette
1987 to 1989 Jaguar XJ-6
1987 & up Mazda
1987 & up Rolls Royce & Bentley
1987 & up Toyota Camry, Celica, Cressida, Supra
1987 & up Volvo
1987 to 1988 Sterling
1989 & up Mitsubishi Sigma
1989 & up Nissan Maxima, 240SX
1990 & up Lexus
1990 & up Nissan Stanza, 300ZX
1990 & up Subaru Legacy
1991 & up Dodge Colt Vista
1991 & up Eagle Summit, Summit Wagon
1991 & up Infiniti Q45
1991 & up Isuzu Rodeo
1991 & up Mazda 929
1991 & up Mitsubishi Diamante, Expo
1991 & up Nissan NX, Sentra
1991 & up Subaru Legacy
1991 & up Suzuki 4DR, Sidekick
1991 & up Toyota MR2, Previa
1992 & up Isuzu Trooper
1992 & up Subaru SVX
1993 & up Mazda MX-3
1993 & up Mitsubishi Mirage
1993 & up Nissan Altima

BOSCH 2E ABS (Nonintegral)
1991 & up Plymouth Laser
1991 & up Eagle Talon
1991 & up Dodge Stealth
1991 & up Mitsubishi 3000 GT, Eclipse and Galant

BOSCH 2S MICRO ABS (Nonintegral)
1990 to 1991 Chevrolet Corvette

BOSCH 2U ABS (Nonintegral)
1990 to 1993 Cadillac Brougham
1991 & up Buick Estate Wagon, Reatta, Riviera, Roadmaster
1991 to 1993 Cadillac Eldorado Touring Coupe, Seville
1991 & up Chevrolet Caprice, Classic wagon
1991 & up Oldsmobile Toronado, Trofeo
1992 & up Oldsmobile Custom Cruiser Wagon
1993 & up Mercury Villager
1993 & up Nissan Quest
1994 & up Cadillac Deville Concours, Fleetwood
1994 & up Ford Mustang

BOSCH ABS/ASR (Nonintegral ABS with traction control)
1992 to 1994 Corvette
1993 & up Cadillac Allante, Brougham, Eldorado, Seville
1994 only Cadillac Deville Concours
1994 only Cadillac Eldorado, Fleetwood, Seville

BOSCH 3 ABS (Integral)
1987 to 1992 Cadillac Allante
1988 to 3/90 Chrysler Fifth Avenue, Imperial, New Yorker
1988 to 3/90 Dodge Dynasty

BOSCH 5 ABS (Nonintegral)
1995 & up Buick Estate Wagon, Roadmaster
1995 & up Cadillac DeVille, Eldorado, Fleetwood, Seville
1995 & up Chevrolet Caprice, Caprice Wagon, Corvette, Impala
1995 & up Porsche 911 Carrera
1996 & up Ford Taurus, Mercury Sable

BOSCH REAR WHEEL ABS (Nonintegral)

1983 to 1990 Dodge & Plymouth Conquest
1983 to 1990 Mitsubishi Galant, Starion
1991 to 1992 Daihatsu Rocky

DELCO MORAINE POWERMASTER 3 ABS (Integral)

1989 to 1991 Buick Regal
1989 to 1991 Oldsmobile Cutlass
1989 to 1991 Pontiac Grand Prix
1990 & up Lotus Esprit
1990 to 1991 Pontiac Grand Prix GTU

DELCO MORAINE ABS-VI (Nonintegral)

1991 & up Buick Skylark GS
1991 & up Oldsmobile Cutlass Calais International
1991 & up Pontiac Grand Am SE
1991 & up Saturn
1992 & up Buick Regal
1992 & up Chevrolet APV, Beretta, Cavalier, Corsica, Lumina
1992 & up Geo Prizm
1992 & up Oldsmobile Achieva, Cutlass, Silhouette
1992 & up Pontiac Grand Prix, LeMans, Sunbird, Transport
1993 & up Chevrolet Camaro
1993 & up Pontiac Firebird
1994 & up Oldsmobile Delta 88, 98

DELCO MORAINE ABS-VI (Nonintegral) with TCS (traction control)

1994 & up Buick Park Avenue & Ultra
1994 & up Chevrolet Camaro Z28
1994 & up Olds 88, 98 & Silhouette,
1994 & up Pontiac Bonneville & Firebird w/5.7L V8

HONDA ABS (Nonintegral)

1988 & up Acura Legend
1990 & up Acura Integra GS, NSX
1991 & up Acura Vigor

KELSEY-HAYES RWAL & RABS REAR-WHEEL ABS (Nonintegral)

1987 to 1991 Ford F Series trucks, Bronco, Bronco II
1988 to 1991 Chevrolet & GMC C/K pickups, R/V trucks
1989 to 1990 Chevrolet & GMC Astro vans
1989 to 1990 Chevrolet S-Series trucks & Blazer
1989 & up Dodge Ram pickups, Ramcharger
1989 to 1992 Dodge Dakota
1989 to 1992 Ford Ranger
1989 & up GMC Safari, S/T Series, S/T Jimmy
1990 to 1992 Chevrolet G-van, Suburban
1990 to 1992 Ford Aerostar & Econoline vans
1990 to 1992 GMC Safari cargo van, Suburban
1990 & up Isuzu Amigo, Pickup, Rodeo
1990 & up Mazda MPV, Navajo, Pickup
1990 & up Subaru Sidekick
1990 to 1991 Isuzu Trooper
1991 to 1992 Ford Explorer
1991 & up Geo Tracker
1991 & up Nissan Pathfinder, Pickup
1992 & up Chevrolet C/K Series pickup
1992 to 1993 Ford Bronco
1992 & up Ford Bronco II, F-Series
1992 & up GMC Sierra
1993 & up Ford Ranger
1993 & up Ford F450, 500, 5500 HD

KELSEY-HAYES 4WAL (4-WHEEL) ABS (Nonintegral)

1990 & up Chevrolet Astro

1990 & up GMC Safari
1990 & up Subaru Legacy
1991 & up Chevrolet S/T Blazer
1991 & up GMC Jimmy 4-door, Syclone
1991 & up GMC S-Series pickups
1991 & up Chevrolet Syclone pickup
1992 & up Oldsmobile Bravada
1992 & up Chevrolet S-Series Blazer, Suburban
1992 & up GMC Jimmy (2-door), Suburban, Typhoon, Yukon
1994 & up Chevrolet S/T-Series pickup

KELSEY-HAYES EBC-5 ABS (Nonintegral)

1993 & up Dodge Dakota
1994 & up Dodge Ram & Ram van
1994 & up Ford Aerostar, Econoline

KELSEY-HAYES EBC-10 ABS (Nonintegral)

1994 & up Ford Windstar

NIPPONDENSO (Nonintegral)

1990 & up Infiniti
1990 & up Lexus

SUMITOMO 1 ABS (Non-integral)

1987 to 1991 Mazda RX-7
1988 to 3/91 Mazda 626
1989 to 3/91 Mazda MX-6
1989 to 3/91 Ford Probe
1990 to 1991 Honda Prelude Si
1991 & up Honda Accord

SUMITOMO 2 ABS (Non-integral)

1990 & up Mazda Miata
3/91 & up Ford Probe
3/91 & up Mazda MX-6 & 626
1992 & up Mazda MX-3
1994 & up Ford Escort GT
1994 & up Mercury Tracer LTS

ANTILOCK BRAKE SYSTEMS

TEVES MARK 2 ABS (Integral)
1985 to 1989 Lincoln Continental
1985 to 1992 Lincoln Mark VII
1986 to 1989 Buick LeSabre
1986 to 1990 Buick Electra, Park Avenue
1986 to 1989 Cadillac Fleetwood Brougham
1986 to 1990 Cadillac DeVille
1986 to 1990 Oldsmobile 98
1986 to 1990 Pontiac 6000 STE
1987 to 1992 Ford Thunderbird
1987 to 1992 Mercury Cougar
1987 & up Saab 9000
1988 to 1989 Cadillac Eldorado, Seville
1988 to 1989 Buick Reatta, Riviera
1988 to 1989 Merkur Scorpio
1988 to 1990 Oldsmobile Delta 88, Toronado
1988 to 1991 Peugeot 505

1988 to 1990 Pontiac Bonneville & SSE
1991 & up Saab 900
1991 & up Volkswagen Passat

TEVES MARK 4 ABS (Nonintegral)
1990 to 1995 Ford Taurus SHO
1990 & up Lincoln Continental, Town Car
1990 & up Volkswagen Corrado & Jetta
1991 & up Buick LeSabre, Park Avenue & Ultra
1991 & up Cadillac DeVille
1991 to 1995 Ford Taurus
1991 to 1995 Mercury Sable
1991 & up Oldsmobile 98 & 88
1991 & up Pontiac Bonneville & SSE & SSEi
1992 & up Ford Crown Victoria

1992 & up Jeep Cherokee, Grand Cherokee, Wrangler
1992 & up Mercury Grand Marquis
1992 & up Oldsmobile Royal LS
1993 & up Chrysler Concorde
1993 & up Dodge Intrepid
1993 & up Eagle Vision
1993 & up Ford Explorer, Thunderbird
1993 & up Mercury Cougar
1994 & up Chrysler LHS, New Yorker
1994 & up Ford Bronco
1994 & up Lincoln Mark VIII

TOYOTA REAR-WHEEL ABS
1990 & up Toyota Pickup & 4Runner
1993 & up Toyota T-100 pickup

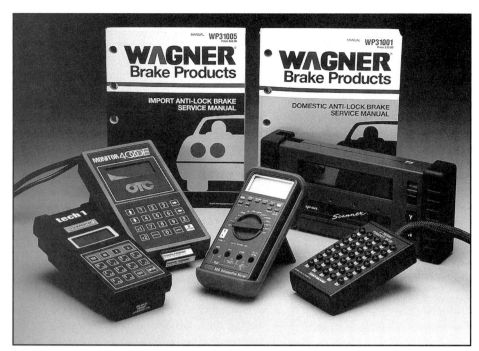

To diagnose ABS problems, you need a scan tool, multimeter, pinout box and the proper reference manuals.

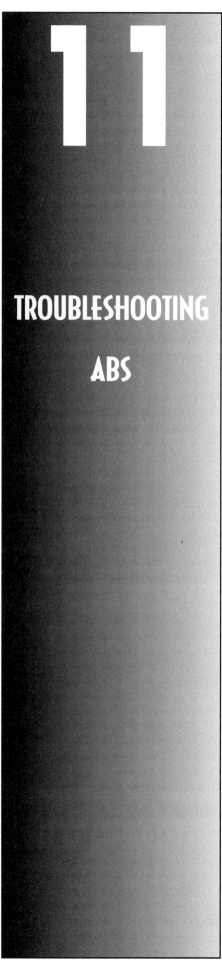

ABS diagnosis and trouble-shooting requires an in-depth knowledge of the system you're working on as well as a scan tool in many instances, so this job might be best left to a professional. But if you want to do your own diagnostic homework, keep the following in mind any time you encounter a suspected ABS problem:

• Don't blame the ABS system for ordinary brake problems. Remember, the only time an antilock brake system does anything at all is when a wheel speed sensor tells it one or more wheels are slowing too quickly and starting to skid. The rest of the time the ABS system is passive and is just along for the ride. Except for power assist on integral ABS systems, it has no effect whatsoever on normal braking. So if your brakes are grabbing, pulling, dragging, making noise, leaking, etc., don't blame the antilock system. Conventional brake problems must always be addressed and corrected first before attempting to diagnose a suspected antilock brake problem.

• Vehicles with ABS generally use the same brake linings, calipers, wheel cylinders and brake shoes as similar models that do not have ABS. On ABS-equipped vehicles that have a conventional master cylinder and vacuum booster, these components are often the same as models that do not have ABS—but there are exceptions! So make sure you have the correct parts before you replace anything! Other parts that may be different on an ABS-equipped vehicle are the rotors and drums because they frequently have a tone ring for the wheel speed sensors.

• Basic brake service procedures on ABS-equipped vehicles are essentially the same as those on vehicles without ABS—with two exceptions. You may have to use a somewhat different bleeding procedure or sequence on some ABS applications because air can become trapped in the ABS modulator solenoids. You must also depressurize the accumulator(s) if your vehicle has an integral ABS system with a combination master

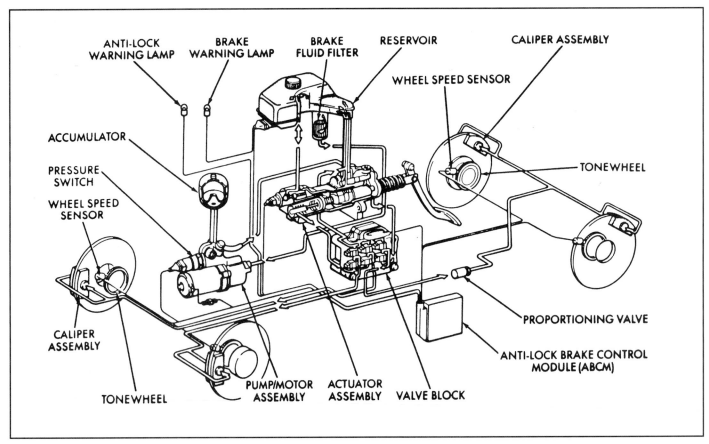

ANTI-LOCK WARNING LAMP
BRAKE WARNING LAMP
BRAKE FLUID FILTER
RESERVOIR
CALIPER ASSEMBLY
WHEEL SPEED SENSOR
ACCUMULATOR
PRESSURE SWITCH
WHEEL SPEED SENSOR
TONEWHEEL
CALIPER ASSEMBLY
TONEWHEEL
PUMP/MOTOR ASSEMBLY
ACTUATOR ASSEMBLY
VALVE BLOCK
PROPORTIONING VALVE
ANTI-LOCK BRAKE CONTROL MODULE (ABCM)

All ABS systems have onboard self-diagnostics to detect faults that might interfere with the safe operation of the ABS system. Self-checks are usually performed as soon as the vehicle is started, and repeated as soon as the vehicle reaches a few miles per hour. If a problem is detected, the ABS warning light will come on. Most systems also log a "fault code" in memory that can be retrieved to help diagnose the problem. Courtesy Chrysler.

cylinder and modulator assembly.

Warning: High pressure accumulators may contain up to 2700 psi of internal pressure. To relieve this pressure, depress the brake pedal 30 to 40 times with the ignition off. Once all the pressure has been drained out of the accumulator, the pedal will take more effort to push. Then and only then is it safe to proceed with any brake repairs or to open the brake lines.

• ABS equipped vehicles generally use the same type of brake fluid as those without ABS (DOT 3 or 4 fluid). Always use the type of fluid specified by the vehicle manufacturer. DOT 5 silicone fluid is not recommended for ABS applications because it contains too much dissolved air and may

aerate, causing a loss of pedal during ABS braking.

• The operation of the ABS system can often be affected by electrical problems in the vehicle as well as the ABS system itself. Underlying conditions that may cause trouble include:

Low Battery Charge—A low charge can interfere with the operation of the antilock control electronics. Blown fuses—Check the brake control module fuse, main relay fuse and pump motor fuse.

Corroded or Loose Connectors—The main relay, pump motor and motor relay, pressure switch, main valve, valve block, fluid level sensor, and control module connectors must all be tight and correctly installed.

Bad Grounds—Check for good body grounds, especially on the hydraulic unit.

• If the ABS warning light remains on after you've started your vehicle or it comes on while driving, it usually means the system has self-diagnosed a fault and has deactivated the ABS system. Normal braking should be unaffected—unless the problem is related to the pump or accumulator on an integral ABS system, in which case power assist may be lost. In any event, the cause of the ABS warning light should be investigated as soon as possible.

• A brake warning lamp that remains on or comes on while driving usually indicates a problem with the hydraulic

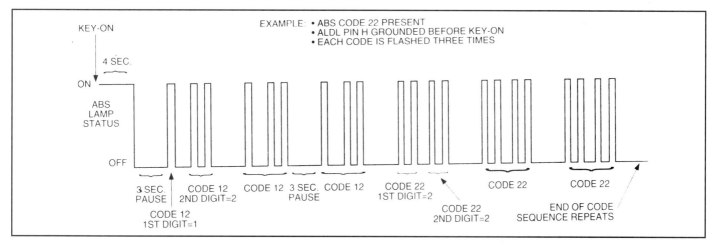

This chart shows how a manual flash code will appear as blinks of the ABS warning light. Shown is a code sequence for a Bosch 2U and 2S Micro application. Code 12 (one flash followed by two quick flashes), repeats three times, followed by a code 22.

system, not the ABS system. Your vehicle may have a fluid leak or loss of pressure, either of which pose a danger to safe braking. The cause of the brake warning light should be investigated immediately.

SCANNING FOR ABS FAULT CODES

If your ABS light is on or is flashing, it means something is wrong. Other clues might be ABS feedback such as solenoid noise and pedal pulsation during normal braking, or a problem with rear wheel lockup when braking on wet or slick roads. But even if your vehicle is showing no symptoms whatsoever, it's still a good idea to scan the ABS system for fault codes when servicing the brakes. Why? Because some codes on some systems won't necessarily illuminate the ABS light and disable the ABS system. These are "nonlatching" faults that are not considered serious enough to interfere with the system's ability to do its job. Even so, a fault is a fault and should always be investigated.

It's also possible that the ABS light itself is burnt out—which is why you

should always check it first. The bulb should come on and remain on for a few seconds when the ignition is first turned on, then go out if no initial problems have been detected. On Delco Powermaster III or Teves 2 integral ABS systems, the ABS warning light will remain on while the pump motor builds up accumulator pressure. This may take up to 30 seconds if the accumulator has become discharged because the vehicle hasn't been driven for a number of days, or because the accumulator has discharged by pumping the brake pedal while the ignition was off.

If the ABS warning light goes out as it should after a few seconds, it doesn't necessarily mean all is well. Many key system self-checks like wheel speed sensor inputs and solenoid cycling are not performed until the vehicle is in motion. So a short test drive may be necessary to verify whether or not the light remains out or comes back on.

When There's A Code

If your ABS light is on, you'll have to use a "manual flash code" procedure to retrieve the code, or plug

a scan tool into the system to read the code. Many applications do not provide manual flash codes so your only option is to use a scan tool. Professional grade scan tools are very expensive, but there are less expensive "read only" scan tools designed for do-it-yourselfers. So if you're serious about doing any ABS diagnostics and your vehicle does not provide manual flash codes, you'll have to rent or buy a scan tool.

On some vehicles (Buick, Corvette and others), fault codes can also be accessed through the climate control system by pushing the appropriate buttons in a specified sequence. The diagnostic information is then displayed on the vehicle's information center or digital speedometer.

The manual flash code procedure generally involves grounding the ABS diagnostic connector, then counting flashes of the ABS light. Reading codes this way is like deciphering Morse code. Was that a long blink or a short blink? Did you miss a pause or was that another flash? Flash codes can be confusing, especially when there's more than one code. And the way in which the flashes are read varies from one ABS system to

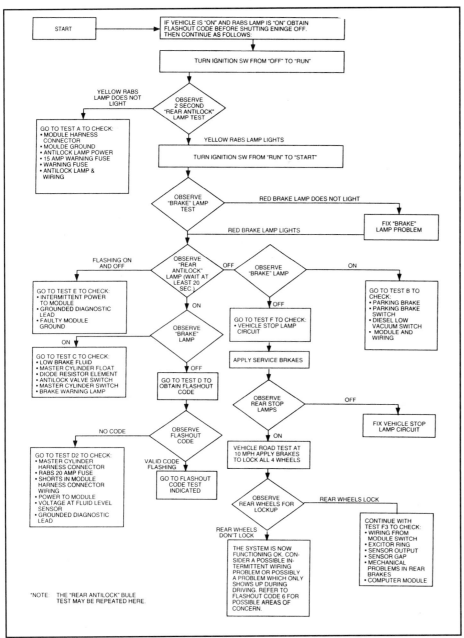

This is a typical diagnostic tree for an ABS fault code. Shown is a Ford rear wheel ABS (RABS) application.

What happens next will again depend on the application. Some systems generate a numeric code that corresponds to a specific fault. Others will give you an actual message which is displayed or scrolls across the display on your tool.

Either way, pulling the code is only the first step in diagnosing the problem. The diagnostic chart that corresponds to the code in a shop manual will give you direction on what checks you need to perform to isolate the fault. The manual will also give you the specific resistance, voltage or other test spec values you need to check the individual components in question. You'll also need a multimeter and possibly a breakout box to make the specific circuit and component checks.

False Codes

ABS systems will sometimes generate "false" codes. Such a code would seem to indicate a fault has occurred, but there's really nothing wrong. You can waste a lot of valuable time chasing ghosts and replacing parts needlessly in an attempt to fix this kind of code. These kinds of problems are often described in "technical service bulletins" (TSBs) issued by the vehicle manufacturers. TSBs are not generally available to the general public but are available from various aftermarket sources including Alldata, Chilton, Mitchell and Motor.

Software Glitches—In some instances, false codes are the product of "glitches" in the ABS software. On Jeep Cherokees, Wagoneers and Grand Cherokees, for example, a wheel speed sensor code may be set if the rear wheels break traction while accelerating on ice or mud in the two-

another. So a scan tool is usually the preferred method for reading ABS codes. You'll make fewer mistakes with a scan tool. And on some of the newer ABS systems, a professional grade "bidirectional" scan tool can also be used to initiate various self-tests.

Scanning For Codes

Depending on the application, you either plug your scan tool into a diagnostic connector on the ABS module itself, or into the vehicle's data communications link (DCL) connector. You then enter the vehicle application info (year, make and model) so your scan tool will know how to read the electronic signals. You then check for any codes following the directions that came with your scan tool.

When diagnosing an ABS fault code, you often have to perform voltage and resistance checks on various components to determine if they're good or bad. This man is checking the resistance of the ABS solenoids in the ABS modulator.

wheel drive mode.

False wheel speed sensor codes on some vehicles can also be triggered in some applications if a wheel is rotated or spun while the ignition is on (as when changing or balancing a tire, working on the brakes, etc.). The ABS module sets a code because the speed signal received from the one wheel does not agree with that from the others. Consequently, it thinks something is amiss with the speed sensor circuit.

False wheel speed sensor codes as well as ABS performance problems can also be triggered by changes in tire size. If replacement tires or wheels have a larger or smaller diameter than the original equipment tires and wheels, it will affect the wheel speed sensor readings—especially if there's a difference in tire size between the front and rear axles. For this reason, the vehicle manufacturers do not recommend changing tire sizes on most ABS equipped vehicles.

ABS FAULT CODES

Now comes the part you've been waiting for, instructions on how to scan various ABS systems for codes, and what the codes mean. What follows is a brief summary for how to access codes on each of the major ABS systems. Each system is in its own box for easy reference. The technology is constantly changing, so always refer to a current shop manual for the latest procedures and information.

Bendix 9

The Bendix 9 system on 1989 through 1991 Jeep Cherokee and Wagoneer models does not provide manual flash codes, so a scan tool must be used. The scan tool can also be used to perform a series of ABS electrical checks. If a failure or problem is detected during these tests, the scan tool will display a fault code indicating which circuit the problem is in. The scan tool can also be used to monitor various system inputs and outputs, including the wheel speed sensors, the ABS solenoids and the operation of the pump motor. Codes on this system can be cleared by removing the ABS BAT fuse from the fuse panel for 10 seconds.

The Bendix 9 fault codes are:
800–No voltage at ECM
801–No serial data from ECM
802–No parking brake signal
803–Warning lights inoperative
804–Yellow ABS warning light inoperative
805–Differential pressure fault
806–Boost pressure fault
807–Low accumulator pressure
808–Pressure modulator fault
809–Self-test failure
810–Solenoid under voltage
811–Relay fault
812–Pump/motor fault
813–Stoplight circuit fault
814–Low fluid
815–Right rear wheel speed sensor
816–Left rear wheel speed sensor
817–Right front wheel speed sensor
818–Left front wheel speed sensor
819–Open circuit at diagnostic connector

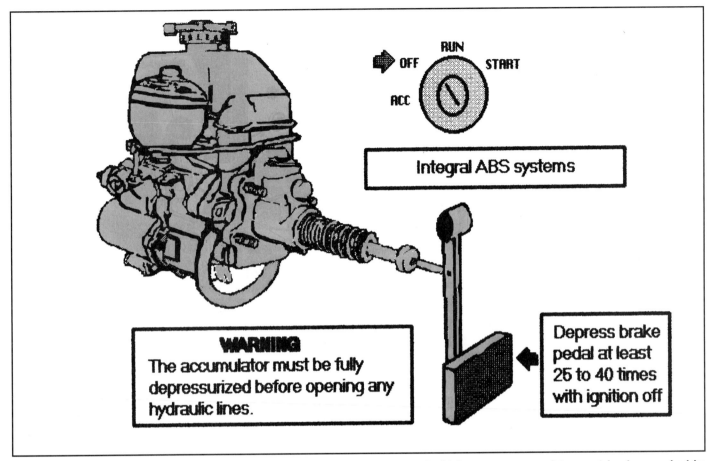

RUN
OFF START
ACC

Integral ABS systems

WARNING
The accumulator must be fully depressurized before opening any hydraulic lines.

Depress brake pedal at least 25 to 40 times with ignition off

Before doing any work that involves opening up lines on an integral ABS system, the high pressure accumulator must be depressurized by pumping the brake pedal 25 to 40 times with the ignition off.

Bosch 2

Bosch 2 ABS systems are found on most import models as well as some domestics. Domestic applications include 1986 & up Corvette, 1991 & up Dodge Stealth, and 1991 & up GM full-size rear-wheel drive passenger cars (Cadillac, Buick, Oldsmobile, Chevy Caprice, etc.)

The Bosch 2 controller on many older import applications has only a limited self-diagnostic capability and cannot generate fault codes like the later Bosch 2U and 2S Micro ABS systems used on domestic cars. But it can still detect a variety of faults that interfere with the safe operation of the ABS system. These older applications require a special dedicated Bosch ABS tester, which in most instances can only be found at a new car dealer. Many Bosch 2 import applications (Lexus, Mazda, Nissan and Toyota) can generate manual codes, but not scan codes.

On the GM applications, the scan tool is plugged into the ALDL connector under the dash while the ignition is off. The key is then turned on so the system can be accessed for any codes. The Bosch 2 codes are:

11–Left front wheel speed sensor
12 –Right front wheel speed sensor
13 –Left rear wheel speed sensor
14 –Right rear wheel speed sensor
15 –Sensor fault
21–G-Force sensor
22–Stoplight switch circuit
41–Left front ABS solenoid
42–Right front ABS solenoid
43–Rear ABS solenoid
51–ABS solenoid valve relay
52–Motor relay
56–Control module

Bendix 10

Bendix 10 ABS is found on 1990 to '93 Chrysler New Yorkers, Imperial, Fifth Avenue and Dodge Dynasty, and the 1991 to '93 minivans. This system has two types of faults: latching and nonlatching. Latching faults are ones serious enough to prevent the ABS system from functioning properly (like a controller, modulator or wheel speed sensor failure). When a latching fault is detected, the ABS light comes on and remains on. The ABS system is also disabled. A nonlatching fault (such as low boost or accumulator pressure, low system voltage, etc.) is considered less serious and will illuminate the ABS and/or brake warning lights as long as the fault exists. But the lights will go out once the fault no longer exists. In most cases, a fault code will be logged.

There are no manual flash codes with this system either, and access is the same as Bendix 9. But this system displays "error messages" rather than three-digit fault codes.

Fault codes in Bendix 10 are also stored in a nonvolatile memory which means they can't be erased by pulling the ABS fuse. The only way they can be cleared is with a scan tool. If a fault does not repeat within 50 ignition cycles, it will be automatically erased.

The diagnostic connector on Bendix 10 applications is located under the dash, left of the steering column. It is a 6-way blue connector. The Codes are:

Component	ABS light	Brake Light	Type
CAB fault	ON	OFF	Latching
Modulator fault	ON	OFF	Latching
Solenoid undervoltage	ON	OFF	Non-latching
Low fluid/parking brake	ON(1)	ON	Non-latching
ABS system relay	ON	OFF	Latching
Wheel speed sensor	ON	OFF	Latching
Boost pressure	ON(2)	ON	Non-latching
Low accumulator pressure	ON(2)	ON	Non-latching
Excessive decay	ON	OFF	Non-latching
Primary/Delta pressure	ON	OFF	Non-latching

Notes: (1) The brake light comes on immediately, and the ABS light comes on when speed reaches 3 mph. (2) Both lights come on when the brakes are applied.

Bendix 6

This system is found on 1991 through '93 Dodge Daytona and Spirit, Chrysler LeBaron and Plymouth Acclaim and Laser. Like Bendix 10, faults are classified as either latching or non-latching. Code access is with a scan tool through the blue, 6-way diagnostic connector located under the fuse box access cover to the left of the steering column. The fault messages for Bendix 6 are the same as for Bendix 10. Codes are also logged in a nonvolatile memory and can only be cleared with a scan tool.

Kelsey-Hayes RWAL & RABS

This rear-wheel ABS system is found on 1987 and up Ford F series trucks (including Bronco & Bronco II), 1988 & up Chevy & GMC pickups and vans, and 1989 & up Dodge trucks. The self-diagnostic capability of this system is limited to one fault code. When a fault is detected, the amber ABS warning light on Ford and Dodge applications, or the red brake light on GM applications, will come on and the ABS function will be disabled.

On GM vehicles, fault codes can be read manually or with a scan tool. To manually access codes, jump terminals "A" and "H" (or ground terminal "H") on the ALDL connector under the instrument panel. If using a scan tool on a GM application, plug the tool into the ALDL connector, turn the ignition on and read out the code. A scan tool with a dealer cartridge can also be used to perform additional system checks such as the system voltage at the ALDL connector, solenoid valve hold and release tests, brake switch function, DRAC output and the vehicle speed sensor signal.

On Ford and Dodge trucks, fault codes can be accessed manually by grounding the diagnostic pigtail connector on the ABS control module.

Manual flash codes are read by counting the first long flash, then adding the short flashes that follow. The total of the long flash plus any short flashes that follow equals the number of the fault code.

Beginning in August 1990, a software change was made in the ABS controller on all General Motors RWAL-equipped vehicles. The change transforms codes 6, 9 and 10 into "soft" (non-latching) codes that only illuminate the warning light as long as the fault is present. If the fault is intermittent and no longer exists, the light will go out with the next ignition cycle. A scan tool must be used on the newer GM applications to read any soft (non-latching) codes that might be present because grounding the "H" terminal on the ALDL connector erases soft codes.

To manually clear a stored fault code on GM and some Dodge trucks with RWAL, remove the ABS fuse or disconnect the battery for 5 seconds. Ford RABS codes will automatically clear when the ignition is turned to the off position. To clear codes on '92 & up GM applications, pull the stop/hazard fuse, turn the ignition on and jump terminals "A" and "H" on the ALDL connector (or ground terminal "H" for one second). Remove the jumper connection or ground for one second, then ground terminal "H" again for one second.

The RWAL & RABS fault codes are:

1–This code should not occur (replace the controller if it does)

2–Open isolation valve circuit or defective ABS module

3–Open dump valve circuit or defective ABS module

4–Grounded or closed RABS or RWAL valve switch

5–Excessive actuations of dump valve during ABS braking

6–Erratic speed sensor signal

7–Shorted isolation valve or defective ABS module

8–Shorter dump valve or defective ABS module

9–High resistance or open speed sensor circuit (resistance should be 1000 to 2500 ohms)

10–Low speed sensor resistance (Dodge & Ford only)

10–Open speed sensor circuit (GM only)

11–Stop lamp switch circuit (Dodge & Ford)

13–ABS module speed processor (Dodge & Ford only)

14–ABS module program (Dodge & Ford only)

15–ABS module RAM memory failure (Dodge & Ford)

Teves Mark 4

Teves Mark 4 is a nonintegral ABS system that's used on 1990 and up Taurus and Lincolns, 1991 & up Buicks, Cadillacs, Oldsmobiles and Pontiacs, 1992 & up Jeep Cherokee, Grand Cherokee and Wrangler, 1993 & up Chrysler Concorde, Dodge Intrepid and Eagle Vision, 1993 & up Ford Explorer and Thunderbird, and 1994 & up Ford Bronco.

Fault codes are retained in a non-volatile memory so they cannot be erased by disconnecting the battery or removing the ABS module's power supply fuse. Faults remain in memory for 50 ignition cycles and can only be cleared with a scan tool. If the fault does not repeat after 50 cycles, it will be automatically erased—except in the case of a failure of the hydraulic unit or the controller, in which case the code will remain until repairs have been made.

All faults except an open fluid level switch will cause the ABS and traction control lights to remain on for the duration of the ignition cycle. An open fluid level switch will only cause the light to remain on as long as the condition exists, but the fault code will be retained even after the light goes out.

If the ABS module itself is defective (code 11), the code cannot be cleared with a scan tool. The only way to clear the code is to replace the ABS module.

No manual codes are provided by the Mark 4 system, so a scan tool must be used. On Ford applications, the ABS diagnostic connector may be located under the hood or in the trunk depending where the module is located. Any 20 series code (any code from 22 to 29 that relates to the modulator solenoid valves) will override any other stored code and will not allow other codes to be output during the system self-test. On Ford applications with traction control, codes 18 and 19 (which relate to the isolation valves) as well as the 20 series codes will override all other codes.

If the vehicle has a 18, 19 or 20 series fault code, service these faults first. Then repeat the self-test to determine if there are any additional codes in memory. The previous codes will not be erased until all faults have been serviced and the vehicle has been driven faster than 25 mph.

The Teves Mark 4 codes are:

11–ABS module
17–Traction assist reference voltage
18–Traction assist isolation valve #1
19–Traction assist isolation valve #2
22–Left front inlet valve
23, 51–Left front outlet valve
24, 52–Right front inlet valve
25–Right front outlet valve
26–Rear inlet valve
27–Rear outlet valve
28–Left rear inlet valve
29, 54–Left rear outlet valve
31, 35, 41, 55, 71, 75 –Left front wheel speed sensor
32, 36, 42, 56, 72, 76– Right front wheel speed sensor
33, 37, 43, 57, 73, 77–Right rear wheel speed sensor
34, 38, 44, 58, 74, 78 –Left rear wheel speed sensor
53–Right rear outlet valve
54–Left rear outlet valve
61–Fluid level indicator circuit
62–Pedal travel switch
63–Pump motor speed sensor
64–Pump motor pressure
66–Pressure switch
67–Traction assist pump motor relay

Delco Powermaster III

The Powermaster III system, which you'll find on 1989 to 1991 Buick Regal, Oldsmobile Cutlass and Pontiac Grand Prix, has the unique ability to partially disable itself when certain faults occur. A code 4, 5, 6, 9, 10, 12, 13, 23, 24, 26 or 27, which relate to the front wheel circuits, will cause the ABS warning light to come on. But only the front ABS circuits will be disabled, not the rear.

A flashing ABS warning light occurs when less serious faults that do not affect the operation of the ABS system occur. These include codes 3, 31, 34, 35, 37, 38, 39, 40, 42 or 62. The ABS system remains fully operational when these codes are present.

The Delco Powermaster III ABS system does not provide manual flash codes, so a scan tool must be used to access fault codes.

To access the codes, a scan tool must be plugged into the ALDL connector located under the instrument panel. The codes are:

1, 2 & 3–ABS warning light circuit
4 –Relay or solenoid fault
5, 6, 37 & 39–Front enable relay
7, 8, 38, 40 & 54–Rear enable relay

9, 17 & 26–RF hold solenoid
10, 18 & 27–LF hold solenoid
11, 19 & 28–Rear hold solenoid
12, 20 & 23–RF release solenoid
13, 21 & 24–LF release solenoid
14, 22 & 25–Rear release solenoid
15–Front systems shorted to battery
16–Rear system shorted to battery
30–Open wheel speed sensors
31–Open pump motor feedback circuit
32, 33, 34 & 41–Brake switch
35 & 36–Pump motor
42–Low brake pressure circuit open
43–Low system voltage
44 & 48–RF wheel speed sensor
45 & 49–LF wheel speed sensor
46 & 50–RR wheel speed sensor
47 & 51–LR wheel speed sensor
52–EEPROM failure
55 & 60–ABS control module failure
56–Test 32 failed or current ignition cycle
59–Low pressure reading on ABS stop
62 –Low accumulator precharge
63–Open rear wheel speed sensor 4-pin connector

KELSEY-HAYES 4WAL

This four-wheel ABS system is found on 1990 & up Chevy Astro, 1991 & up Chevy S-Series pickups and Blazers, and 1992 & up Suburbans. This system can log and display multiple fault codes, and provides manual or scan tool access. The manual flash code and scan procedures are essentially the same as with RWAL. The codes for this system are:
12–System normal (2WD)
13–System normal (brake applied - 2WD)
14–System normal (4WD)
15–System normal (brake applied - 4WD)
21, 22, 23-Right front wheel speed sensor
25, 26, 2–Left front wheel speed sensor
28–Erratic sensor
29–No input all four wheel speed sensors
31, 32, 33 Right rear wheel speed sensor
35, 36, 37 Left rear wheel speed sensor
38– Wheel speed sensor error

41, 43   Right front ABS isolation valve
42, 44–Right front ABS pulse-width modulation valve
45, 47–Left front ABS isolation valve
46, 48 –Left front ABS pulse-width modulation valve
51, 53 –Rear ABS isolation valve
52, 54 –Rear ABS pulse-width modulation valve
61–Right front reset switch
62–Left front reset switch
63–Rear reset switch
65, 66 –Pump motor relay
67, 68 –Pump motor
71, 72 –ABS control module
73, 74 –ABS control module
81– Brake switch circuit
85, 86   ABS warning light circuit
88– Brake warning light circuit
   Codes, 43, 44, 47, 48, 53, 54 and 68 indicate a power or ground circuit fault.

Teves Mark 2

This integral ABS system is used on 1985 to '89 Lincoln Continental, 1985 to '92 Mark VII, 1987 to '92 Thunderbird, 1986 to '89 & '90 GM full-size rear wheel drive cars (Buick, Cadillac & Olds) and 1986 to 1990 Pontiac 6000 STE.

The Teves Mark 2 ABS module can't store more than one fault code with the same first digit at the same time (a code 23 and a code 24 simultaneously, for example). It can, however, store codes with different first digits or last digits (a code 23, 33, 43, 44 etc.). So it may be necessary to recheck the system for subsequent fault codes after the initial code has been retrieved and the problem repaired. Driving the car faster than 25 mph will erase any stored codes and allow the system to rediagnose any faults that still remain.

On Ford applications, fault codes can be read manually by grounding the underhood diagnostic connector and counting the flashes of the warning lamp, or with a scan tool. On GM applications, only 1988 to 1990 applications can generate fault codes. The earlier 1986 and 1987 applications did not provide codes. On these older applications, faults are diagnosed by noting whether or not the ABS and/or red brake warning lights are on and under what driving conditions, then comparing the lights to a "light sequence chart" in a service manual. The chart will tell you which circuits to check.

On the 1988 to 1990 GM applications that do provide codes, they can be read manually or with a scan tool. Grounding pin G on the ALDL connector under the instrument panel (1988 models), or pin H (1989 & 1990 models), then turning the ignition on will cause the ABS light to flash out the codes.

The number of times the ABS light flashes corresponds to the first digit of the code. There will then be a 3 second pause followed by more flashes that correspond to the second digit of the code. The last pulse, when the lamp remains on, should not be counted as a flash. If no codes are present, the light will come on for 4 seconds, then go out. Like the Ford applications, only one code at a time can be generated. Once a fault has been diagnosed and corrected, the code can be cleared by driving 18 mph or faster. If the ABS light comes back on, read out the next code, isolate and repair the problem, and repeat until no more codes are present.

On Buick Riviera/Reatta models with CRT display instrumentation, ABS codes can also be read through the CRT display by selecting the "climate" screen, then touching "off" and "warm" simultaneously. This puts the system into the service mode. Select the Body Control Module (BCM) antilock tests. If there are no stored codes, the CRT will display "no BCM codes."

Codes that indicate antilock problems include B482 (low brake accumulator pressure), BI18 (low brake pressure), BI21 (low brake fluid) and BI22 (parking brake applied). The Buick system differentiates between "old" and "new" fault codes. If the antilock lamp is on before the diagnostic mode is entered, at least one of the stored codes is current. If the antilock lamp is off before entering the diagnostic mode, none of the stored codes are current.

The fault codes for Ford and GM Teves Mark 2 applications are:

11–ABS module
12–ABS module
21–Main valve
22–Left front inlet valve
23 & 51–Left front outlet valve
24–Right front inlet valve
25 & 52–Right front outlet valve
26–Rear inlet valve
27, 53 & 54–Rear outlet valve & ground
31, 35, 41, 55 & 75–Left front wheel speed sensor
32, 36, 42, 56 & 76–Right front wheel speed sensor
33, 37, 43, 57 & 77–Right rear wheel speed sensor
34, 38, 44, 58 & 78–Left rear wheel speed sensor
45–Left front wheel speed sensor & one other
46–Right front wheel speed sensor & one other
47–Both rear wheel speed sensor signals missing
48–Missing three of four wheel speed sensor signals
61–Fluid level indicator and PWC circuit (Ford)
61–EBCM loop circuit (GM)
71–Left front wheel speed sensor (Ford)
71–Left front outlet valve (GM)
72–Right front wheel speed sensor (Ford)
72–Right front outlet valve (GM)
73–Right rear wheel speed sensor (Ford)
73–Right rear outlet valve (GM)
74–Left rear wheel speed sensor (Ford)
74–Left rear outlet valve (GM)
88–ABS module (Ford only)
89–ABS module (Ford only)

Delco ABS-VI

This ABS system is found on a variety of GM vehicles starting in 1991. If a fault is detected, the controller will either flash or illuminate the ABS warning light. Like the Powermaster III system, a flashing light indicates a problem that does not affect the operation of the system. On this application, ABS remains active in spite of the flashing warning light. A steady or continuous ABS warning light, however, indicates a more serious problem and disables the ABS system. There are no manual flash codes provided, so to access the codes a scan tool must be plugged into the ALDL connector. Codes are stored in nonvolatile memory and can only be cleared with a scan tool. If a fault does not repeat for 50 ignition cycles, it will be automatically cleared from memory.

Professional grade scan tools can provide additional diagnostic information such as:

Data Inputs—The scan tool can display data from individual wheel speed sensors, the vehicle speed sensor, battery voltage, the ABS warning light, brake switch, solenoid status, amp readings for each of the three motors, electromagnetic brake status, enable relay status and brake telltale status.

Code History—This mode provides a brief history of up to five trouble codes as well as the last one set.

ABS Snapshot Mode—Captures system data to help detect intermittent ABS problems that occur while driving.

ABS Function Tests—This includes both automatic and manual tests of individual components in the Delco VI system. The gear tension relief procedure must be used when replacing the motor pack assembly on the modulator to prevent damage or injury that might otherwise occur if you attempt to remove the gears without relieving tension.

When checking fault codes, read current trouble codes first, then history codes. If you find more than one code, start with the lowest number first. The Delco ABS-VI codes are:

11–ABS light open or shorted to ground
13–ABS light circuit shorted to battery
14–Enable relay contacts or fuse open
15–Enable relay contacts shorted to battery
16–Enable relay coil circuit open
17–Enable relay coil shorted to ground
18–Enable relay coil shorted to B+ or 0 ohms
21 & 25 Left front wheel speed sensor
22 & 26–Right front wheel speed sensor
23 & 27–Left rear wheel speed sensor
24 & 28–Right rear wheel speed sensor
31–Two wheel speed sensors open
36–System voltage is low
37–System voltage is high
38–Left front EMB will not hold motor
41–Right front EMB will not hold motor
42–Rear axle ESB will not hold motor
44–Left front EMB will not release motor, gears frozen
45–Right front EMB will not release motor, gears frozen
46–Rear axle ESB will not release motor, gears frozen
47–Left front nut failure (motor spins free)
48–Right front nut failure (motor spins free)
51–Rear axle nut failure (motor spins free)
52–Left front channel in release too long
53–Right front channel in release too long
54–Rear axle in release too long
55–Motor driver interface fault
56–Left front motor circuit open
57–Left front motor circuit shorted to ground
58–Left front motor circuit shorted to battery
61–Right front motor circuit open
62–Right front motor circuit shorted to ground
63–Right front motor circuit shorted to battery
64–Rear axle motor circuit open
65–Rear axle motor circuit shorted to ground
66–Rear axle motor circuit shorted to battery
67–Left front EMB release circuit open or grounded
68–Left front EMB release circuit shorted to battery
71–Right front EMB release circuit open or grounded
72–Right front EMB release circuit shorted to battery
76–Left front solenoid circuit open or shorted to battery
77–Left front solenoid circuit grounded
78–Right front solenoid circuit open or shorted to battery
81–Right front solenoid circuit shorted to battery
82–Calibration memory failure
86–ABS controller turned on BRAKE warning lamp
87–Red BRAKE warning light circuit open
88–Red BRAKE warning light circuit shorted to battery
91 & 92–Open brake switch contacts
93–Test 91 or 92–failed last or current ignition cycle
94–Brake switch contacts shorted
95–Brake switch circuit open
96–Brake lights open

This 1997 30th Anniversary Camaro Z28 convertible has ABS-IV with ASR (automatic slip regulation). ABS-IV was first offered on the Camaro and Firebird in 1993, but ASR traction control didn't become available until mid-1994, and then only on V8 F-bodies.

In 1991, General Motors introduced a new antilock brake system called "ABS-VI." Manufactured by GM's Delco Moraine NDH Division in Dayton, Ohio (which has since changed their name to Delphi), the new ABS-VI system was initially offered on a number of GM models before it became available on the restyled Chevy Camaro and its sister F-body Pontiac Firebird in 1993. Traction control wasn't offered until mid-1994, and then only as an option on the Z-28 and Trans Am.

ABS-VI

ABS-VI is a nonintegral add-on system with a conventional master brake cylinder, vacuum power booster and separate ABS modulator. It's a four-wheel, three channel system that provides independent ABS braking for each front wheel, with the rear brakes sharing a common ABS control circuit.

The hydraulic modulator is located in the left front area of the engine compartment. The electronic brake control module (EBCM) that controls the ABS system is located inside the passenger compartment above the driver's side kick panel. The "enable" relay for the ABS modulator is located with several other relays in the engine compartment on the left front fenderwell. The ABS-IV system has three wheel speed sensors, one for each front wheel and a common sensor for both rear wheels. The front sensors are built into the sealed front wheel bearing assemblies and are not adjustable or replaceable. If the sensor is bad, you have to replace the entire wheel bearing assembly. The rear wheel speed sensor is mounted on the differential and is serviceable.

Features

The ABS-VI system has some unusual and unique features. Like other ABS systems, wheel speed is monitored via individual wheel speed sensors. When one wheel starts to decelerate faster than the others while braking (indicating the wheel is starting to lock up), the ABS control

Delco's (now called Delphi) ABS-IV is a very compact and efficient ABS system. It is also totally unique from other ABS systems in its design and operation. Instead of using solenoids to hold, release and reapply hydraulic pressure in the individual brake circuits, it uses a solenoid to isolate the circuit and a screw-driven piston to modulate brake pressure.

module signals the hydraulic modulator assembly to reduce pressure to the affected brake. That's the standard operating principle for all ABS systems. But the ABS-VI system works in an entirely different way than other ABS systems. Instead of using solenoids to hold, release and reapply hydraulic pressure in individual brake circuits, ABS-VI uses motor driven pistons to cycle hydraulic pressure up and down. Here's how it works:

The ABS-VI modulator contains three screw driven pistons, one for each front brake circuit and one for the common rear brake circuit. Each piston sits atop a threaded shaft that is

gear driven by its own electric motor. At the top of each piston cavity is a check ball that controls hydraulic pressure within the brake circuit.

During a normal non-ABS stop, each piston is all the way up at the "home" position, and is held in place by the expansion spring brake (ESB). The check ball at the top of the piston chamber is unseated and the bypass solenoid is normally open. This allows brake pressure from the master cylinder and power booster to apply the brakes in the usual manner.

When ABS is needed, brake pressure must be controlled to prevent wheel lockup. This is done by closing the normally open bypass solenoid to

isolate the brake circuit and then turning the screw so the piston can slide down to reduce brake pressure. As the piston moves down, it increases the volume of the piston chamber causing a drop in pressure in the brake circuit. Easing off the pressure this way keeps the wheel from locking up and skidding. As the wheel regains traction, brake pressure is reapplied by running the piston back up. This decreases the volume of the piston chamber and restores pressure to what it was before. The ABS-VI system continues to cycle the piston up and down to modulate brake pressure until ABS braking is no longer needed or the car comes to a stop.

One of the advantages of modulating the brakes this way is that it allows hydraulic pressure in the individual brake circuits to change more gradually. This creates a "softer" ABS braking effect that reduces noise and the amount of feedback you feel in the brake pedal. The ABS-VI system has a maximum cycling frequency of up to seven cycles per second, which isn't as fast as some ABS systems but fast enough to prevent wheel lockup under most circumstances.

The ABS-VI system is also simpler than some other ABS systems because it has no high pressure accumulators or pump. In other systems, these components are used to apply pressure in the individual brake circuits during an ABS assisted stop. But the ABS-VI system can't do this so it cannot increase brake pressure on its own during an ABS stop or apply more pressure to the brakes than that which is generated by the driver's foot on the brake pedal through the master cylinder.

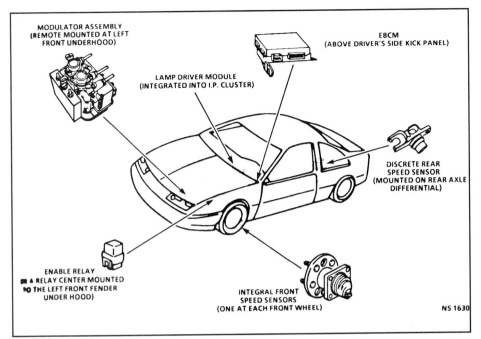

MODULATOR ASSEMBLY
(REMOTE MOUNTED AT LEFT
FRONT UNDERHOOD)

LAMP DRIVER MODULE
(INTEGRATED INTO I.P. CLUSTER)

EBCM
(ABOVE DRIVER'S SIDE KICK PANEL)

DISCRETE REAR
SPEED SENSOR
(MOUNTED ON REAR AXLE
DIFFERENTIAL)

ENABLE RELAY
(IN A RELAY CENTER MOUNTED
TO THE LEFT FRONT FENDER
UNDER HOOD)

INTEGRAL FRONT
SPEED SENSORS
(ONE AT EACH FRONT WHEEL)

NS 1630

ABS-IV component locations on the F-body. On cars with rear drum brakes, a single rear wheel speed sensor mounted on the differential as shown is used. But on cars with four-wheel disc brakes, each rear wheel has its own speed sensor. Courtesy Delphi Chassis Systems.

Traction Control & ASR

When traction control became available as an option mid-year in 1994 on the Z-28 and Trans Am with four wheel disc brakes, Chevrolet called their version "ASR" (Acceleration Slip Reduction) while Pontiac went with "TCS" (Traction Control System). Both ABS-VI systems use the same hardware, which includes a throttle relaxer similar to the one used on Corvettes with Bosch ABS/ASR.

Wheel spin is controlled three ways: by the throttle relaxer which pushes back against the driver's foot, by braking both drive wheels, and by reducing engine torque (spark retard). A light on the instrument panel signals when the ASR or TCS system is doing its job.

The traction control applications also have four rather than three wheel speed sensors. Each rear wheel has its own separate speed sensor instead of a common sensor in the differential. The EBCM needs to monitor the speed of each rear wheel separately in order to provide traction control, but the ABS-VI system still functions in the same three-channel mode when called upon for ABS braking.

SERVICE & BLEEDING THE BRAKES

The ABS-VI system is designed for easy service. The motor pack as well as the solenoids on the hydraulic modulator assembly are all replaceable.

The ABS-VI system can be manual or pressure bled. Use DOT 3 brake fluid only. But prior to bleeding, the rear displacement cylinder piston in the ABS modulator must be returned to its home position using a Tech 1 or similar scan tool. This is done by entering the manual control mode. Make sure the enable relay is on, then apply the rear motor to run the piston to the upper home position. The recommended bleeding sequence is right rear, left rear, right front, left front.

If you don't have a scan tool, use

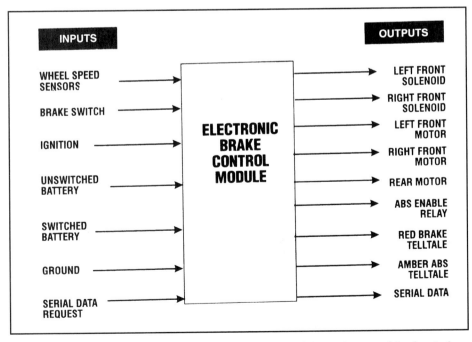

INPUTS		OUTPUTS
WHEEL SPEED SENSORS		LEFT FRONT SOLENOID
BRAKE SWITCH		RIGHT FRONT SOLENOID
IGNITION	ELECTRONIC BRAKE CONTROL MODULE	LEFT FRONT MOTOR
UNSWITCHED BATTERY		RIGHT FRONT MOTOR
		REAR MOTOR
SWITCHED BATTERY		ABS ENABLE RELAY
		RED BRAKE TELLTALE
GROUND		AMBER ABS TELLTALE
SERIAL DATA REQUEST		SERIAL DATA

The Electronic Brake Control Module (EBCM) is the brains of the system, receiving inputs from the wheel speed sensors and other items shown. When ABS (or ASR/traction assist if available) is needed, the EBCM generates the appropriate outputs. Courtesy Delphi Chassis Systems.

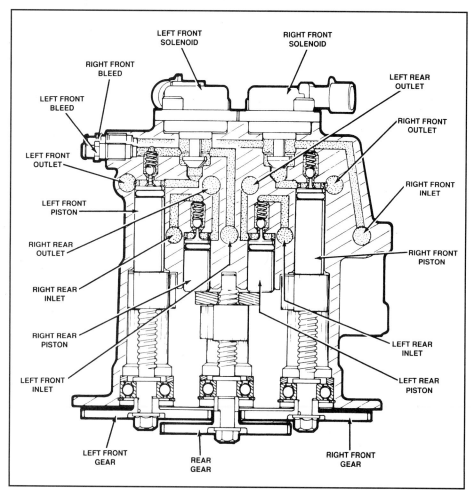

LEFT FRONT SOLENOID

RIGHT FRONT SOLENOID

RIGHT FRONT BLEED

LEFT FRONT BLEED

LEFT REAR OUTLET

RIGHT FRONT OUTLET

LEFT FRONT OUTLET

RIGHT FRONT INLET

LEFT FRONT PISTON

RIGHT REAR OUTLET

RIGHT FRONT PISTON

RIGHT REAR INLET

RIGHT REAR PISTON

LEFT REAR INLET

LEFT FRONT INLET

LEFT REAR PISTON

LEFT FRONT GEAR

REAR GEAR

RIGHT FRONT GEAR

Cutaway of the ABS-IV modulator. ABS-IV is a three-channel system so three piston assemblies are used. The left and right pistons are for the left and right front brakes, while the center dual piston controls the rear brakes. Courtesy Delphi Chassis Systems.

the following procedure: First, bleed the two front brakes. Make sure you have enough pedal to apply the brakes, then drive the vehicle at a speed of at least 4 mph. This will cause the ABS system to home the rear modulator piston. The rear brakes can now be bled.

Diagnostics

To diagnose the ABS-VI system on the Camaro and Firebird, you'll have to use a scan tool since no manual flash codes are provided. Chevrolet and Pontiac dealers use a "Tech 1" scan tool, but any scan tool with the proper calibration and adapters can access the system to retrieve fault

codes (see Chapter 11 for a list of codes). Additional data that can also be accessed with a scan tool includes wheel speed sensor readings, vehicle speed, battery voltage, individual motor and solenoid command status, warning light status and brake switch status.

The ABS-VI system can generate up to 58 different codes. When the control module detects a problem in the system, the amber ABS warning light on the dash will flash if the problem does not immediately hamper the operation of the system. If the problem affects the operation of the system, then the warning light will remain on continuously and the ABS

system will be disabled. The corresponding trouble code(s) that is set is then stored in a "nonvolatile" memory so it won't be lost if the battery is disconnected — which means the only way you can erase a code is with a scan tool. Disconnecting the battery or pulling the EBCM fuse won't do it.

A scan tool can also access the history of up to five trouble codes. For each of the first five codes that are logged (which are stored in the order in which they occurred), the module keeps track of the number of failure occurrences and the number of drive cycles since the failure first and last occurred (a drive cycle occurs when the key is turned on and off and the vehicle is driven faster than 10 mph). This kind of information can help determine whether or not an earlier fault is linked to the most recent fault (like an intermittent wheel speed sensor which has later become completely open).

A scan tool can also be used with this system to capture ABS data before and after a fault occurs (like taking a "snapshot" of the data) to aid in the diagnosis of a problem.

Finally, a scan tool can be used to initiate both automatic and manual tests of individual components such as cycling the individual piston motors and control solenoids.

Electrical Checks

If you suspect an ABS problem and don't have a scan tool, there are some voltage and resistance checks you can make that may help you identify the problem. First, check for a blown EBCM fuse. The 5-amp fuse is located in the underhood electrical center. There is also a fusible link (identified as fusible link "K" in the

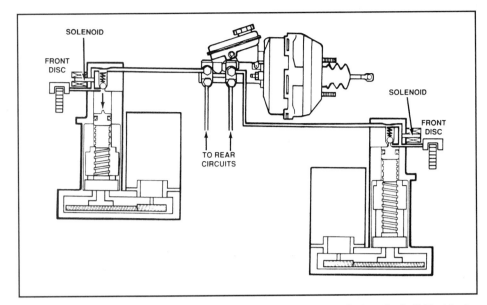

If ABS braking is needed at one or both front brakes, the solenoids isolate the individual brake circuits while their respective pistons in the modulator are driven down to reduce pressure, then driven back up to reapply brake pressure. **Courtesy Delphi Chassis Systems.**

The front sensors should have 1020 to 1137 ohms. The rear sensor should have 969 to 1185 ohms.

Between each wheel speed sensor and the main wiring harness is a jumper harness made of highly flexible twisted pair wiring. The up and down motions of the suspension create quite a bit of flexing, so a "bad" sensor reading may actually be due to damaged wiring. If the jumper harness wiring is damaged, however, don't try to repair it. Replace it with a new jumper harness. Soldering, splicing or taping the wires may temporarily solve your problem but usually won't last because of all the flexing these wires receive.

car's wiring diagram) between the battery and electrical center to protect the system against overloads, and a second fusible link (identified as fusible link "B") between the battery and enable relay to protect that circuit. If the fuse and fusible links are okay, the 32-pin EBCM connector may be loose or corroded. You can also disconnect the EBCM connector and measure voltage between ground and terminal "B10" to see if it is at least 10 volts. If it isn't, there's an open or excessive resistance in the ABS fuse circuit.

The electric motors in the modulator pack should each have 0.4 to 1.5 ohms of resistance (measuring across terminals "A" & "B" for the left front brake circuit motor, "C" & "D" for the rear brake circuit motor, and "E" & "F" for the right front motor). If any motor is bad, the motor pack needs to be replaced.

The left and right front solenoids should have 2.5 to 5.0 ohms of resistance. An open, grounded or shorted to battery solenoid circuit will not allow ABS operation.

If you find a wheel speed sensor code or suspect a bad wheel speed sensor, you can check the resistance of the sensors through the wiring harness or at the sensor connectors.

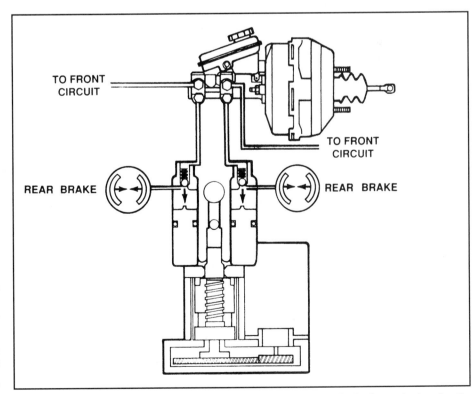

When ABS braking is needed at the rear wheels, the dual pistons for both rear brake circuits are driven down simultaneously to reduce pressure, then driven back up to reapply pressure. **Courtesy Delphi Chassis Systems.**

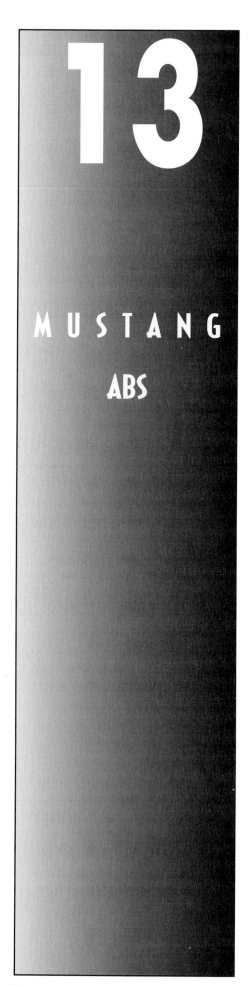

13

MUSTANG

ABS

When Ford introduced the restyled Mustang in 1994, it offered ABS for the first time as an option.

Despite Mustang's reputation as a performance car, Ford did not offer ABS until the introduction of the restyled 1994 model. Even then ABS was offered only as an option, not standard equipment.

The ABS system on the Ford Mustang is a four-wheel, three-channel Bosch 2U system. It is a nonintegral add-on ABS system with a conventional master brake cylinder, vacuum power booster and separate ABS hydraulic modulator. The ABS control module is mounted on the modulator, which is located in the right front of the engine compartment next to the coolant recovery reservoir.

The modulator contains 3 three-way ABS solenoid valves, one for each front brake and one for both rear brakes. Each front brake is controlled individually but the rear wheels are controlled as a pair. The ABS control module uses the "select low" principal of operation for the rear brakes. The ABS module monitors the speed of both rear wheels and reacts to the one that is slowing (decelerating) the fastest. So if either rear wheel starts to lock up during a hard stop, the module activates the rear brake ABS circuit and cycles the pressure to both rear brakes to prevent wheel lock up.

The Mustang has a separate wheel speed sensor for each wheel. The front sensors are built into the front hub assembly with the wheel bearings and are not adjustable. The rear sensors are mounted on the brake caliper anchor plate, with the sensor tone rings pressed on the rear axles. The rear sensors are replaceable but do not require adjustment.

BOSCH ABS OPERATION

The three ABS solenoids inside the ABS modulator (which Ford refers to as the "hydraulic control unit" in their service manuals) each have three positions: a normally open position which passes pressure to the brakes, a closed position which isolates and holds pressure within the brake circuit, and a release position which vents pressure from the brake circuit. The position of each solenoid is determined by how much voltage is applied to it through a relay. With no voltage applied, each solenoid is open. A current of 1.9 to 2.3 amps will pull a solenoid part way closed to the intermediate position that isolates the brake circuit. If the current is then increased to 4.5 to 5.7 amp, it pulls the solenoid all the way closed to the release position that uncovers a port that vents fluid in the brake circuit back to the master cylinder.

The fluid that flows back through the release port is routed into a spring-loaded accumulator. There are two accumulators in the modulator, one for the front brakes and one for the rear brakes. The accumulators hold the fluid that is released from the brake circuits until the return pump can pump it back to the master cylinder. The return pump receives its power through a pump relay mounted on the modulator. The ABS control module switches the pump relay on when the return pump is needed during ABS braking. The pump can generate up to 2900 psi, which is necessary to overcome brake pressure from the master cylinder.

Of all the components in the modulator assembly, only the relays and pump motor are serviceable. If one of the solenoid valves is defective or if the modulator assembly is leaking, the entire modulator assembly must be replaced.

The ABS control module monitors inputs from all four wheel speed sensors along with the status of each ABS solenoid and battery voltage. Outputs go to the pump motor, solenoid relays and ABS warning light. The system is capable of cycling the ABS solenoids continuously from 4 to 10 times per second until ABS braking is no longer needed or until the vehicle comes to a stop, whichever occurs first. At that point, the

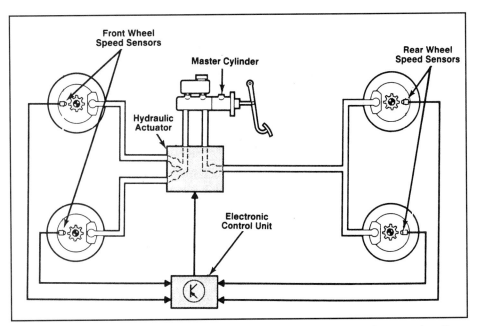

Schematic of Bosch 2U ABS system on the Mustang. The Mustang's ABS system has three channels, though each wheel has its own speed sensor. If ABS braking is needed at the rear wheels, both rear brakes are modulated simultaneously. Courtesy Bosch.

controller deenergizes the solenoid and pump relays and reverts back to its standby mode.

ONBOARD DIAGNOSTICS

Like most ABS systems, the Mustang ABS system has a built-in "Quick Test" that checks for faults when the ignition is first turned on. The ABS warning lamp on the dash should come on for about three seconds for a bulb check, then go out if no faults are detected. But if the ABS warning light remains on or comes on while driving, it tells you a fault has been detected. The ABS system is deactivated when the lamp comes on. This should not affect normal driving but you won't have any ABS braking should you need it.

The Bosch system can store up to three fault codes in memory. The codes will be retained in memory until they are erased by a scan tool, by disconnecting the battery or by removing the ABS fuse.

Ford provides a manual flash code

procedure for retrieving codes on the Mustang, or you can use a scan tool. To retrieve the codes manually, locate the ABS diagnostic connector near the power distribution panel in the engine compartment. The connector is a rectangular shaped plug with six terminals. Hold the plug so the row of four terminals are under the row of two terminals (four on bottom, two on top). The second terminal from the right on the bottom row is terminal "K." The right terminal on the top row is ground. With the key off, use a jumper wire to connect terminal "K" to the ground terminal on the connector. This will put the system into the diagnostic mode when you turn the ignition on. The ABS warning lamp on the instrument panel will begin to flash when the key is turned on signaling you that the system is okay (code 12) or that it has detected a problem, in which case you'll see the codes displayed as a series of flashes separated by half second pauses. A code 12 will appear as one flash followed by two quick

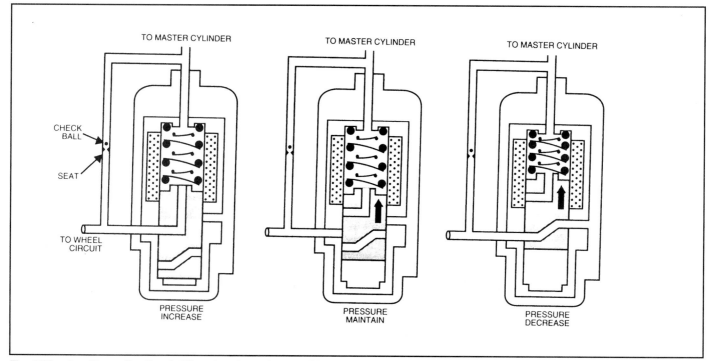

The ABS solenoids on the Bosch 2U system have three positions. At rest (left) with no current applied, they are normally open and pass hydraulic pressure from the master cylinder directly to the brake. When a small current is applied (center), the solenoid slides up partway to block the ports and isolate pressure in the brake circuit. When more current is applied (right), the solenoid valve pulls all the way up opening a vent port to release pressure from the brake circuit. Courtesy Bosch.

flashes, followed by about a half second pause. Any other codes will appear as a series of flashes (the first digit of the code followed by the second digit), separated by a half second pause.

Mustang Fault Codes

12—System OK
19—ABS control module
22—Right front ABS solenoid
24—Left front ABS solenoid
26—Rear ABS solenoid
31—Right front wheel speed sensor
32—Right rear wheel speed sensor
33—Left front wheel speed sensor
34—Left rear wheel speed sensor
41—Right front wheel speed sensor
42—Right rear wheel speed sensor
43—Left front wheel speed sensor
44—Left front wheel speed sensor
69—Low battery voltage (less than 10 volts)
78—ABS sensor frequency fault

Electrical Checks

If you get a fault code for an ABS solenoid, the resistance of the solenoids in the modulator can be checked with an ohmmeter. To do this, pull the 6-pin connector off the modulator. The terminal pins are numbered consecutively from 1 to 6. To check the right front solenoid, measure the resistance between pins 3 and 4. To check the left front solenoid, measure the resistance between pins 1 and 2. To check the rear solenoid, measure the resistance between pins 5 and 6. If a solenoid is good, it should have 1.0 to 1.5 ohms of resistance. If it does not fall within this range, the solenoid is bad and the modulator needs to be replaced.

Wheel speed sensor resistance checks can be made through the wiring harness or at the sensor connectors. The front sensors should have 1015 to 1245 ohms of resistance. The rear sensors should have 2187 to 2673 ohms of resistance.

Bleeding the Brakes

Manual or power bleeding can be used. Use DOT 3 fluid only. If bleeding the brake manually, do the rear brakes first, followed by the front brakes. If using a power bleeder, bleed in the following sequence: right rear, left rear, right front, left front.

Corvette has been through four generations of ABS, starting in 1986 with Bosch II, then Bosch 2S Micro in 1990, followed by Bosch ABS/ASR with Acceleration Slip Regulation in 1992, and then Bosch 5 in 1995.

Who would have dreamed that an American sports car with Australian disc brakes would be equipped with a German antilock brake system? That's what happened in 1986 when Chevrolet engineers offered antilock brakes for the first time on the Corvette. The system was a four-wheel Bosch II ABS system similar to the Bosch ABS systems used on Audis, BMWs, Lexus, Mazda, Mercedes, Porsche, Volvo and Rolls Royce. The same system was used through the 1989 model year.

Like all non-traction assist ABS systems, the Bosch II system on the Corvette only came into play during hard braking so it had no effect on normal braking, driving or acceleration. It did improve the car's ability to stop straight on wet or slick surfaces, and came in handy during panic stop situations. But it didn't make the Corvette "spin-proof." The physical laws of traction and inertia still held, so if a driver exceeded the limits of adhesion going into a turn, the tires would still break loose.

BOSCH II ABS

The Bosch II ABS system on the Corvette is a nonintegral system with a conventional master cylinder and vacuum brake booster. The Bosch II system provides four-wheel ABS braking with three hydraulic control channels. Each wheel has its own speed sensor, but the rear brakes share a common ABS hydraulic circuit.

The system uses the "select low" principle of control. The ABS module monitors the speed of both rear wheels and reacts to the one that is slowing (decelerating) the fastest. Consequently, if either rear wheel starts to lock up during a hard stop, the module activates the rear brake ABS circuit and cycles the pressure to both rear brakes to prevent wheel lock up.

The front wheel speed sensors are part of the wheel bearing and hub assembly, and are not replaceable or adjustable. The rear wheel speed sensors are mounted on the rear suspension knuckles. The left and right sensors are different and are not interchangeable. The sensor rings are pressed onto the ends of the drive shaft spindles, and are not serviceable. If damaged, a new drive shaft spindle must be installed.

The hydraulic modulator assembly, which is located in a small

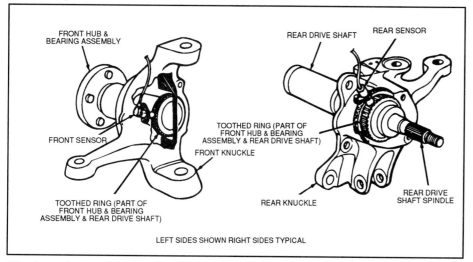

FRONT HUB & BEARING ASSEMBLY

FRONT SENSOR

FRONT KNUCKLE

TOOTHED RING (PART OF FRONT HUB & BEARING ASSEMBLY & REAR DRIVE SHAFT)

REAR DRIVE SHAFT

REAR SENSOR

TOOTHED RING (PART OF FRONT HUB & BEARING ASSEMBLY & REAR DRIVE SHAFT)

REAR KNUCKLE

REAR DRIVE SHAFT SPINDLE

LEFT SIDES SHOWN RIGHT SIDES TYPICAL

Wheel speed sensor locations on the Corvette. Courtesy Bosch.

compartment behind the driver's seat, has three, 3-position ABS solenoids (one for each front brake and one for the combined rear brake circuit), a high pressure return pump, two fluid accumulators, and pump and solenoid relays.

Each of the ABS solenoid valves in the modulator is normally in the open position. Voltage is supplied through a relay on the modulator assembly. When a small current (1.9 to 2.3 amps) is applied to one of the ABS solenoids, it pulls the valve up to its second or intermediate position which isolates the brake circuit and prevents any additional pressure from reaching the brake. When the current to the solenoid is increased (4.5 to 5.7 amps), it pulls the valve to the third position which opens a port and releases pressure from the brake circuit.

The fluid that flows back through the release port is routed into a spring-loaded accumulator. There are two accumulators in the modulator, one for the front brakes and one for the rear brakes. The accumulators hold the fluid that is released from the brake circuits until the return pump can pump it back to the master

cylinder (which produces the pulsations that are felt in the brake pedal during ABS braking). Each of the accumulators can hold about 2 cc of brake fluid, and are designed to operate at pressures of less than 148 psi (10 bar).

The return pump receives its power through a pump relay mounted on the modulator. The ABS control module switches the pump relay on when the return pump is needed during ABS braking. The pump draws about 45 amps and is capable of moving 3.5 cc of brake fluid per second at 2,900 psi (200 bar). High pressure is needed to overcome brake pressure from the master cylinder.

Of all the components in the modulator assembly, only the relays and pump motor are serviceable. If one of the solenoid valves is defective or if the modulator assembly is leaking, the entire modulator assembly must be replaced.

Lateral Acceleration Switch

The ABS control module is located just ahead of the modulator behind the driver's seat. The module monitors the inputs from the four wheel speed sensors, the brake pedal switch, and a

"lateral acceleration switch" mounted under the front of the console behind the A/C control head. The purpose of this switch is to signal the control module when the car is cornering hard and is experiencing high G-loads (side forces). Hard cornering produces body roll or yaw in the chassis which changes the loading on the tires. To compensate, the control module changes its ABS braking characteristics slightly when it receives a signal from the lateral acceleration switch.

The lateral acceleration switch contains two mercury switches connected in series. One switch opens when making hard left turns (over 0.6 G) and the other when making hard right turns. Both switches are normally closed. When the car goes into a hard turn, the appropriate switch opens and causes a voltage loss to module terminal #13. This triggers the control module to switch to the modified ABS programming in case antilock braking is needed. This improves the car's overall braking performance and also handling stability in such situations.

Operation

When you apply the brakes, a brake pedal switch alerts the ABS control module to get ready. As the car begins to slow, the ABS control module compares each wheel's speed to the others. If one wheel starts to decelerate more quickly than the rest and is in danger of locking up, the ABS control module initiates antilock braking.

Outputs from the ABS control module go to the pump motor relay and solenoid relays, the three three-way ABS solenoid valves and the ABS warning light. The system is

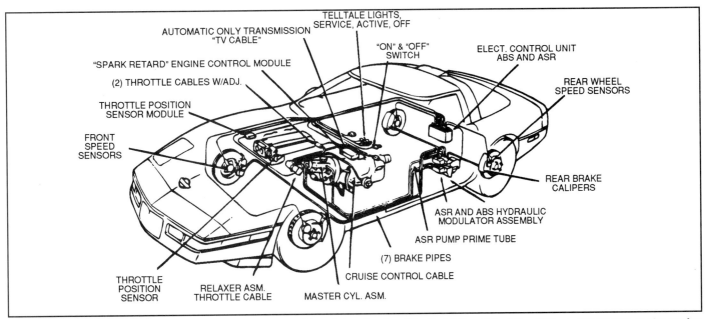

Bosch ABS/ASR components on a 1992 Corvette. The addition of Acceleration Slip Regulation linked the ABS control module to the engine computer. By communicating with the engine computer, the ABS system could reduce engine torque to minimize wheel spin. Courtesy Bosch.

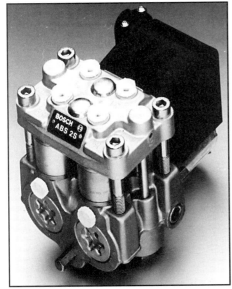

Bosch 2S Micro hydraulic modulator unit. This second generation ABS system was functionally identical to the first, but much more compact. Courtesy Bosch.

capable of cycling the ABS solenoids continuously from 4 to 10 times per second until ABS braking is no longer needed or until the vehicle comes to a stop, whichever occurs first. At that point, the ABS module deenergizes the solenoid and pump relays and reverts back to its standby mode.

Note: A black wire attached to the modulator valve pump motor goes to a connector inside the storage compartment. This wire is grounded to the left bird-cage pillar behind and near the courtesy light. The control module and all relays also ground to the left pillar, so corrosion in this area may cause the ABS system to malfunction.

BOSCH 2S MICRO ABS

In 1990, the Corvette antilock brake system was upgraded to the next generation Bosch "2S Micro" ABS system. Functionally, the two systems are the same (four-wheel, three-channel ABS), and performance wise there's no difference. What is different is the hydraulic control hardware and the ABS control module.

The older Bosch II system had adequate self-diagnostic capability but could not generate "trouble codes" to help you diagnose faulty sensors and other components in the system. So troubleshooting an ABS problem on a Bosch II equipped Corvette required the use of a special (and expensive) dedicated Bosch ABS tester that only the car dealer had. The 2S Micro system changed all that. The new control module added the capability to generate and store trouble codes, which can be retrieved using either a plug-in "scan" tool or a manual flash code technique that causes the ABS warning light to flash out a numeric sequence.

The lateral acceleration sensor on the Bosch 2S Micro applications was also changed to a Hall effect switch to provide an analog or graduated reading of progressively higher side loads, starting at 0.4 G.

BOSCH ABS/ASR

In '92, Corvette switched to a "third generation" Bosch ABS system that included traction control capabilities for the first time. The new system was dubbed "ABS/ASR" with ASR standing for "Acceleration Slip Regulation." Chevrolet's decision to add the ASR traction control system to the '92 Corvette was prompted in part by the addition of 55 more

Here's what the BOSCH ABS/ASR system looks like if you lift the body off the frame. The hardware is packaged right next to the axle just aft of the drivers seat, and can be easily accessed through a panel.

horsepower (300 total) in the '92 LT1 engine. Adding traction control to the existing ABS system was fairly easy because most of the hardware was already in place.

The only changes that were needed for the ABS/ASR system were to add an additional solenoid valve in the modulator so that each rear wheel can be braked independently (which only occurs during traction control, not ABS braking). The module was also reprogrammed and linked electronically to the engine's computer so spark retard could become part of the traction control strategy. Chevy engineers also added an annoying little gadget called the "throttle position relaxer" to the throttle cable linkage so the ABS module could back off the throttle opening to reduce torque when the rear wheels started to spin.

Though some people thought the idea of adding traction control to a Corvette was akin to putting training wheels on a Harley, it actually turned out to be a good thing. If you've ever driven a Corvette on a rainy day, you'll know why. Wide tires and wet pavement do not exactly create ideal conditions for traction. The ASR system means you don't have to baby the throttle when starting out from a stop light even if there's a Mustang in the next lane. ASR makes the car safer to drive, especially in the hands of novice drivers (or girlfriends) who may not be used to the way a Corvette handles in wet weather, even with the Goodyear GS-C directional asymmetric Eagle tires. Fortunately, Chevy engineers included a push button on the instrument panel to deactivate the ASR system so you can still burn rubber if the mood strikes.

How ASR Works

The ASR system works by continuously monitoring the speed of the drive wheels via the rear wheel speed sensors. When the car is accelerating, it compares the speed of the rear wheels to those up front to determine whether or not the rear wheels are starting to spin. A difference in acceleration rates triggers the ASR mode to come into play.

The first thing that happens is that the ASR controller signals the engine computer to disable cruise control (if in use). If the car has an automatic transmission, it also signals the engine computer to disengage the torque converter lockup clutch. The ABS/ASR control module then has three options from which to choose. It can signal the engine computer to momentarily back off or retard spark timing. This reduces torque output, which may be enough to prevent the rear wheels from breaking loose. The ABS/ASR control module can also back off the throttle opening by using the "throttle cable relaxer" to push back against the throttle linkage. Besides reducing power, it gives you a tactile cue which you can feel through the gas pedal to ease up on the gas. A third option, which may be exercised independently or in conjunction with either of the other two, is to apply the brakes on either rear wheel. Rear braking is only used at speeds below 50 mph. Above 50 mph, spark retard and throttle reduction are the only control strategies used.

One of the advantages of using braking to control wheel spin is that it can split torque side-to-side like a limited slip differential. In other words, the ABS/ASR system can route engine torque away from the wheel that has the least traction to the one that has the most traction. By braking the wheel that's slipping, torque is shifted through the differential to the other side—which makes a world of difference in traction, acceleration and tracking stability when one wheel is on a wet or slick surface and the other is on dry pavement.

Disabling—Disabling the ASR system by pressing the dash mounted button has no effect whatsoever on antilock braking. It merely puts the ASR system into a passive mode. Turning the ASR system off illuminates the "ASR OFF" lamp on the instrument panel driver information center. When the ASR

This button on the instrument panel deactivates the ASR system in case you want to have some tire-spinning fun. But for normal driving or even road racing, leaving the ASR system active enhances handling and traction.

system is activated, you'll see an "ASR ACTIVE" message if ASR comes into play while accelerating.

Warning Lamps—The ASR system also has its own separate warning lamp to indicate any faults that have been detected by the onboard self-diagnostics. Like the amber SERVICE ABS warning lamp and red BRAKE warning lamps, the ASR OFF, ASR ACTIVE, SERVICE ASR and ABS ACTIVE messages are all illuminated for a bulb check when the ignition is turned on. The ABS lamp will remain on as the engine is cranked, and should go out once the engine starts.

If the "SERVICE ASR" message remains on or appears while driving, it signals that a problem has been detected and that the ASR system has been disabled. This will have no effect on normal vehicle operation or antilock braking—if the faulty component isn't also involved in the ABS system. If the problem is common to both systems, then the SERVICE ABS message will also appear and the ABS system will also

be disabled.

Note: On the '92 to '94 Corvettes with ABS/ASR as well as the Bosch II and 2S Micro systems on the earlier models, installing the spare tire will deactivate both antilock braking and traction control. This is necessary because the spare has a different diameter, width, and different traction characteristics than the standard tires on the car.

Caution: If you replace the original equipment tires with ones of a different size or aspect ratio, it may upset the calibration of the ABS or ABS/ASR system. For this reason, Chevrolet does not recommend changing tire sizes when tires are replaced.

BOSCH 5 ABS

In 1995, Chevrolet went to its fourth generation ABS system on the Corvette: Bosch 5 ABS (which was also offered the same year on the Porsche 911). Unlike all the earlier ABS systems, the Bosch 5 system is a

four-channel ABS system with separate hydraulic circuits for each wheel. It also uses a pair of inlet and outlet ABS solenoid valves for each brake circuit instead of a single 3-position ABS solenoid valve for each circuit.

Features

The Bosch 5 system features a compact "unitized" design. The "Electronic Brake Traction Control Module" (EBTCM) is mounted right on the "Brake Pressure Modulator" (BPM) valve body, which is located behind the driver's seat the same as before. The lateral acceleration sensor is retained to keep the control module informed about G-forces.

The Bosch 5 hydraulic unit contains a pair of ABS valves for each circuit (one normally open inlet solenoid and one normally closed outlet solenoid) for a total of eight. Even though Bosch 5 is a four channel system, it continues to respond like the earlier three channel systems in the ABS mode using the "select-low" principle of reacting to rear wheel lockup. If either rear wheel starts to lockup and skid while braking, both rear brake circuits are cycled simultaneously to provide antilock braking.

When the control module senses wheel lockup is about to occur, the inlet solenoid is energized to close and isolate the brake circuit (or both rear brake circuits in the case of the rear wheels). This prevents any further pressure increase to the brake. If the speed of the wheel does not increase and match the reference speed of the other wheels, the control module energizes the outlet solenoid to open it so fluid pressure can escape from the circuit. This relieves brake pressure and allows the wheel to regain

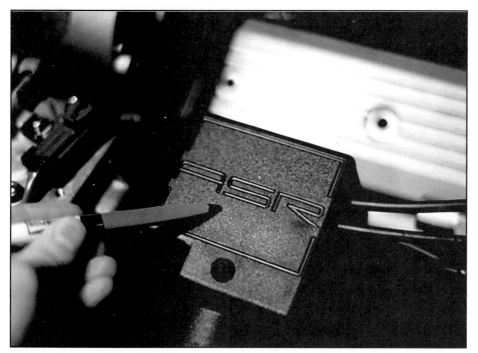

The plastic cover marked "ASR" in the engine compartment on '92 and newer Corvettes hides the Bosch throttle relaxer.

traction. When the reference speed is obtained, the control module opens the inlet valve allowing pressure to be reapplied to the brake. The cycle is repeated continuously as long as needed or until the vehicle stops.

The pump motor is used for fluid return during ABS braking and to generate rear brake pressure on applications that have traction control. On the latter, an extra pair of solenoid valves are used for controlling rear braking during acceleration.

Like the earlier Bosch ABS/ASR system, the Bosch 5 system uses braking to reduce wheel spin but only at slower speeds (below 50 mph). Throttle reduction and spark retard are again used to reduce engine power as needed.

When traction control braking is needed, the ABS module energizes the pump and the two extra solenoids: the "ASV" Prime Line Solenoid Valve, which opens a circuit that allows fluid to flow to the return pump so it can generate brake

pressure, and the "USV" Traction Control Solenoid, which closes to prevent pump pressure from returning to the master cylinder. A relief valve in the USV solenoid valve also limits the maximum pressure that the pump can apply to the rear brakes in an effort to control wheel spin.

If engine power needs to be reduced, spark retard and/or throttle reduction via a throttle "Adjuster Assembly" attached to the throttle linkage may also kick in. The throttle adjuster assembly consists of a small electric motor and a control cable cam assembly. The unit is attached to three cables: the accelerator pedal cable, the cable to the throttle body and the cruise control cable. The adjuster only moves in one direction, which is to pull the throttle closed. When the unit is engaged to reduce power, the driver will feel the accelerator pedal pushing back against his foot.

Like the Bosch ABS/ASR system, an indicator light signals the driver when the traction control system is

active. A switch is also provided on the Corvette to deactivate the traction control system.

SERVICE

An ABS equipped Corvette requires no special maintenance, but annual brake fluid changes are recommended to prolong the life of ABS hydraulic control unit. Brake fluid is hygroscopic and absorbs moisture over time, which can corrode the solenoids in the ABS modulator. Chevrolet recommends using DOT 4 brake fluid in Corvettes, not DOT 3. Silicone brake fluid is not recommended.

Brake Bleeding

The brakes can be bled manually, or with power or vacuum equipment. The recommended bleeding sequence for '91 and earlier Corvettes is right front, right rear, left rear and left front. Raising the front of the car so the bleeder screws on the rear calipers are at the 12 o'clock position will help prevent air from being trapped inside the calipers. The sequence for the '92 Corvette with ABS/ASR and the '95 and up Bosch 5 applications is: right rear, left rear, right front, left front.

ABS Diagnostics

All Corvette ABS systems constantly monitor input from all four wheel speed sensors, and perform an automatic self-test every time the car is driven. As soon as the car's speed reaches 4 miles-per-hour in forward or reverse, the ABS control module cycles the solenoids, relays and pump motor to check their operation. You may hear or feel the self-test while it is taking place, but don't be alarmed: the system is just checking itself.

If a problem is detected during the self-test or while the car is being driven, the ABS and/or ASR warning lamps will come on and the ABS and/or ASR systems will be disabled. On the 1990 and later Bosch systems, a numeric trouble code will also be logged in the ABS module's memory that corresponds to the problem. The ABS and/or ASR warning light will remain on as long as the key is on, and will come on again the next time the engine is started as long as the problem is present. If the problem is intermittent, the warning light will not come back on until the problem reoccurs. Then the ABS or ASR light will come on and remain on for the duration of the ignition cycle.

The only condition that can cause an intermittent ABS or ASR warning light while driving is low system voltage. Low battery voltage or intermittent wiring problems in the controller, solenoid relay or pump relay harness may cause the light to flicker on and off.

General diagnostic tips are covered in Chapter 11, but 1986-89 Corvettes require a special Bosch J-35890 ABS tester to perform detailed system diagnostics. On 1990 and later Corvettes, trouble codes can be retrieved using either a manual procedure or a special "scan" tool that plugs into the ALDL connector. For specific circuit checks, a J-35592 pinout box (1990-91 models) or a J-39700 pinout box (1992 models) and digital volt/ohm meter are also needed.

We're not going to go through the detailed diagnostic procedures here because you need a service manual for the specific diagnostic flow charts once you've obtained a trouble code. See Chapter 11 for a list of Bosch 2 fault codes.

Bosch 2S Micro Flash Codes

The manual procedure for retrieving a trouble code on a 1990-91 Corvette with the Bosch 2S Micro ABS system goes as follows:

1. Ground pin "H" on the ALDL connector and turn the ignition on. This puts the system into the self-diagnostic mode.

2. Stored codes can then be read by counting flashes of the ABS warning light. These are referred to as "flash codes." The first will be a code 12, followed by any remaining ABS codes. A maximum of three codes can be displayed at one time. Code 12 will flash three times — flash, pause, flash, flash, followed by a longer pause, then repeat. Each additional code will then be displayed three times.

Though this technique can reveal whether or not there are certain fault codes in memory, it won't reveal all possible codes. Some hard codes can only be accessed by using a scan tool.

Hard codes cannot be erased by turning the ignition off or pulling the ABS fuse. The codes are stored in a nonvolatile memory, and can only be erased with a scan tool. Codes remain in memory for 50 ignition cycles. If the fault does not reoccur during that time, the code will be automatically erased.

Bosch ABS/ASR Codes

On '92 Corvettes ABS/ASR, you can use the driver information center to display trouble codes. Here's the procedure:

1. Ground pin "G" on the ALDL connector, and turn the ignition on.

2. The CCM (central control module) will display any fault codes

Bosch 5 Fault Codes

21—Right front wheel speed sensor
23—Right front wheel speed sensor
25—Left front wheel speed sensor
27—Left front wheel speed sensor
28—Wheel speed sensor circuit frequency malfunction
31—Right rear wheel speed sensor
33—Right rear wheel speed sensor
35—Left rear wheel speed sensor
37—Left rear wheel speed sensor
41—Right front ABS inlet valve solenoid
42—Right front ABS outlet valve solenoid
45—Left front ABS inlet valve solenoid
46—Left front ABS outlet valve solenoid
47—ASV prime line solenoid
48—USV pilot valve solenoid
51—Right rear ABS inlet valve solenoid
52—Right rear ABS outlet valve solenoid
55—Left rear ABS inlet valve solenoid
56—Left rear ABS outlet solenoid valve
58—ABS control module
61—Pump motor
62—RPM signal
63—Modulator valve power supply
64—Throttle position sensor
65—Throttle adjuster circuit
66—Throttle adjuster malfunction
67—Throttle position sensor comparison malfunction
71—ABS module
72—Serial data line malfunction
73—Spark retard monitoring malfunction
75—Lateral acceleration sensor circuit
76—Lateral acceleratomer signal out of range
85—Low system voltage

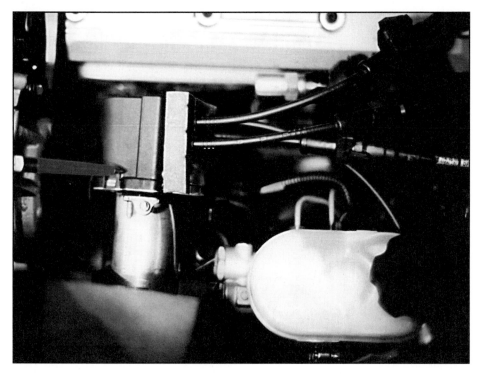

Under the cover is a small stepper motor that pulls back on the throttle linkage when the wheels start to spin to reduce engine power. You'll feel the nudge through the gas pedal.

and the module for which they apply in an automatic sequence. The CCM is module 1, the engine module is 4, and the ABS/ASR controller is 9. The module number will be displayed on the trip odometer while the code will appear on the digital speedometer. Each code is displayed for three seconds, followed by a one second pause before the next code is shown. The end of the code list is indicated by three dashes.

The speedometer will also indicate whether the code is a current one with a "C," or a history code "H," indicating the fault occurred in the past but is no longer present. History codes, by the way, are a good indication of intermittent faults.

Pressing the TRIP RESET button will cycle through the CCM automatic display sequence until the ABS/ASR controller is selected. A 9.0 will show on the trip odometer. Pressing the TRIP/ODO button until 9.1 appears will select the code

display mode. Pressing the ENG/MET button will then allow you to cycle through any additional fault codes until the end message — three dashes — is reached. If more than one code is present, you can go back through the list by pressing the FUEL INFO button.

The CCM diagnostics can also be used to clear codes. This is done by selecting the ABS/ASR controller display using the TRIP RESET button, then pressing the TRIP/ODO button until 9.7 appears on the trip odometer. Then pressing and holding the ENG/MET button until the three dashes appear. This clears any ABS/ASR codes from memory.

Bosch 5 Diagnostics

Diagnosing Bosch 5 problems is no different than the earlier Bosch ABS/ASR systems. You can use a scan tool or read the codes through the Climate Control Module (CCM) by pushing certain buttons in the

proper sequence.

To display CCM fault codes:

1. Ground pin "G" on the ALDL connector, and turn the ignition on.

2. The CCM will display any fault codes and the module for which they apply in an automatic sequence. The CCM is module 1, the engine module is 4, and the ABS controller is 9. The module number will be displayed on the trip odometer while the code will appear on the digital speedometer. Each code is displayed for three seconds, followed by a one second pause before the next code is shown. The end of the code list is indicated by three dashes.

The speedometer will also indicate whether the code is a current one with a "C," or a history code "H," indicating the fault occurred in the past but is no longer present. History codes may indicate intermittent faults.

Pressing the TRIP RESET button will cycle through the CCM automatic display sequence until the ABS controller is selected. A 9.0 will show on the trip odometer. Pressing the TRIP/ODO button until 9.1 appears will select the code display mode. Pressing the ENG/MET button will then allow you to cycle through any additional fault codes until the end message — three dashes — is reached. If more than one code is present, you can go back through the list by pressing the FUEL INFO button.

The CCM diagnostics can also be used to clear codes after repairs have been made. This is done by selecting the ABS controller display using the TRIP RESET button, then pressing the TRIP/ODO button until 9.7 appears on the trip odometer. Then pressing and holding the ENG/MET button until the three dashes appear.

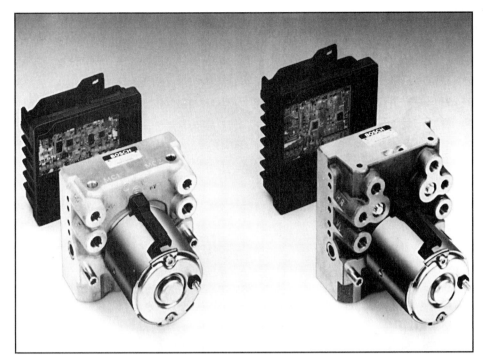

The Bosch 5 ABS system combines the control module and hydraulic modulator into one compact assembly.

line (ASV) valve solenoid, and traction control solenoid on the 1995 and up Bosch 5 systems should all have 8.5 to 9.5 ohms of resistance. The modulator outlet solenoids, though, should read 4.2 to 5.2 ohms.

Wheel speed sensor resistance checks can be made through the wiring harness or at the individual sensor connectors. The front and rear sensors on 1986-89 Bosch 2 applications should have 900 to 1500 ohms resistance. On 1990 Bosch 2S Micro systems, front and rear sensors should read 900 to 1100 ohms. On 1991 Bosch 2S Micro systems, the front sensors should have 1070 to 1170 ohms while the rear sensors should have 900 to 1100 ohms. The 1992 and up ABS/ASR applications should have 990 to 1210 ohms at the front sensors, and 900 to 1100 ohms at the rear. The 1995 and up Bosch 5 systems should also have 990 to 1210 ohms up front, but the rear sensors should read 1600 to 1800 ohms.

This clears any ABS codes from memory.

Electrical Checks

If you find an ABS solenoid code on any Bosch system, or you suspect a bad solenoid in the module, check the resistance of the solenoid to see if it is within specs. On the older 1986-89 Bosch 2 and 1990 Bosch 2S Micro applications, the solenoids should have 0.8 to 1.5 ohms of resistance. On the 1991 Bosch 2S Micro applications, different solenoids with slightly higher resistanced were used. These should measure 0.8 to 1.8 ohms. On the 1992 and up ABS/ASR applications, the solenoids should have 1.7 to 2.1 ohms of resistance. The modulator inlet solenoids, prime

15

R E A R

W H E E L

ABS

Kelsey-Hayes rear wheel ABS was introduced back in 1987, and has been used on a wide range of both import and domestic trucks. It's simple design and low cost made it an ideal ABS system for truck applications.

Starting in 1987, a new rear-wheel antilock brake system called "RABS" appeared on Ford F-series trucks, as well as later model Ranger, Bronco, Bronco II and Explorer trucks and Aerostar vans. Supplied to Ford by Kelsey-Hayes, the same system appeared in 1988 as "RWAL" (Rear Wheel Anti-Lock) on Chevrolet "C" and "K" series pickups. In 1989, the same system was added to Astro minivans and "S" and "T" series pickups, and some "S" series Blazers. In 1990, RWAL became standard on "R" and "V" series light Chevy and GMC trucks and "G" series vans. Dodge also adopted the RWAL system in '89 on its "D" and "W" 150/350, Dakota and Ram pickups.

A variant on the basic RWAL system called "Zero Pressure Rear Wheel Antilock" or "ZPRWAL" system was added in 1992 on 3500 HD model "C" and "K" series GM trucks. But all other '92 "C" and "K" series truck applications still used either the RWAL or the four-wheel drive "4WAL" system. The new ZPRWAL system works in essentially

the same manner as the RWAL system, but components are not interchangeable. The ZPRWAL system is designed to handle the larger volume of fluid that's found in the rear disc brake calipers on the 3500 HD models. The electronic controllers for the RWAL and ZPRWAL systems look the same, the only external difference being a gray electrical connector on the ZPRWAL controller compared to a black connector on the RWAL controller. The two are not interchangeable.

HOW IT WORKS

The Kelsey-Hayes RABS, RWAL and ZPRWAL systems are nonintegral rear wheel only antilock brake systems. The conventional master brake cylinder and power booster supplies brake pressure to a "Dual Solenoid" control valve for the rear brakes. This unit contains only two solenoid valves: an isolation valve to block pressure from the master cylinder to the rear brakes during antilock braking, and a dump valve for relieving pressure. The dual solenoid control valve also contains a pressure accumulator for storing fluid pressure during the dump or release phase of operation, and a reset switch which allows the system to maintain proper brake pressure.

The electronic controller that regulates the operation of the solenoid valves is separate from the control valve, and is located next to the master cylinder on some trucks. On Dodge trucks, you'll find it on the passenger side cowl panel under the dash. On Ford Bronco IIs, it's located under an access panel by the driver's door pillar.

The controller receives a speed signal from a single vehicle speed sensor. On Ford and Dodge applications, you'll find the speed sensor in the differential. The sensor ring is on the ring gear. On GM trucks, the speed sensor is located in the transmission tailshaft.

One problem with differential-mounted speed sensors (and automatic transmission-mounted sensors, too) you should be aware of is that their readings can be adversely affected by the presence of metallic debris in the gear oil. Metal chips from the casting or gear wear (clutch wear in an automatic transmission) can be attracted to the magnetic sensor, causing abnormal readings. So if you get a speed sensor fault code on one of these vehicles, remove and inspect the vehicle speed sensor for metal debris. If metal slivers or chips are stuck to it, the differential will have to be drained and refilled with the specified gear oil. The speed sensor will also have to be removed, cleaned and reinstalled.

On GM applications, the speed sensor signal first passes through an intermediate module on its way to the

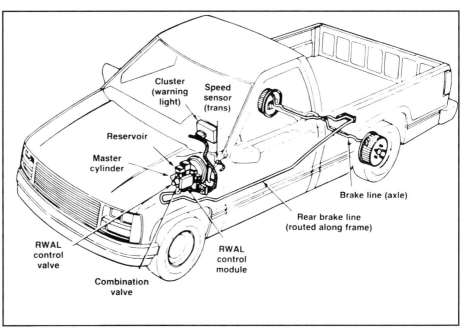

A typical RWAL application. The RWAL control valve may be located near the master cylinder as shown here, or under the chassis.

antilock controller. This module is called the "Digital Ratio Adapter Controller" or "DRAC" for short. The DRAC's job is to translate the analog speed sensor signal into a digital signal that can be processed by the ABS controller. In addition, the DRAC divides the basic speed sensor signal into three separate frequencies of signals that are used by other vehicle systems:

• A 4000 pulse per mile frequency that is used by the cruise control system and electronic instrument cluster on some vehicles.
• A 2000 pulse per mile frequency that is used by the engine control module for various emission and torque converter lockup functions.
• And a 128,000 pulse per mile frequency that's used by the ABS controller.

The DRAC module is calibrated to the final drive ratio and original equipment tire size of the vehicle. Replacing the original tires with ones of a different size or aspect ratio will upset the speed sensor signal, which in turn can adversely affect the operation of the ABS system as well as torque converter lockup and the accuracy of the speedometer and odometer.

If the tire sizes are changed, one of two steps will have to be taken to correct the speed sensor signal: The DRAC module will have to be replaced or recalibrated.

On 1991 and earlier "C" and "K" pickups, the DRAC modules can be recalibrated for different tire sizes and axle ratios by changing the configuration of an 8 pin connector that plugs into the instrument panel circuit board connector. A DRAC recalibration kit from GM is needed for this procedure. By referring to a speedometer calibration chart in the factory service manual, the correct pin positions can be determined for any tire size and gear ratio combination. The specified pins are then broken off the connector. This alters the DRAC circuits when it is replaced in the

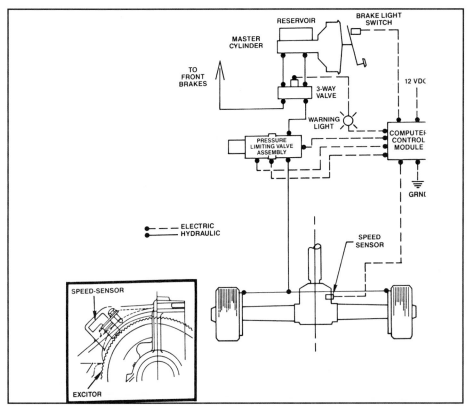

RWAL Schematic for a Dodge truck application. The item labeled "Pressure Limiting Valve Assembly" is the RWAL control valve.

instrument cluster to recalibrate the vehicle speed signal.

The "S" and "T" Blazers and vans as well as '92 "C" and "K" pickup truck applications have a DRAC that is a sealed plug-in module referred to as a "Vehicle Speed Sensor Buffer." It is matched to the original gear ratio and tire size of the vehicle, and cannot be recalibrated. Any changes in tire size or axle gearing requires replacing the DRAC or buffer with one that's correctly calibrated for the application.

RABS/RWAL DIAGNOSTICS

The self-diagnostic capability of the Kelsey-Hayes RABS, RWAL and ZPRWAL systems are limited to one fault code at a time. When a fault is detected, the amber ABS warning light on Ford and Dodge applications, or the red BRAKE light on GM

applications will come on and the ABS function will be disabled. Of course, the red BRAKE warning light can also come on if there's a hydraulic failure in the brake system or the parking brake has been set.

In the GM applications, the BRAKE warning light will be brightest when grounded by the parking brake, a little dimmer when grounded by the hydraulic system and dimmest when grounded by the ABS controller.

To determine what's causing a red BRAKE warning light in a GM application:

1. Set the parking brake. If the light gets brighter, the problem is not the parking brake.

2. Disconnect the connector from the combination valve by the master cylinder. If the light is still on, the problem is in the ABS system.

Both RWAL and RABS

applications provide manual flash codes. On GM trucks, the code can be retrieved by jumping terminals "A" and "H" on the ALDL diagnostic connector. On Ford and Dodge trucks, the code can be retrieved by manually grounding the diagnostic "pigtail" connector on the ABS controller. See Chapter 11 for the diagnostic procedures and list of fault codes.

One point to keep in mind about Kelsey-Hayes rear wheel antilock systems is that the controller can only store one code. So after you've retrieved, diagnosed and repaired a fault code, you should test drive the vehicle to see if any additional codes appear. If the ABS warning light remains out, you've fixed the problem. But if it comes back on, it means there's another fault that needs correcting.

False Codes

Sometimes an RWAL system will set a "false code" when there is no problem. If terminal "H" on the ALDL connector is grounded when the warning light is not on, it will set a code 9. If you've accidentally induced a code 9, simply clear it by disconnecting the battery or pulling the ABS fuse.

On 1989-91 GM "S" and "T" series trucks, and 1988-90 "C" and "K" series trucks with manual transmissions, a false code 7 can be set if the blower motor is set on high, and the ignition is turned off while the brakes are applied and the truck is still moving. This "glitch" was eliminated in August 1990 when a change was made in the ABS controller.

To prevent this condition from occurring, a relay needs to be installed between the blower motor and the resistor block to prevent electrical

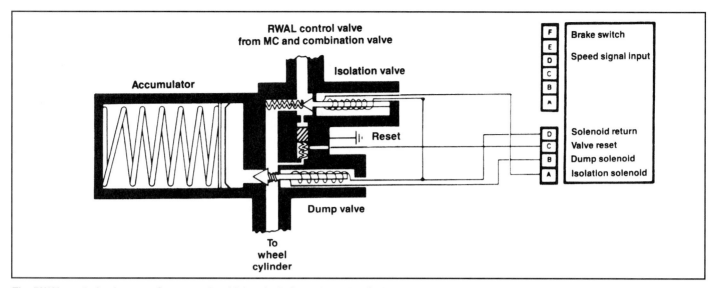

The RWAL control valve contains two solenoids: an isolation valve solenoid (normally open) and a dump valve solenoid (normally closed). If the rear wheels start to lock up, the ABS control module energizes the isolation solenoid to block off and hold pressure in the rear brake circuit. The dump valve solenoid is then opened to vent pressure into the accumulator. Both solenoids are then de-energized so pressure can be reapplied to the brakes. This process is repeated over and over until ABS braking is no longer needed.

feedback that could set the fault code (Chevrolet service bulletin #91-73-5, Oct. 1990).

Another false code problem has been noted on some 1988 and '89 "C" and "K" series GM trucks (Chevrolet service bulletin 89-285-5, Dec. 1989). A code 10 may be set when the vehicle is traveling over 37 miles-per-hour and the ABS controller sees an open circuit or no voltage in the stoplamp switch circuit. GM corrected this problem by releasing a new brake pedal switch (P/N 15607063), and cruise control release switch bracket (P/N 15607068).

In August 1990, a software change was made in the ABS controller on all General Motors RAWL equipped vehicles. The change transformed codes 6, 9 and 10 into "soft" codes which only illuminate the warming light as long as a fault is present. If the fault is intermittent and no longer exists, the light turns off and remains off when the ignition is turned off. The conditions by which these codes are set remains the same, as do the diagnostic procedures.

A condition that causes a code 6 (erratic speed signal) or 9 (open circuit in speed signal) will light the BRAKE light when a fault is detected. The BRAKE light will remain on until the next ignition cycle. If the fault is no longer present, however, the BRAKE light will go out but the code will remain in memory. If the problem reoccurs, the BRAKE light will come back on and remain on until the next ignition cycle.

A code 10 (brake lamp switch circuit) will be set if the brake pedal is depressed or the brake switch circuit is open and remains open until the vehicle's speed passes a predetermined speed. This code along with codes 6 and 9 will keep the BRAKE light illuminated during the existing ignition drive cycle. It will be stored as a history code in memory after the drive cycle in which it occurred. It can only be accessed with a scan tool.

Note: A scan tool must be used to read soft codes on the 1991 and later trucks because grounding the "H" terminal on the ALDL connector

erases soft codes. What's more, grounding terminal "H" will also set a false code 9 on these applications.

RABS/RWAL BLEEDING PROCEDURES

Brakes can be bled in the usual manner using pressure or manual techniques. The wheel bleeding sequence is right rear, left rear, right front, left front. If you're using a pressure bleeder to flush the lines, you'll need a tool to hold the combination valve open.

The best way to bleed this system if there's air in the lines is to do the modulator first, then the wheels, then the modulator a second time. A modulator bleeder screw is provided on older applications, but the screw was eliminated on some of the newer applications. For these, it may be necessary to loosen a brake line to vent bubbles from the modulator. If you don't get all the air out of the modulator, you will have a soft and/or low pedal.

SECTION II
RACING BRAKE SYSTEMS

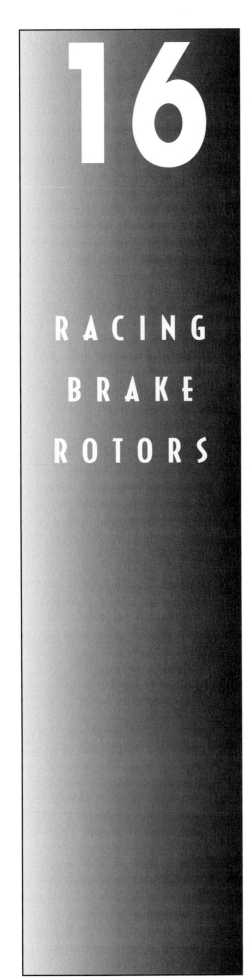

This cast iron racing rotor features curved vanes for superior heat evacuation. If vanes are angled or curved, position rotor so vanes lean to the rear in relation to direction of rotation. This is a right-side rotor.

ROTOR MATERIALS

From a standpoint of acceleration and handling, reducing rotating and unsprung weight is always a good thing to do, in any form of racing. A reduction in rotating weight (wheel, tire or rotor) translates into a 4:1 benefit. In other words, if you reduce rotating weight by 1 pound at each wheel position (for a 4-pound total reduction), it's the same as reducing overall vehicle weight by 16 pounds.

The majority of rotors are machined from cast iron or billet steel. In addition, lightweight materials are often used where racing rules permit. Aluminum and titanium are the two lightweight metals of choice, and some applications exist for the use of lightweight carbon fiber composite rotors as well. However, lighter is not always better, which will be discussed later in this chapter.

Titanium Rotors

A very lightweight alternative is the titanium rotor, with primary applications on sprint cars and DIRT cars, although some late-model oval racers are starting to use these, simply because of the advantage of their lighter unsprung weight.

Titanium rotors have unique properties. When the brakes are applied (hard application), they heat very quickly, and will commonly glow brightly almost immediately upon reaching operating temperature, and will stop glowing almost immediately as the brake pedal is lifted. The visual scenario is akin to the on/off pop of a flash bulb. On a brake dyno, a titanium rotor can be brought to high temperature (in excess of 1,000 degrees F), glowing brightly. When the dyno stops, the glow disappears, and within seconds you can lay your hand on the rotor (although I don't advise trying this, for obvious reasons). It cools that quickly.

Typically, a titanium rotor will be treated with a ceramic coating on the disc faces, which serves two purposes: it acts as a heat barrier, preventing excessive heat from building up within the rotor (since titanium can heat so quickly anyway, you need a barrier to keep the heat absorption

This rotor's ground surface shows angled-intersecting grind marks. Acceptable, but a random finish is best. If the rotors need a fresh finish, the final surface finish should be very random and can be achieved using sandpaper or a rotary abrasive ball surfacer. Naturally, rotors should first be parallel (each side of rotor) and flat, which will be accomplished on a lathe.

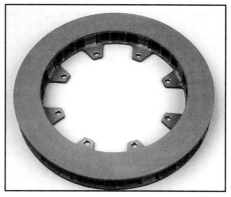

A titanium rotor. The disc faces are ceramic coated to provide frictional bite for the pads. Titanium rotors are very lightweight (and very expensive). They dissipate heat very, very quickly.

Titanium rotor is weld-assembled with two separate discs. Note the solid bridge spacers (these add rigidity and determine thickness) and the thinwall vanes.

down to a manageable level for proper pad performance). The ceramic coating also provides a preparation surface for pad "bedding." The surface may be prepared on the "rough" side, similar to sandpaper. Once ceramic coated, this hard roughness helps to allow pad material transfer from the pad to the rotor (remember, any pad must be able to transfer its material to the rotor, so the end result is pad material-against-pad material for effective braking).

Various pad materials can be used with titanium rotors, but the most effective are an all-metal matrix with a bronze content, bonded to a steel backing plate. Specific compounds are not discussed freely among the folks who make this stuff. They could tell me more, but then they'd have to shoot me.

Since the titanium material dissipates heat so quickly, a heat emitter coating in the vanes usually isn't necessary. The big downside to titanium rotors is their cost: about $600 each. However, in a big-money series where every bit of weight counts, the expenditure can be justified.

Applications for titanium rotors include Indy cars, some dragsters, and various circle track series where rules permit alternate rotor material.

Aluminum Rotors

Aluminum rotors offer a distinct weight savings as compared to cast iron, though not as light as titanium. Aluminum rotors are used in a limited number of applications, including some drag racing situations. Some jet dragsters use aluminum rotors, strictly from a weight standpoint. Since the brakes are primarily used only to hold the vehicle at the starting line, they experience no high levels of abuse. Sprint car applications often use aluminum rotors, at the left front wheel only. Since a sprint car experiences only left-hand turns, no brake is used on the right front. The left-front brake alone helps to bias the car into a left-hand turn, and in a sprint car setup, the left front wheel tends to lift off and unload during a turn anyway, so the demands are not great. The lightweight and relatively

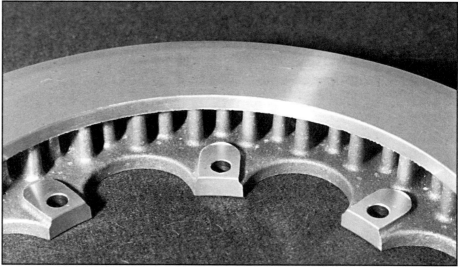

Vented cast aluminum rotors. These are to be used in a Late Model application. Note offset entry location of vanes. This helps promote air flow through rotor.

Thinner aluminum rotor will be used on rear brakes; thicker rotors for fronts. The car builder is considering ceramic coating the front rotors for added protection (since aluminum gets very soft as heat hits the 650 degree range, and can melt at 1000 degrees). Ceramic coating will help to a point, but when 1000 degrees is hit, the base aluminum may soften anyway.

it's difficult to transfer a conventional pad material to a carbon fiber rotor. As a result, the use of a carbon fiber pad against a carbon fiber rotor will create the frictional properties needed to stop the car. However (and this is something that newcomers to carbon fiber may not realize initially), carbon fiber systems only work when hot. The characteristics are such that a cold rotor and pad combination may not be able to produce enough friction to stop the car as it rolls out of its trailer. Also, carbon fiber is extremely unstable in terms of frictional coefficients, largely because they cool so darned fast. Braking performance can be very erratic, from front to rear and even wheel to wheel. Drastic temperature variations (temperature rises and drops quickly) can produce braking results that change every time the pedal is depressed. You can usually tell if a Formula 1 car is equipped with carbon fiber rotors by watching the wheel locations. Similar to the appearance of titanium rotors in use, when the brakes are applied and peak temperature is reached, the

softer aluminum can work in this application, since it's not relied upon for sustained hard braking. Depending on the application, aluminum rotors may or may not be ceramic coated. Sprint cars, for example, generally run them uncoated.

Carbon Fiber Rotors

Carbon fiber rotors offer light weight, but they are limited in their use. Currently, the only applications I'm aware of is in Formula 1 in Europe and in Top Fuel and Funny Car drag race applications in the U.S. (on rear brakes only). The cost is very prohibitive, at close to $1000 per wheel for a rotor and pads. There are a few interesting and unique aspects to carbon fiber rotors worth noting. First of all, you must use carbon fiber brake pads in conjunction with carbon fiber rotors. Nothing else will work properly. Just as the task of any pad and rotor combination is to transfer pad material to the rotor, in an attempt

to "normalize" the frictional properties between the two materials by creating a pad material-to-pad material contact when the pads rub against the rotors, carbon fiber-against-carbon fiber is what makes this system work.

Since carbon fiber is so darned hard,

Carbon fiber rotor and pads. Carbon pads must be used with a carbon rotor, since this is the only material that will work. Carbon rotor/pad assemblies provide very low coefficient of friction when cold. Carbon/carbon systems work only when very hot. This setup is popular on Top Fuel and Funny Car rear brakes. They won't hold the car at the staging lights, but they'll work when trying to haul the car down from speeds of 200+ mph. The big attraction of carbon/carbon is their light weight. Not for all applications, by a long shot!

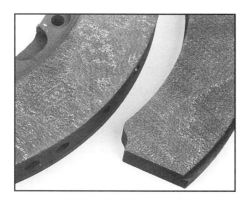

Carbon/carbon rotors dissipate heat very quickly. A series of small holes drilled through the matrix (see edge of rotor disc) is sufficient in evacuating heat. Relief holes are limited in number and size because carbon/carbon rotors only work when hot, so cooling them is not a major concern.

Rotor weight depends on the demands placed on the brake system by the car, track, and driver. Aggressive drivers, with a track with lots of hairpins and short straights, coupled with a heavy Trans Am car like this Roush Mustang, will dictate use of a sturdy rotor. Never select a rotor without considering these factors.

rotors can glow very quickly, almost like the flash of a strobe. Once the pedal is released, they again cool very quickly.

ROTOR SELECTION

Rotor styles are offered in two basic categories: solid and vented. Given similar materials, solid rotors are lighter in weight than vented rotors. Light cars can use lighter/thinner rotors, and heavier cars require thicker rotors. The heavier the car, and the greater the mass to be stopped, the thicker the rotor. A few broad generalizations are as follows: lighter cars such as sprint cars and midgets can use solid rotors. Cars weighing approximately 1600–2000 lbs. running on dirt, a .810" thick vented rotor would be a good choice. Cars weighing up to 2800 lbs. could use a 1.250"–1.380" thick vented rotor.

NEVER select a rotor based on weight alone. A lighter rotor may not be able to handle the heat and stresses that your situation involves. Yes, lighter is better, but only providing it will perform and live under given conditions. If you're thinking of switching to another rotor size or

lighter material, the best thing to do is to use temperature indicating paint to gauge your current rotor temperature under race conditions. Once you have this information in hand, a rotor manufacturer is then able to guide you to the proper rotor type and size. Don't simply scrap your existing rotors in favor of airweight unobtainium just for the sake of spending more money. Do your research first and make an informed selection.

How light you can go depends on the braking demands of the car on a given track. A too-light or too-thin rotor may distort, warp or not be able to soak up sufficient heat from the pads.

The critical points to consider regarding rotors include the mechanical advantage (in other words, how big is the thing in terms of diameter and surface area?), stability of the material (resistance to cracking as it goes through extremes of heat cycling, and stability if thermally shocked when experiencing a sudden change in temperature), the rotor's ability to dissipate heat, and its weight.

Generally speaking, in terms of braking performance, the largest diameter rotor that will fit or is allowed should be used, unless weight or brake balance dictates a smaller diameter. Disc thickness generally increases in proportion to disc diameter, and should increase in proportion to vehicle weight.

Variables To Consider

When considering using smaller, thinner and/or lighter rotors, you have to consider all of the aspects of racing dynamics that ultimately affect the braking system. In basic terms, lighter cars can use lighter brakes because the demands are less, and heavier cars need heavier brakes. This all has to do with heat buildup and heat dissipation.

If the track is not very demanding in terms of braking, thinner rotors can be considered. If the track is nasty on brakes, heavier, thicker rotors may be needed. If the track has a few hard-braking turns, but also features long straights that allow the brakes to cool, the car may be a candidate for thinner rotors. This is a very broad explanation, I know, but the use of thinner and/or lighter weight rotors

Variety of rotor designs shown here, including slotted vented rotors and cross drilled vented rotors. Super lightweight rotor on far right is aluminum slotted. Never cross drill a vented rotor on your own. If the manufacturer deems this necessary, they'll do it. Courtesy Alcon.

can be partially determined by track type and conditions.

Driving style is a variable that is all too often ignored. Some drivers habitually "ride" the brakes, generating heat the entire time the car is on the track. Some pump the brakes halfway down the straightaway in anticipation of the turn, generating heat and preventing the brakes from cooling adequately after the previous turn. Conversely, other drivers accelerate deep into turns, use the brakes to the tire threshold, then lift off of the pedal, allowing the brakes to cool until the next braking demand. If the driver is hard on brakes, moving to lighter/thinner rotors may be a mistake.

Any pre-existing brake system problems may be compounded by lighter and/or thinner rotors. For instance, if the caliper mounts are crooked, or if a caliper piston hangs up, etc., that condition will promote excessive forces and heat buildup that can warp, deflect or even break a too-light rotor. Remember, one of the rotor's main functions is to absorb and dissipate heat. If the rotor is so thin that it cannot absorb the amount of

frictional heat being generated, it may not be able to withstand that level of heat because it just doesn't have enough material to soak up the heat that it sees.

VENTED ROTORS

Vented rotors feature a series of air channels between the two disc faces. These channels (or the separation walls that create the individual channels) are referred to as vanes. Vented rotors are designed to provide maximum cooling. The internal vanes pump cooler air from the center of the wheel, which carries this air through the vanes, picking up heat along the way and removing a percentage of that heat from the rotor. Some vented rotors feature straight vanes and some use curved vanes (variances in rotor design) to disperse this heat away from the rotor. After heavy race use, especially in adverse conditions like offroading, check the vanes to make sure they're clean and free of obstructions.

Rotor Drilling/Slotting

In some cases, rotors are drilled or

slotted. Initially, crossdrilling was done to help reduce the "gas buildup" between the pad and rotor. Granted, when pads begin to squeeze a rotor, heat is generated due to friction. With some pad compounds, the heat would react with the pad, causing the resin binders within the pad material to rise to the surface and "gas," which creates a gas pressure layer between the pad and rotor. This pressure begins just after the point of attack as the pad meets the rotor, and continues to progressively build along the pad until it can escape at the exit end of the pad. We can draw a comparison between this phenomenon and a car's suspension. Let's say the car is driven on a flat, smooth road. Suddenly, the road angles upwards in a quick-ramp fashion. As the front wheels hit this ramp entry, the suspension deflects upwards, towards the body and the body deflects downwards in compression. After the full suspension settles and the entire car is once again stable while it rides up this angle, the suspension rebounds and settles into a steady state once again. A similar event takes place if the pads gas. Using older-technology pads as our

Cross-drilled steel rotor. Cross drilling decreases rotating and unsprung weight, which is always desirable. Multitude of holes can also provide pads with additional "biting edges" for more immediate pad response. In some cases (depending on pad compound and edge-shape of the holes), multiple holes can shorten pad life via accelerated wear. Under the right circumstances, cross drilling can be of benefit. To be honest though, most racers choose a drilled rotor because they like the appearance. Unit in photo is from Aerospace Components.

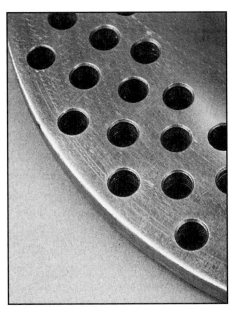

A cross drilled solid steel rotor. Holes have been carefully chamfered to reduce chance of stress cracking. Sharp edges caused by drilled holes can act as stress risers.

example here, as the pads compress onto the rotor, heat builds, resins in the pads react and gases are released to the pad surface, building a sudden "pressure ramp," which forces the pads away from the rotor, which pushes the pistons back into their bores. A staggered piston setup uses the larger diameter piston(s) at the exit portion of the pad to counteract this gas-push by applying greater force behind the pad. By drilling a series of holes in the rotor disc face, this provided a faster escape path for these gas buildups, which worked hand in hand with staggered piston calipers or even reduced the problem on their own when the same size pistons are used in the caliper.

However, with today's carbon pads, this gas buildup does not occur, hence many experts feel that there is no longer a need to drill the rotor (other than for weight savings). The other thing to consider is rotor composition. If it's a cast iron rotor, it should be

obvious that you're dealing with a brittle material. Excessive cross drilling serves to create a bunch of potential stress risers, which could provide the rotor with an excuse to crack. If the rotor is made of steel, which is more malleable, cross drilling does not present the same level of stress-cracking potential.

Also (early in racing brake development), it was assumed that a bunch of holes in the rotor surface would help increase the coefficient of friction between the pads and the rotor because all of the small holes would provide plenty of small edges, which would permit the pads to "bite" more effectively. With today's carbon-type pads, the heat level is higher and the coefficient of friction higher, and the hole edge "bite" isn't necessary. Besides, a bunch of small holes provide a bunch of small edges to nibble away at the pads, which can shorten pad life.

In summary, don't cross drill a cast

iron rotor on your own. For that matter, you probably shouldn't cross drill any rotor. If the rotor maker drilled the part, then assume that it's a move for the better. If it wasn't drilled when you took it out of the box, don't drill it on your own.

Slotting, however, does provide a benefit that few can argue with. The purpose of these slots or grooves is to improve braking bite and to ensure that, as the pad friction material wears, the debris particles are cleared away from the face of the pad and rotor. These shallow slots or grooves are machined into the rotor face in either a series of straight lines that are angled (at an angle not perpendicular to the radius of the rotor), or in a series of curved lines. These help to reduce brake dust buildup. Their shape and number will vary depending on the design whims of the maker. These grooves do not "cool" the rotor. Grooved or "slotted" rotors are directional. The rotor should be mounted so that in the direction of rotation, the grooves sweep rearwards

Indy Car slotted rotors. Slots are designed to self-clean rotors/pads, removing pad dust/debris during use. Slots have nothing to do with rotor cooling. Rotor on left is "standard" out-of-the-box, while rotor on right has been pre-bedded. Pre-bedded rotor has been stabilized through heat cycle and can now be used to bed new pads. Courtesy Alcon.

at the outer perimeter of the rotor.

ROTOR BEDDING

Just as pads need to be "bedded" before being used under racing conditions, rotors require their own "seasoning" in order to provide optimum friction and longevity, stability and resistance to cracking. This is probably most important with cast iron rotors.

If the race car is equipped with brake cooling ducts, these should be partially blocked off (block off 1/2 to 3/4 of the duct openings), because during the bedding process, you want to let frictional heat work to your advantage in seasoning the rotors. When bedding new rotors, use only pads that have already been bedded. Use the brakes gently at first from initially low speeds, and progressively increase to normal racing speeds, but continue to use gentle braking pressure when applying the brakes.

Do this for about 8-10 miles or so. After this, apply the brakes hard for 2 or 3 applications. During this final braking, you want to raise rotor temperature to at least 600 degrees F, and possibly up to about 800-1000 degrees. Naturally, you need to apply temperature indicating paint for this procedure.

New rotors are referred to as "green" rotors, and require a slow break-in period. Don't go out and hammer new rotors on the first few laps. Allow them to build heat slowly, eventually up to race temps, then allow them to cool completely.

ROTOR INSTALLATION

Rotor runout is a critical factor in your setup and should always be checked on every new installation. What you're concerned about is axial runout...rotor walk or wobble as you view the rotor from the disc edge, as the rotor turns. Excessive runout can

cause a number of problems, including pedal bounce, tapered pad wear, piston kickback (where the high spot on the rotor continually hits the pad and pushes it outboard, whacking the piston back into its bore), and brake pad drag.

If the rotor is spindle-mounted, and there's only one center attachment of the rotor to the hub or spindle, runout will indicate either a bent spindle or a warped rotor. If the rotor is bolted to a separate mounting hat, it's possible to correct the runout by shimming the rotor at its hat attachment points.

Whenever installing a rotor and hat assembly, rotor runout should always be checked as a matter of routine. With the rotor/hat assembly securely installed onto the hub (make sure there's no slop that would allow the rotor to wiggle in/out from the hub. Install lug nuts on the hat face to secure the assembly in a rigid position), position a dial indicator (secured on a dial indicator mount which is clamped or magnetized on a nearby non-moving part such as the frame) at the rotor face, and zero the dial. Place a chalk mark on the rotor to indicate a starting point, then slowly rotate the rotor a full 360 degrees, monitoring the dial in the process. If more than .005" runout is displayed, the rotor may need to be shimmed at the hat.

Adjust this by shimming between the rotor and the hat mounting face using decreasing thickness shims, to create a full contact at all bolt locations. Don't just shim two or three bolts, because this can create an air gap at the adjacent bolt locations, preventing metal-to-metal mating of the hat/rotor mounting ears. Attempting to tighten these remaining bolts to achieve full mating will

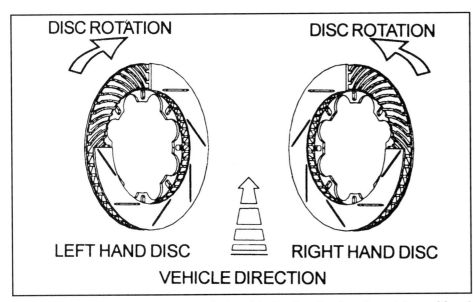

Any vented and/or slotted rotors are designed to be directional, and must be positioned appropriately on the car. Slots and vanes always angle to the rear. Angled vanes must sweep rearwards to evacuate heat from the rotor, and slots must angle rearward to evacuate brake pad dust. Courtesy AP Racing.

Rotor and caliper being run on brake dyno at Wilwood. In addition to using dyno for testing and development purposes, rotor manufacturers can also use dyno to pre-bed rotors. Courtesy Wilwood.

further distort the hat and rotor, and you'll create a worse runout problem than you started with. If the hat is lifted away from the rotor at any point, each of those points must be filled with a shim of the appropriate thickness.

Any rotor assembly that features a separate disc bolted to a mounting hat features a series of mounting bolts placed around the perimeter of the hat. It is highly recommended that each of these bolts is safety-wired to prevent loosening. You can run a safety wire at each adjacent pair of bolts (wiring two bolt heads together at a time).

Rotor hats (also called bells) are generally machined from aluminum, though some late model classes demand the use of a steel hat. Hats are available in a wide range of diameters, bolt patterns, stud patterns and offsets to accommodate rotor and hub applications. Some rotor hats will feature a black coating. Don't be tempted to remove this or paint over this coating. Black will help to promote heat dissipation from the hat. Also, this may be a special heat emitter coating designed to pull heat from the hat. So, don't blindly disrupt this finish just because you want to change its color.

RIGID vs. FLOATING DISCS

There are essentially two methods of attaching the rotor to the hat...bolted and floating. A bolted mounting is generally preferred for strength and security, where the rotor disc is bolted to the hat with a series of fasteners. A floating attachment allows the disc to move in an axial direction (inboard and outboard) in order to "find" a centered home when the clamping force of the pads acts upon the rotor.

A floating system either allows the rotor to move independently of the hat because the bolts can slide in-out of the hat holes; or the rotor can move axially because the rotor-to-hat bolts can slide in the disc's mounting holes. Either way, the rotor is allowed to move in an axial direction (inboard or outboard) to center itself each time the brakes are applied, in much the same way as a single-piston "sliding" caliper can float axially to center itself over the rotor. A floating disc might offer advantages in certain conditions.

A floating design can be handy when caliper piston knockback takes place, since the rotor can continually "center" itself relative to the caliper pads. This can reduce pedal travel. A floating disc might also feature a small amount of radial float as well (allowing the rotor to move eccentrically) in order to avoid stresses caused by thermal expansion of the hat and rotor (to avoid cracking the hat or rotor where they bolt together).

ROTOR WARP MEMORY

By the way, if a rotor does become warped through excessive heat exposure, etc., your first impulse may be to resurface the rotor to correct the

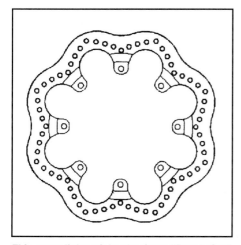

This super lightweight aluminum "Revolution" rotor from The Brake Man is a good example of how skeletonized a rotor can be and still perform. This style rotor can be used in some midget and sprint applications. Naturally, due to its light weight and minimal mass, this style of rotor is only suited to braking applications where braking demands are relatively light. Courtesy The Brake Man.

problem. While resurfacing the rotor on a lathe will regain a "flat" disc surface, the problem may not be solved. When a rotor distorts due to excessive heat/pressure, the metal may acquire an internal "memory" (stresses that are induced in the metal). Even though resurfacing may at first regain a flat and parallel disc surface, once the rotor is again exposed to operational heat, it is possible that the internal stresses may draw the rotor into a warped state once again. This won't happen every time, and you may get lucky by simply resurfacing. Just be aware that it might happen. If you suspect stress-induced warpage, and you want to save the rotor, consider having the rotor stress relieved with either a cryogenics or vibratory stress relief process. Once treated, then resurface the rotor. That way, you have a much better chance of keeping the flat/true disc state. On the other hand, if it's an inexpensive rotor and it's seen better days anyway, you may be better off

by simply replacing it.

STRESS RELIEVING ROTORS

Even though a cast iron or steel rotor is theoretically normalized during manufacture, there may be an advantage to having your rotors stress relieved, depending on the application and the severity of rotor use. There are two processes which have risen dramatically in popularity within the racing community, including cryogenics and vibratory stress relief. While some racers may view these practices with a healthy dose of skepticism, others firmly believe in the benefits that can be achieved. While each process uses a different approach, they are essentially intended to obtain the same goal: to make the metal stronger and more stable, and to reduce the potential for cracking, breakage and warpage.

Metals (especially castings) commonly feature microscopic internal areas that are weak, and other areas that are stronger. Stress relieving attempts to make the metallurgical composition more uniform (improving the "grain" structure, to put it one way), and thereby more stable.

My personal experience with stress relieving has made me a believer. In preparation for a 24-hour race at Moroso Motorsports Park, we had our road racing front hubs cryo treated (Dodge Neons, an application known for front hub failure). Although we were warned that our hubs would probably require replacement halfway through the race, both cars finished (one of our cars won its class as well) on the same hubs, requiring no hub changes at any time during the event. After the race, we mag'd them, and

they revealed no fractures.

As an experiment at the same race, we decided to run stock/out-of-the-box front rotors on one car, while the other car's front rotors were VSR-treated (the vibratory process). While the braking performance was essentially identical on both cars, an after-race inspection told the tale: the untreated rotors were covered with heat-check cracks (minor surface cracks in the steel, which is normal and expected after being subjected to 24 hours of race-speed braking). However, the VSR-treated rotors were virtually heat crack-free! While VSR didn't make the brakes work any better, it was obvious that the treatment made the metal more stable, which should provide longer life and a greatly reduced risk of failure.

I'm sure that there are plenty of folks who think this is all hogwash, but I'm also sure that there are plenty of folks who have tried these treatments and have become believers. As far as cryo and VSR is concerned, I'm sold. These processes work, and in my opinion, you should take advantage of what they offer. As a natural part of racing, there's always going to be a lot of B.S., old wives' tales and snake-oil floating around, but this stuff is legit.

CRYOGENIC STRESS RELIEF

Hang onto your mittens. If you want to stress-relieve a brake rotor (or hub, or spindle, upright or any other suspension or engine piece), consider cryogenic stress relief.

A relatively new science has emerged within the racing community involves freezing metal parts to make them stronger. Cryogenic tempering isn't a completely new idea. The

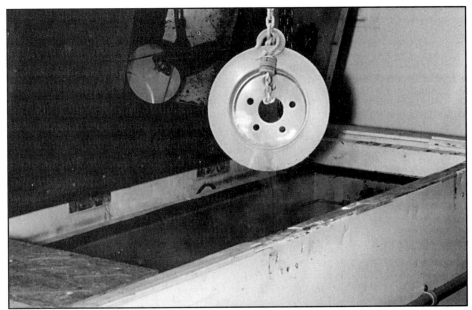

This rotor is being cryogenically treated. The parts are frozen to -300 degrees F. using liquid nitrogen, then brought back to ambient temperature. This entire process, from start to finish, is computer-controlled. When the part is removed from the freezing cabinet, there's no frost on the part. For purposes of this photo however, we shot the rotor at the point where it was frozen just so you could get an idea of how cold the part is at this point. Cryogenics alters the grain structure of the metal, making the part more stable and much stronger. In the case of a brake rotor, this makes the rotor less prone to warpage and potential cracking.

freezing of metal in an effort to increase its durability and strength has been practiced for some thirty years within various factions of science and industry. In fact, the tool & die industry regularly uses this approach to temper and extend the life of steel tooling bits. More recently, with the advent of "deep cryogenics," entirely new possibilities are emerging in the field of race car parts.

What It Does

The condensed explanation of this process, in terms of automotive applications, is this: by cryogenically tempering (deep-freezing) a metal part, the internal structure is made more uniform, more durable and stronger.

In the "conventional" sense, we're accustomed to using heating ovens to stress-relieve a metal part. While ovens will maintain their usefulness, the addition of cryogenics offers far-reaching benefits for racers.

The process of deep cryogenic freezing changes the structure of the metal being treated. Inside the metal, areas of weaker, potentially brittle deposits called "austenites" may exist. These are flaws that create the potential for cracking. Deep cryogenics changes these areas into harder, more uniform "martensites." The process also creates a vast distribution of very fine carbide particles throughout the metal. The result is increased strength and structural uniformity. These particles are responsible for the exceptional wear characteristics imparted by the process, due to a denser molecular structure.

The Cryogenic Unit

In simplified terms, this is a big freezer that's controlled by a computer program. The system consists of a freezer cabinet, a computer system with highly specialized software, and a storage tank filled with liquid nitrogen.

One of the cryo shops that I've visited is Advanced Cryogenics, near Pittsburgh, Pennsylvania. This shop has conducted an enormous amount of research in the field of cryogenic tempering of engine parts, brake rotors and suspension parts, with a high level of success. By the way, these guys have operated in the hi-tech industrial tooling industry for years, so they definitely know their way around metals. These guys live and breathe ultra-tight tolerances.

In all, Advanced Cryogenics' race-testing program has involved the component treatment of some 15 cars, in D.I.R.T., Busch Grand National, NASCAR, and a few SCCA road racing applications. They're also performing cryo testing for a few aftermarket parts manufacturers.

Benefits

Cryogenic treatment will find an internal flaw that would be missed by external mag bench detection. Obviously, a magnetic particle inspection station or dye penetrant process is used to locate surface flaws in metal. However, an internal pocket-flaw may actually cause the part to snap open during freezing. Certainly, any race car builder would agree that it's better to find a bad part now as opposed to discovering the problem during a race. What I'm driving at is this: if the part is already badly flawed, this process may break it. But, it's better to find out now as opposed to later.

With this process, you'll improve the tensile and ductile strength of the part. Cryogenic treatment will also improve the bond of a weld, by producing a more uniform metallurgy structure. Since this treatment

143

Rotors being vibratory stress-relieved with Bonal's Meta-Lax system. This process subjects the rotors to a series of sub-harmonic vibrations, in effect "seasoning" the rotor. The entire process is computer controlled and monitored for precise and repeatable results. As with cryo treatment, sub-harmonic vibratory stress relief (VSR) makes the part more stable, changing the molecular structure of the metal to better align the grain pattern. The process also changes "weak" spots in the metal to create a more uniform matrix. This process is completely non-destructive and can be reapplied as often as you like. Courtesy Bonal Technologies.

stabilizes the metal, it also improves the machinability of the part.

Cryo treatment is a one-time, permanent process. Unlike treatments that are designed to increase only the surface hardness of metal, cryo treatment changes the metal structure throughout the part. Once a part has been cryo treated, there's no surface layer to break through during future rotor machining.

This subzero metal treatment may be just the ticket to cure a rotor's tendency to warp. While cryo treatment isn't likely to straighten a warped rotor, once the rotor is remachined flat and then cryo treated, the chances of future warping are drastically reduced.

What Parts Apply?

Regarding what types of materials are compatible with this type of structural treatment, any cast, forged or billet metal can be treated, and will

benefit from the treatment. If the rotors are carbon fiber, this process won't be of benefit.

While the process will create a slightly higher Rockwell hardness, that isn't the real directive. Cryogenic processing benefits a part by stabilizing the metal structure, creating a stronger molecular "grain" pattern uniformity within the metal.

As far as cost is concerned, it's primarily based on the amount of nitrogen used. The larger the part, the more nitrogen is used. Treating aluminum sometimes uses less nitrogen (due to the higher conductivity of alloy). However, this work is very reasonably priced. Expect to pay something in the neighborhood of $30 - $50 to have a set of rotors cryo treated.

The Process

In a nutshell, the temperature of the part is reduced, gradually, to -300 degrees F, then gradually allowed to return to ambient temperature. Although that sounds simple enough, the real magic involves the way in which the temperature cycles occur.

It's best to have the parts cryo tempered before any machining takes place. Once the parts have been cleaned, the cooling can begin.

Specific metals require specific procedures. For example, a part might be cooled to -100 degrees F within a 60-minute period, then reduced to –180 degrees within the next 120 minutes, then held at -187 degrees for the next three-hour period, then reduced to -279 degrees within the next hour, then to -300, where it stays for sixteen hours. Then temperature may be increased to -248 degrees for a specific time, then -205 degrees, then -154 degrees, etc., until ambient

temperature is achieved. The entire cold-cycle process may take twenty-four to thirty hours to complete.

Following the end of the cryo process, the part may then be subjected to a gradual rise of heat in a convection oven (at a specific temperature, and for a predetermined time period) in order to finalize the part's "triple temper" stability. Again, the exact cycle steps, both in the freezer and in the oven, will vary according to the type of material involved and its intended use.

The number of shops performing this work and offering the service to racers is gradually increasing (the equipment costs around $30,000 or so), so you shouldn't have too much trouble finding a cryo service. The two shops that I'm familiar with are Advanced Cryogenics, Leechburg, Pennsylvania, 412-845-8708; and Cryogenic Tempering near Akron, Ohio, at 330-665-5424.

VIBRATIONAL STRESS RELIEF

It may initially sound like a black-magic formula, but inducing a controlled series of vibrations to brake rotors can provide a safe, effective and non-destructive method of stress relief. The end results: longer life and greater rotor efficiency.

Bonal Technologies (to my knowledge, the only manufacturer of this technology that offers this service to the automotive racing industry) designs and makes a complete system for subharmonic vibrational stress relief.

The system includes a force-inducer (this unit attaches to the workpiece and creates the vibrations), a transducer (this sends a feedback signal from the workpiece to the controller), and the controller console unit (an electronic head that tells the force inducer what to do, based on the operator's input and information it receives from the transducer). This stress relief system can be used on-site as a portable setup, or in the shop as a permanent fixture. The force inducer can be attached directly to the piece being treated. For example, the inducer can be clamped to a rotor while the rotor is on the vehicle. Or, the rotors can be rigidly mounted to a heavy steel platform table, with the force inducer mounted to the table top instead of directly to the parts being treated. The objective is to transmit the vibrations to the rotors, however that is best accomplished.

As long as the vibrations can be transmitted to the rotors (or whatever parts are being treated) in direct fashion (by either direct attachment to the force inducer or by direct, rigid mount to the tabletop, when the inducer is secured to the table), the vibrational force will affect the part's internal stress.

How Does It Work?

There are two forms of stress that can exist within a metal part: mechanical and thermal. "Sub-harmonic vibratory stress relief," as it's officially known, is a method that relaxes metal (hence the brand name Meta-Lax), but only in terms of the metal part's thermal stress, leaving the mechanical stresses unchanged.

In other words, vibrating a part serves to relieve any stresses that were created due to the heat involved in welding, casting, machining or forging, but it does not change the metal's strength. Vibrational relief does not generate heat, and won't alter the part's hardness. As a result, it's

Rotors are clamped to a steel table (small portable size table shown here, which can be used in shop or at track). Large unit located at rear of table induces vibrations to the table and the rotors. Small unit clamped to right side of table is transducer, which feeds signals back to computer. Courtesy Bonal Technologies.

safe to use on a repeated basis, since it can't harm the part involved.

The vibration process searches for the harmonic peak of the workpiece by vibrating it (the peak is where the piece tends to create the maximum harmonic disturbance, just as a tuning fork vibrates when subjected to force, or as a fishing rod tends to whip and vibrate when dynamic force is present).

As a harmonic disturbance is sent through the workpiece, those signals are sent back to the system's console. The force inducer (the machine that creates the vibrations) is then adjusted to vibrate the workpiece in a frequency range that begins just before the peak. This energy area at the base of the peak is where maximum damping energy occurs. Sending vibrations through the workpiece with this adjustment serves to relax the workpiece.

Subharmonic vibratory stress relief simply serves to "season" a part on an accelerated basis. After all, the theory of vibration stress relieving isn't new. Part of the reason that a "seasoned"

engine block is favored by many race engine builders is because it's been subjected to harmonic vibration and has "settled" and relaxed, which makes it a good candidate for precision machining to create a stable race engine block. In fact, if a part is "natural aged" next to a set of railroad tracks, its seasoning is accelerated, due to the heavy vibrations that occur. This high-tech process accomplishes the same thing...it accelerates the seasoning process, by dissipating the stored thermal energy within the part.

When Should It Be Used?

Thermal stresses cause three basic problems: distortion immediately after grinding or machining, delayed distortion following grinding or machining, and a tendency to prematurely crack.

According to Bonal, the process will benefit the part in either case, and since it can't hurt anything, there's really no bad time to use it.

All four types of stress relief, including heat treating, cryogenic freezing, vibratory relief and natural seasoning, address the issue of

Indy car rotors have diameters that range in size from 12 5/8" to 14". Rotors sizes and types vary according to the type of track they'll be running. Indy cars run on superspeedways, where little braking is used, to tight street circuits, where drivers are on the brakes all the time. Matching rotor size and materials is critical.

thermal stress. Subharmonic vibration relieving apparently offers an advantage, in that it doesn't affect the mechanical stresses, and it's appreciably faster. Vibratory relieving takes an average of 45 minutes, as compared to cryo freezing at about 24 hours and oven relieving at maybe 8 hours. Of course, natural seasoning might take 6 months to 2 years.

While I'm not trying to push anybody's product or service, if you're interested in having your rotors treated, contact Meta-Lax System, Bonal Technologies, Inc., 21178 Bridge St., Southfield, MI 48034, or call them at 800-META-LAX (800-638-2529). This is neat stuff and it won't damage the rotors.

INDY CARS

Indy type cars might use a rotor diameter in any size ranging from 12 5/8" to 14". Thickness might vary from 1 1/4" to even 1 1/2" thick. All rotors will feature curved vanes for greater heat dissipation, due to the larger surface area a curved vane offers as opposed to a straight vane.

WINSTON CUP

Winston Cup, Busch Grand national and Craftsman truck series cars are mandated to use 15" wheels, and as a result are limited with regard to rotor diameter. Generally, front rotors are 12 5/8" x 1 3/8". Rear rotors are generally 12.19" x 1 1/4". On most tracks, NASCAR teams run 12.72 inch diameter vented cast iron rotors But at Daytona and Talladega, some teams actually run solid rotors to save a few pounds of weight. Some teams may also switch to a slightly larger diameter rotor to increase braking leverage, which comes in handy on the higher speed tracks.

In a race where a driver is constantly on the brakes, like Martinsville or Richmond, the rotors are always hot and can sometimes reach as high as 1400 degrees F! Under these conditions, the rotors will glow bright orange. So for these kinds of tracks, vented rotors are a must to manage heat.

Most NASCAR teams run vented rotors made by Wilwood Engineering of Camarillo, CA. The rotors have 48

to 60 curved cooling vanes to draw air from the hub area and force it outward. Rotors are cast from a special grade of cast iron that allows the vanes to be relatively thin to reduce weight, increase surface area and maximize airflow. The rotors are not a one-piece design like those used on passenger cars, but bolt to an aluminum mounting "hat" that attaches to the hub. Some of these mounting hats also have "thermal insulator" shims that fit between the rotor and hat to reduce heat transfer to the hub.

Another difference between NASCAR rotors and the ones on your vehicle is that race rotors usually have small grooves machined into their faces. Racers used to cross drill their rotors to increase cooling and reduce weight. But at high temperatures spider cracks can form and spread outward from drilled holes, which under extreme conditions may cause a rotor to fail! That's one thing you certainly don't want to happen when entering a corner at high speed. So most racers today have shallow surface grooves machined into their rotors to help clean the pads and allow hot gases that build up under the pads at high temperature to escape.

Before a NASCAR team goes racing with a new set of rotors, the rotors are broken in. This process is called "bedding in" the rotors before they're used under actual racing conditions. Doing this prolongs the life of the rotors and makes them more resistant to thermal checking or cracking under severe braking conditions.

Race rotors are usually bedded in with used pads (not new ones), and done gradually so as not to heat the rotors too quickly. The first step in

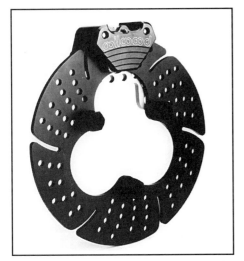

Left front disc and single-piston caliper for sprint car. This lightweight rotor will bolt to hat. Courtesy Wilwood.

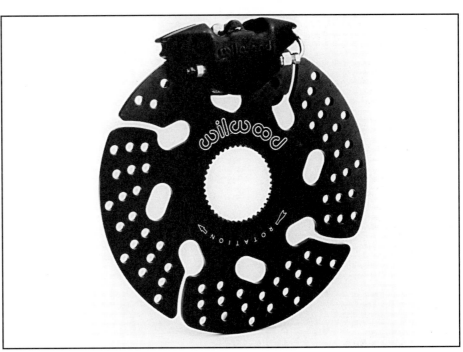

Right rear sprint car rotor. This is designed to slip over axle splines. Note direction of rotation marked on rotor. Cross drilled holes and large cutouts reduce weight and provide additional biting edges for pads. Courtesy Wilwood.

the break-in procedure is to restrict air flow in the brake cooling ducts by about 75%. Next, several stops are made from a moderate speed (60 mph or so) to gradually heat up the rotors. Once this has been done, several high speed slow downs from 100 to 150 mph down to 30 to 60 mph are made to heat the rotors up to approximately 1000 degrees F. The car is then driven back to the pits and the rotors are allowed to air cool back down to ambient temperature.

Because many racers prefer to install rotors that have already been bedded in, some suppliers use a computerized brake dynamometer to bed in new rotors. The brake dyno gives more consistent results and eliminates the need to use up valuable practice laps when a team is under time pressure to qualify before a race.

LATE MODEL

Late Model asphalt cars tend to run 11 3/4" x 1 1/4" front rotors, but they really should run 12 3/16" x 1 1/4" rotors (the smaller diameter is popular because of a weight savings, but these racers tend to sacrifice braking

performance for reduced rotating weight. Rear rotor size of 11 3/4" x 1 1/4" is fine. Rotor manufacturers generally would like to see Late Models run larger fronts, but it's difficult to talk these guys into adding more weight. Late Models running on dirt tend to use 11 3/4" x 1 1/4" rotors on all four wheels. These are generally cast iron rotors, with some teams using titanium rotors treated with ceramic coating.

SPRINT CARS

Left front rotors are 10" diameter aluminum rotors with a thickness of 1/4". The rear inboard rotor is generally 12.19" x .810" thick, and are made of standard cast iron. A lot of World of Outlaw cars will use titanium rotors with a ceramic coating, with some using aluminum rotors with a metal matrix for rear inboard locations. However, this poses a problem. Since there's very little airflow under a sprint car, the rear

inboard brake is deprived of cooling air. A very common rotor temperature for these cars is 1000-1100 degrees F, and once aluminum reaches this temperature range, it tends to melt. Even though the World of Outlaw "big boys" tend to use these lightweight rotors, the average Saturday night racer should probably avoid using alloy rotors. They're expensive and they do have problems at very high temperatures. The only sensible application is for the left front brake location on a sprint car.

DRAG RACING

The standard is steel rotors on the rear, typically in a 11.4" x 3/8" size. Front rotors are generally 10 3/4" x 1/4"-3/8", depending on the caliper size. Top Fuel cars run carbon/carbon rear rotors and pads, with no front brake.

ROAD RACING

Typical dragsters do not use front brakes, but use carbon rotors and pads in the rear. Doorslammers definitely use front brakes, however.

Just as with caliper sizing, a wide variety of rotor sizes can be used in the various categories and classes of road racing. As a result, no "standard" formula can be followed. Both cast iron or steel rotors might be used, as well as titanium rotors in certain instances. Where a choice is available, the biggest rotors that will fit behind the wheel will be used. Road racing places enormous demands on rotors, depending on the track and driver style. I've driven cars at 24-hour races where the rotors get so hot during hard braking at the end of a long straightaway, that they glow to the point of illuminating the corners, almost acting as additional momentary driving lights. Depending on the track, the brakes may be applied hard within 5 more seconds or so, or may not be applied (hard) for another 30 seconds to a full minute.

Where brake cooling is allowed, this should always be taken advantage of. Duct work should be directed to the center of the rotor, using ducting of at least 3" diameter, up to as large a size as the chassis allows. To aid rotor heat dissipation and to promote rotor stability under ever-changing conditions, two treatments can be employed. First of all, a heat emitter coating can be applied to the vanes (this is a heat-shedding coating that helps the rotor to evacuate internal heat more quickly). Secondly, the rotors can be treated with a stress relief process such as cryogenics or vibratory stress relief, as we mentioned earlier in this chapter. This will help to prevent rotor warping and heat-cracking.

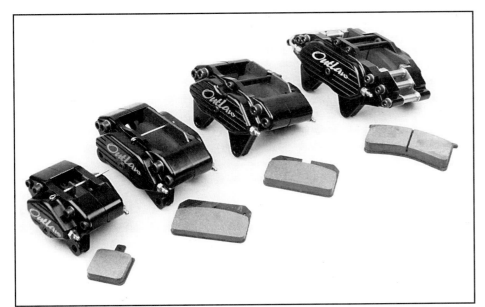

Sample variety of calipers. From left: two-piston caliper; four-piston caliper "medium body" four-piston caliper with single bridge support tube for higher stress applications where caliper flex is a concern; and four-piston "large body" caliper with twin bridge tube supports and open bridge ends for added cooling.

CALIPERS

Racing disc brake calipers can vary in several areas, including weight, overall size, number of pistons, size of pistons, piston diameter relationships, method of fluid transfer from one side to the other, reinforcement design and cooling efficiency (in terms of heat dissipation).

The majority of dedicated "race" calipers will be of aluminum construction. The majority will also be designed to bolt solidly to a caliper bracket, so in most cases you won't be dealing with a "sliding" style caliper. Each caliper half will feature its own pistons (opposing setup, where each pad is activated by its own dedicated pistons). However, for applications that do use a slider style (Late Model Dirt and Asphalt racing and some drag racing stock applications), a single-piston sliding type caliper may be used. Single-piston calipers are only used where the rules dictate, or where light braking applications are the norm, and light weight is more of an issue as opposed to heavy braking demands.

Single- Or Dual-Piston Disadvantages

The big disadvantage of a single piston caliper, or a two-piston caliper for that matter, is the fact that only one piston is pushing on the brake pad backing plate, in a centered location. If the application doesn't call for heavy braking use, and if the pads are relatively short in length, this may not be a problem. However, if demand is high and the pad is long, as temperatures and braking pressures rise, the single centered piston (since it's only pushing the pad at the middle of the backing plate) can allow the pad/backing plate to deflect outward at the ends, as the backing plate steel becomes more malleable.

The result is a minimized area of contact between the pad and the rotor, and likely promotion of pad cracking and chunking. Backing plate deflection is a bad thing in any racing brake setup.

Multi-Piston Calipers

Multiple piston calipers address this issue by spreading the clamping

This Sierra four-piston caliper features staggered pistons. Note rotation direction inscribed on caliper body. This indicates mounting position of caliper, so that rotor rotates in proper direction. This is essential so that smaller diameter pistons are placed at rotor entry side and larger pistons are placed at rotor exit side.

As caliper pad opening becomes longer, certain high-demand applications require additional caliper support to prevent unwanted caliper "spread" as brakes are applied. This additional center tube (with bolt running through) prevents caliper top area from flexing inboard or outboard.

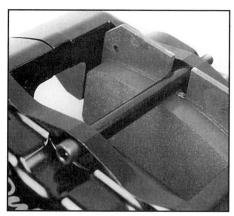

Note that where center bridge support tube is used, pad backing plate is notched to clear tube. Tube also provides centering orientation for pads.

Twin-piston calipers (using one piston per side) will normally use the largest diameter piston that will fit the body size, to provide the largest footprint behind the pad backing plate. Larger surface area provides more support for the pad. Larger diameter piston also provides more hydraulic clamping force, which helps the smaller caliper do more work.

forces more evenly along the entire surface area of the pad backing plates. A wider footprint of support means less pad flexing and more consistent and evenly distributed pad clamping force against the rotor.

This concern will only be a critical issue where racing rules dictate the use of a single-piston caliper (for instance, where road racing showroom stock rules don't allow a change to aftermarket calipers, and the stock OEM caliper must be used). If that design uses a single piston caliper in conjunction with relatively long pads, the pads will likely be prone to excessive flexing. For multi-piston race calipers, where sufficient thrust force from pistons to the pad backing plates is evenly distributed across the backing plates, and the pads are designed to a length that works in conjunction with the piston surface area, pad flexing becomes much less of a concern.

Race caliper makers are aware of this potential problem, so they tend to design a caliper/pad size fitment that will provide the pad-to-rotor frictional surface area required for the car weight and application, and will use the number, placement and size of pistons to provide adequate support at the backing plates for a given size pad.

Caliper Pistons

Caliper pistons may be constructed of steel, stainless steel, aluminum, titanium or phenolic resin, and will vary in terms of piston diameter. The caliper may feature as few as one piston or as many as twelve tiny pistons. Piston quantity and size is dictated by the overall size of the pads and by the type of application. While a small diameter bore size will produce more pressure in a master cylinder than a larger diameter master cylinder bore, caliper bores/pistons are just the opposite...the larger diameter caliper piston will provide more "push" or clamping force than a smaller caliper piston.

Some multiple-piston calipers (for example, a caliper that features two pistons per side) may feature all four pistons of the same diameter, or two different sized pistons. When piston diameter varies in a caliper, this is referred to as a "staggered" piston design. The smaller piston is located at the entry of the disc, while the larger piston is positioned at the exit. As a result, a staggered piston caliper is directional—it must be mounted so that the disc is grabbed by the smaller piston on its entry through the caliper body, while the larger piston handles the exit point of the disc. Some caliper bodies will feature a stamped or etched indicator of rotor direction (an arrow, the word "rotation," etc.) to indicate how the caliper must be

External brake fluid crossover tube, which is the route for brake fluid between caliper halves, must be isolated from harmonic vibrations. If not dampened, vibrations can eventually crack the tube. This tube is nestled in a bead of RTV silicone, which works very well to protect the tube from vibrational fractures. You can also insulate it with a high-heat insulated plastic sleeve.

mounted on the car. Always position the caliper so that the smaller pistons are located towards the rear and the larger pistons are located towards the front. Where the caliper is mounted in a vertical position, just remember that as the rotor turns, it should rotate past the smaller piston first, and then pass the larger piston. The larger piston always indicates the "exit" point in terms of rotor rotation.

The reason that a four-piston caliper may feature a staggered piston format is primarily to reduce the chance of taper-wear on the pads, and to maximize braking efficiency in certain applications. As the brakes are applied, the disc enters the caliper body and is acted upon by the pads, which are pushed against the disc under hydraulic pressure. As the pads push against the disc, the point of caliper entry (where the disc first experiences clamping force) starts performing most of the work. As the disc continues to rotate and leave the pressure point of the first pair of pistons, the exit-position pistons are trying to play catch-up. They may

experience added demands, since the pads are being "pushed" by exit heat (the friction between pad and rotor) and possible evacuation of gasses created by pad heat. As a result, in some cases where the pads are relatively long and pedal application is heavy, a taper wear may start to occur at the entry side of the pads (if the entry pistons are more efficient at pushing the pad than the exit pistons). In order to balance the clamping force, and in an attempt to keep pad-to-disc pressures constant throughout the travel length, a larger diameter piston may be used at the exit point, to exert more pressure against the exit portion of the pads.

While pad "gassing" (see p. 161) is an issue of some debate (some say this does occur and some say it doesn't), the fact remains that the exit portion of longer pads do sometimes tend to provide less clamping force as compared to the entry portion of the pads. The added clamping force pressure afforded by larger diameter pistons addresses this issue. With that said, why do some four-piston

calipers feature the same size pistons on both entry and exit areas? Because the caliper maker, through its own research and development, has concluded that this particular caliper (given its size and the length of its pads) does not create a tapered-wear problem for its pads, and therefore doesn't need a staggered piston setup.

Caliper Design & Operation

A two-piece aluminum caliper (the majority of racing calipers) features two body sections that bolt together. This design makes it easier to manufacture (in terms of casting or milling, and machining piston bores). Since this is a two-piece sectional design, the two halves can be bolted directly together, or can be assembled with the addition of "bridge" spacers, to accommodate thicker pads and/or thicker rotors. In this way, one caliper body can be used to construct several thickness configurations.

Brake fluid enters the caliper from one side only (where the flexible brake hose fitting attaches to the caliper for fluid feed). Since these calipers feature pistons in both sides of the caliper body, brake fluid naturally has to access the side opposite from the initial fluid entry side. This is handled in one of two ways: the use of internal transfer orifices, or external fluid transfer tubes. Since it's easier to manufacture and service, and less prone to leakage, external transfer tubes are the norm on custom racing calipers. This transfer tube connects each half of the caliper body and is easily removed for caliper service.

Most racing calipers will feature either a small-diameter section of rubber or silicone hose that's placed over the transfer tube or the transfer

151

Some caliper halves are bolted directly together. Where the same caliper body is used for thicker rotor/pad combinations, a solid aluminum spacer may be used to tailor caliper to exact width needed.

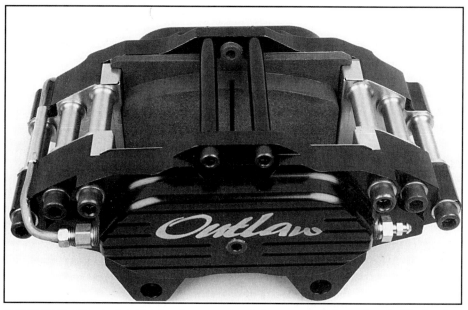

In large-body calipers where long pads are used and stresses are high, such as in Winston Cup or Trans Am, for instance, two bridge support tubes/bolts may be used. This more evenly distributes load as hydraulic force (as pistons clamp against rotor) tries to flex caliper. Note center ear on pad backing plate locates between the two support tubes. This aids centering of pad. Also, there are six individual bridge support tubes instead of two bridge spacers. This open effect permits faster heat evacuation.

Caliper bridge support is an important aspect of caliper design in terms of strength and resistance to flexing under high-demand racing conditions. The more attachment bolts are used (to secure the two caliper body halves together), the better. Bolt locations are designed to spread load over as large an area as possible. Here three bolts are used at each end.

tube may be embedded in a layer of RTV silicone, where the tube runs along the caliper bridge area. The reason for this is to provide a damping isolation for the tube. When brakes are applied under racing conditions, an initial harmonic vibration commonly occurs in the caliper body. You may not feel this, but the harmonics can be so severe that the

tube can crack. The damping insulation prevents these harmonics from vibrating the tubes, thus preventing tube damage.

When a caliper is constructed of two sections, the attachment point where the two halves meet is called the "bridge." This mating can feature the two aluminum bodies flush against each other, or this may involve solid spacers, as we noted earlier, to create the correct width needed to accommodate pad and/or rotor thickness. In some applications, such as NASCAR Winston Cup, Busch Grand National, road race or Indy car setups where heat buildup is extreme, some caliper designs may incorporate a series of individual tube bridge spacers. This creates an air gap between the caliper body halves, allowing increased heat evacuation.

Caliper Reinforcement

When the brakes are applied in a severe-duty situation such as is

encountered in road racing and in many Winston Cup, Busch or Supertruck applications, for instance, the caliper body halves are subjected to an enormous strain. As pedal effort increases, the hydraulic force being applied to the pads attempts to pull the caliper halves apart. The result is that the caliper halves may deflect somewhat under severe conditions. To address this, manufacturers of racing calipers continually look for ways to provide maximum rigidity of the assembly. You'll note that at each end of the caliper body (on a sectional two-piece caliper body), there may be two, three or even four bolts that secure the halves together. The idea is to spread the clamping force of the two caliper body sections over as wide an area as possible to increase rigidity. In addition, some caliper designs may feature centered bridge bolts instead of long cotter pins (in some caliper designs, this center pin is used to mount/hang the pads, as some

Small-bodied 2-piston caliper uses small pad pucks. Pad center width area is relatively narrow, so no center bridge support tube is needed. Four bridge bolts are placed to spread load evenly. Smaller size caliper doesn't require additional bracing due to lighter demands and smaller size.

Not all calipers feature staggered piston layout. In sizes and applications where the caliper maker sees no performance benefit by staggering piston sizes, caliper pistons will be the same diameter. When pistons are all the same size in a given caliper, this is referred to as a "symmetric" caliper.

pad backing plates feature a centered eyelet for this purpose). The use of one or two bolts in this location provides additional bracing at the caliper center, preventing the halves from spreading apart at this area.

Caliper Alignment

When installing a racing caliper, strict attention must be paid to caliper alignment in relationship with the rotor. If the caliper is positioned in a non-parallel angle to the rotor, tapered pad wear is assured. Plus, since a crooked caliper simply won't allow the pads to achieve full surface contact with the rotor, braking efficiency will be greatly compromised.

Before checking caliper alignment, perform an axial runout check of the rotor on its spindle/hub. This means that you want to check the rotor "wobble" or deviation as viewed from the front or rear of car. Put another way, you're looking for "camber"

angle changes of the rotor as it rotates. Mount a dial indicator on the rotor disc surface, zero the gauge, and monitor the reading as you slowly rotate the rotor through a full 360-degrees. Although a zero runout is naturally preferred, use a target of .005" or less as your goal. While as

much as .018" runout might be acceptable in a street car, under high speed racing conditions, that much runout might cause enough pedal oscillation and caliper chatter to disturb the car's braking forces to the point where the car is less controllable, or is prevented from

Staggered pistons in a 4-piston caliper. This arrangement allows greater clamping force at the exit portion of the rotor/pad area. Initially, a staggered piston layout was performed to compensate for pad "gassing," a phenomenon that occurred as friction-generated heat caused a pad's binder resins to "gas." This gas layer, which tended to build from the midpoint of the pad to the exit area, caused a wedge effect, pushing the exit portion of the pads away from the rotor. Since a larger diameter caliper piston creates more clamping force, the larger pistons are placed at the pad exit area to keep clamping force relatively equal from the start to the end of the pads. Today, pad gassing isn't a factor due to the carbon pads being used. However, staggered pistons still have their place, to maintain clamping force on long pad lengths and high stresses.

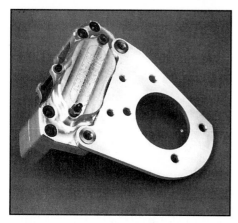

Caliper mounting bracket bolts to axle flange. Caliper mounting brackets are available in a wide variety of designs and sizes to accommodate different calipers and mountings.

stopping in the distance required. If excessive runout is encountered, check the spindle/axle hub, and check the rotor hat itself (in the case of a modular rotor/hat assembly). It could be that the rotor isn't warped, but needs to be shimmed at the hat mounting bolts.

Once rotor runout has been checked, mount the caliper and check the gap between the caliper body and the rotor surface, on both sides of the rotor. The caliper should be centered in relation to the rotor, within .020" of being parallel. After centering the caliper, check pad fit. Pads should drop into place easily (with the pistons fully retracted). If the caliper is crooked, you can use shim washers to adjust this angle (placing shims between the caliper mounting ears and the caliper mounting bracket). ALWAYS check any newly installed caliper for alignment to the rotor! never assume that the caliper will bolt-on and is already pre-aligned. When you're building a race engine, you wouldn't assume that the crankshaft or the block's main bores are aligned, so why assume the same when it comes to the brakes, which are the most important components on

the car?

Caliper Mounting Brackets

You can either buy steel or aluminum brackets or you can make your own. Considering their relatively low cost, it doesn't make much sense to bother making your own, unless you own a machine shop or if none of your suppliers make a bracket for your application (which would be rare). The brackets should be rigid enough to prevent deflection when the brakes are applied. If they distort, pads will taper-wear, pistons can become cocked, the caliper mounting ears can fracture, etc. When it comes to caliper brackets, the thicker and tougher, the better. If made of mild steel, thickness should be at least 5/16". Don't drill the hell out of the bracket to provide a bunch of "lightening" holes, either. The object is to maintain as much structural rigidity as possible. The calipers have enough work to do without moving around every time you nail the pedal.

Rear Brake Floaters

Brake floaters (also called "birdcages") remove torque from suspension components by directing the braking forces through separate radius rods. By adjusting the angle of the brake radius rods, brake influence and handling can be tuned. These are popular on late model dirt cars and sprint cars.

The floater bracket features a large main bore that slips over the axle tube. This bore sometimes includes a nylon bushing sleeve to reduce friction and allow unrestricted rotation on the axle tube during adjustment. The assembly features a caliper mounting bracket and an adjustment arm that attaches to one end of the

radius rod.

This approach completely separates braking forces from the suspension components. This enables braking influence to be individually tuned to track conditions, without compromising handling.

By placing the calipers on their own separate radius rods, the point at which the brake forces act on the chassis can be adjusted. Since the rear axle assembly is free to move up and down, the angle of the brake rod can cause the brake force to push up, straight forward or down on the chassis. Due to the weight difference between the rear assembly and the car itself, the resulting pressures exerted by the brakes are felt at the tire's contact patch. When the brake rod pushes up on the chassis, downward pressure is realized at the tire. When the brake rod pushes down on the chassis, tire contact pressure is reduced. When the brake rod is level, no pressure difference is realized at the tire.

According to Carl Bush at Outlaw Brakes, floaters are used primarily to control the effects of braking and deceleration torque to the chassis. This isolates brake torque from the deceleration torque that's already in the rear end, which also helps to eliminate unwanted pinion angle changes. Floaters can be used to achieve certain handling characteristics by changing the loading effects seen by the tires. If the floater's radius rod is positioned fairly level from the birdcage to the chassis, brake torque would be fairly neutral. If you angle the radius rod, say, upwards (from the birdcage to the chassis), under braking the rod would push up on the chassis, and push down on the wheel, providing greater tire loading for increased bite. So, you can adjust the assembly to neutralize the effect of brake torque, or to unload the tire or to load the tire. Many racers will adjust each side to differentiate the torque changes at each rear wheel, to change the turn-in of the car under braking or deceleration. If you place more load on the right rear, this creates additional traction on the right rear tire, and will tighten the car on corner entry. Conversely, if you adjust for less load on the right rear, the car will be more loose at corner entry. The primary purpose, however, is to neutralize brake torque so the car isn't upset during braking and deceleration.

Caliper Position

When a caliper is located at the forward side of the rotor, this is a "leading" or a "front-mount" location, in front of the axle. When a caliper is installed on the rearward side of a rotor, behind the axle, this is a "trailing" or a "rear-mount" location. In either case, the bleed screws must be positioned as close to the 12 o'clock position as possible to avoid trapped air.

The primary reason a caliper is mounted to the front or rear of a rotor is because of chassis components clearance (clearance at spindle, shock, etc.), as the caliper really doesn't care where it's located in terms of clock position on the rotor. In terms of clamping performance, the caliper will function regardless of clock position. Granted, some chassis builders will locate the caliper in a front or rear mount because of perceived load forces, but the main reason that a chassis builder might locate calipers (aside from a clearance standpoint) is to help distribute weight more efficiently. Towards this end,

Caliper/rotor mounted inboard on a sprint car. Only single left rear brake and left front brake are used on this car. Courtesy Wilwood.

some builders will try to position their calipers closer to the center of the car for theoretically better weight distribution, by placing the front calipers as rear-mounts and the rear calipers as front-mounts. Does this really make a difference? Maybe, and maybe not. However, anything you can do to move weight closer to the car's center is always a good thing.

The most critical aspect of caliper positioning, aside from making sure the caliper is "square" to the rotor, is the position of the caliper's bleed screws. We can't stress this too strongly. BLEED SCREWS MUST BE IN THE UP POSITION. Air runs upwards. If the bleeder isn't positioned at the top, you simply cannot evacuate air from the system!

Caliper Sizing/Selection

How do you choose the correct caliper size and design for a specific application? Actually, the best approach is to follow the recommendations of the caliper manufacturer, because they'll know what works based on years of experience and field testing. There are many variables to consider when selecting a caliper, including weight

of the car, its racing application (short track, super speedway, drag racing, oval track, road racing short course or long course, etc.), the type of track surface (dirt, asphalt), and driver characteristics (whether or not the driver is traditionally hard or easy on brakes).

Various caliper sizes will be designed to accommodate thicker or thinner rotors, some will feature additional bridge reinforcements and some will feature a great number of smaller pistons, all depending on the caliper maker's engineering efforts to maximize caliper performance. It's really difficult to make standardized recommendations for specific calipers in specific situations, because there are so many variables involved, many of which are based on different caliper manufacturers' design ideas.

Some caliper makers dedicate their calipers for rotation (where staggered pistons are used), and may dedicate a leading or trailing position caliper due to bleed screw locations. Other caliper makers may offer calipers that can interchange for left-right and leading/trailing positions by changing bleed screw locations. If the caliper has staggered bores, though, it will be dedicated as a left- or right-hand position.

We can make some very broad generalizations in terms of caliper type and size for various applications. Bear in mind that the actual selection will depend on the rotors being used, the weight of the car and the braking demands. Following are some generalizations for racing categories, following the advice of Mark Woods at Outlaw Disc Brakes.

Sprint Cars—Sprint cars on dirt tracks will use a smaller-body two-piston caliper on the left front, with

Note the stainless steel heat shielding installed in this Winston Cup caliper. This shielding extends along the inboard faces of each caliper half, and along the inboard faces of the bridge sections as well. This acts as a barrier to reduce the rotor heat from being transmitted through to the caliper body, thereby reducing the heat soaked by the brake fluid.

Wilwood's midget caliper is a small, four-piston unit mounted inboard in the rear. Courtesy Wilwood.

piston sizes of 1 7/8" and 1 3/4". A larger body four-piston caliper on the rear single inboard brake. Depending on driver preference, some applications will also use a small two-piston caliper on right rear to help set up the chassis for left turns. The rear of these cars use a live axle that spins, so the caliper is mounted to a rigid point directly on the side bell of the rear end.

Sprint cars on paved tracks will generally use the same rear inboard brake setup, but may use smaller-piston sizes in the front calipers, with 1 3/8" 4-piston calipers.

Midgets—Midget cars generally run a small four-piston on the rear inboard brake and two-piston caliper on the left front. When these cars run on pavement, teams will add a 2-piston caliper on the right front.

IMCA Modifieds—These cars must run a completely original equipment (OEM) GM type cast iron stock caliper, since rules dictate that it's not legal to run aftermarket calipers. On dirt, larger-diameter piston calipers are used on the rears and the left front, while a smaller GM caliper is used on

the right front. IMCA Modifieds that run on asphalt tend to run the bigger GM calipers on both fronts and a small piston GM caliper on both rears.

Drag Racing—Drag car brakes are predominantly rear-oriented. A "standard" size caliper for the bulk of drag applications can use a caliper featuring 1 3/4 & 1 5/8" pistons. As far as front brakes are concerned, cars that weigh 2000 lbs. or more can use the same caliper. If the car weighs under 2000 lbs., a smaller 2-piston caliper is used, such as Outlaw's series 1000. Top Fuel cars do not feature front brakes at all, instead relying on rear brakes alone, usually a carbon fiber rotor and pad setup. Funny Cars tend to use a small single-piston floating style caliper on the front spindles.

Winston Cup—Caliper sizes become more specialized on a per-track basis, with some teams experimenting with multi-pad 8-piston calipers in order to improve initial pad bite (the more pads, the more leading pad edges you have for additional bite at the rotor). But, the bulk of Winston Cup cars are running

a 4-piston caliper. Because of the heavier weight of the vehicle, and because of more severe rotor temperatures experienced at tracks such as Martinsville, brake pads are 1 1/8" thick, requiring a wider caliper. After 500 laps at Martinsville, it's common for these thick pads to wear down to the backing plates. As the brakes on these cars are used about every 6-7 seconds at a track like Martinsville, rotor temperatures are elevated to a range of 1400-1500 degrees F. Piston sizes are generally a staggered combination of 1 7/8" and 1 3/4".

For super speedway applications, these cars generally run 3/8" to 1/2"-thick steel rotor (not cast iron). The brakes are generally only touched when the car enters the pits. Since braking demands are reduced, cars will still run the big pistons (1 7/8" & 1 3/4"), but in a smaller caliper housing.

Indy Car—There is no standard setup that's used in every car. Indy car teams tend to perform a lot of experimentation. Some prefer to use 6-piston calipers, and some will use 8-piston calipers. The intent when using a multi-pad system (where you have a number of smaller pad pucks instead of one large pad per caliper side) is to reduce the chances of pad taper, and to provide added initial "bite" at the pad-to-rotor.

Note: Change caliper seals regularly for optimum caliper performance. The rule of thumb is to change seals every time you change pads!

Road Racing—This opens up a big can of worms, since there's no one caliper design suitable for all forms of road racing, and since this type of competition involves a wide range of vehicle types and weights, from Trans Am and large GT cars to mid-size and compact GT and production cars to showroom stock classes and a wide array of formula cars. In road racing, there are no standardizations, as everybody tends to use a variety of setups based on their own needs and the chassis builder's recommendations. Road racing represents a very diverse range of braking system applications.

However, we can make a few general observations. Road racing applications generally require the biggest, baddest calipers and pads that will fit behind the wheels, since braking is performed (depending on the individual track) very frequently under a range of conditions. That's the unique aspect of road racing: no two tracks are identical in terms of lap length, road camber, number of turns or elevation changes, all of which can effect the pressure application and duration of the system. If the application involves endurance racing (this could involve any duration of race from 3 hours to 24 hours), the calipers, brake pads and brake fluid will be exposed to a prolonged period of heat and application. The only lapses in terms of use will be on

This large Winston Cup caliper features individual bridge bolt tubes. While a solid aluminum spacer could have been used to create the appropriate width spacing for the rotors and pads being used, this caliper uses individual bridge bolt tubes. This accomplishes the same task in terms of joining the two caliper halves and providing the needed structural strength, but has the added benefit of providing air passages to enhance heat evacuation from the rotor.

straights and while in the pits. Brake setups may, because of the specific track layout, duration of the event, or a combination of these two factors, require changes in terms of caliper bore size and type of pad.

D.I.R.T.—D.I.R.T. series cars tend to run one of two setups for front brakes: either 2-piston calipers with 1 3/4" pistons, or small-body 4-piston

This NASCAR rear setup features a 4-piston caliper with 1 1/8" and 1 1/4" pistons. Courtesy Alcon.

This Alcon caliper built for NASCAR road course application features stick-on temperature indicating card. Courtesy Alcon.

calipers with 1 3/4" and 1 5/8" pistons on the left front wheel; and smaller-bodies caliper with 1 3/8" piston sizes on the right front. Rear brakes tend to use 4-piston calipers with 1 3/4" and 1 5/8" pistons. The rear caliper setup doesn't change, but front setups may change depending on the track conditions.

Late Model Oval—A standard setup for Late Models on asphalt involve two options for front calipers: 4-piston calipers with 1 7/8" and 1 3/4" pistons, or with 1 3/4" and 1 5/8" pistons. On the rear, 4-piston calipers with 1 3/8" piston sizes are the norm. The NASCAR class Winston Series is mandated to use a GM style single-piston caliper, but this can be made of aluminum. Generally, a 2 3/4" piston will be used in front calipers, while rears will use a 2 3/8" piston. The NASCAR Northeast Modified series (running in upstate NY, NJ, PA and the New England states tend to run staggered bore 4-piston calipers using 1 3/4 and 1 5/8" pistons on all four wheels, though some racers will use rear calipers with 1 3/8" pistons.

Late Model Dirt—Four-piston calipers with piston sizes of 1 3/4 & 1 5/8" will be used on the rears and the left front, while the right front may use a 4-piston caliper with 1 3/8", to create a differential under braking to bias the car for turns.

Busch Grand National & Craftsman Truck—A standard setup for all tracks involves the use of a 4-piston caliper with 1 7/8" and 1 3/4"

pistons. Since the use of a minimum thickness of 1 1/4" rotor is mandatory, the caliper is a standardized size in terms of width as well. Rear calipers are standard as well, using 1 1/4" pistons. At certain tracks however, some teams may use rear calipers with 1 3/8" or 1 1/8" piston sizes.

RACING BRAKE PADS

Brake pads are available in a wide variety of materials and compounds. Some pads are ideal for lower-temperature/high friction applications on less demanding tracks (such as dirt), while others are better suited to provide the needed frictional characteristics under more demand-ing, higher-heat conditions. Leading pad brands for competition use at the time of this writing include Performance Friction, Outlaw, Hawk and The Brake Man.

Pad Recommendations

There are a bunch of pads out there today, some great, some good, and

A wide array of pad materials/compounds are available for specific racing applications, from "soft" to "hard" depending on rotor material, weight of car, duration and frequency of braking and, most importantly, rotor temperatures. A selection of Hawk pads are shown in this example.

Temperature range of rotor operation is absolutely critical in pad selection. As this example shows, pads are temperature rated for a specific range of operation.

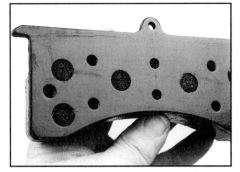

Race pad are generally bonded to the backing plates, since rivet holes may provide stress areas for potential of pad cracking. This pad is also extruded to the backing plate (pad material is pressure formed into holes in backing plate for strong bond).

Factory-burnished pads are cure-treated, but still require bedding to rotor for optimum performance and long life.

some that are very mediocre. We're not going to get into a war of words and opinions here, debating how good one brand of pad is over another. Some deliver what they promise and some don't. The primary things to remember are that you want to match the pad type and compound to your car and the specific racing conditions that you face. You also want a pad that provides a consistent coefficient of friction, every time the brake pedal is depressed. From experience, you'll find that a specific pad that works great for one team won't produce the same results for your application. When that happens, it's not the fault of the pad. Chances are, other variables are controlling the situation, such as master cylinder size, master cylinder-to-cylinder balance, overall brake system condition, driver style, car weight and chassis setup.

Variables To Consider

The only way to find the best pad for you is to test on your specific vehicle. Here's a good example of how the variable of driving style can affect pad performance: at a 24-hour race a few years ago, we had four drivers for our car. Two of those drivers had very similar driving styles, and they knew how to make

equipment live. When one of those guys drove the car, a front pad change was needed about every 3 hours. When another guy drove, fresh pads were needed every hour and a half. When the fourth guy drove, the pads lasted an average of 20 minutes. By the way, the guys with the fastest lap times were the two who made the pads live the longest. My point is that you can't perform an apples-to-apples comparison between your race car and other race cars when there are so many other variables that can enter the picture. At that same race, some weasel that owned another team was telling everybody that he had a magic brake pad that would last an entire 24-hour race. He offered them, in an unmarked box, at $400 per axle set. Sound silly? Of course, but a bunch of guys bought them anyway. They lasted every purchaser an average of 1-2 hours. As it turns out, they were off-the-shelf semimetallic replacement pads probably bought for $20 or so. By the way, all of the pads we used didn't "wear" down to require placement, rather, they chunked apart because we were forced to use single piston calipers with a long pad shape. The pads flexed and they blew the friction material off.

There were only two times when I personally witnessed surprisingly long life coupled with consistent performance in a 24-hour race: once when we ran a Mustang at Watkins Glen and once at Moroso in a pair of Dodge Neons (both races were for showroom stock classes. I know they're not "real" race cars, but bear with me). At the Glen, we ran an experimental pad that we obtained via the backdoor from an engineer at a well-known pad maker. They were made of a ceramic-metallic material (secret stuff, and to this day the engineer won't tell me the whole story). They looked like slabs of cast iron, and scared the hell out of us, but we tried them anyway. To our surprise, they stopped the car when they were cold, and they worked incredibly well at high temp, with really consistent brake force. They lasted the whole race, and wore evenly without chunking apart. Even though they seemed hard as a rock, they only wore the rotors an additional .012" or so as compared to the pads we had been using. At the 24-hour race at Moroso, we ran Hawk Blue pads with the same results. We never had to perform a pad change, and stopping power was solid and repeatable. Again, I know that these are not as fast or as heavy as some of

Some pads may feature one or more vertical slots in the friction material. These serve to allow pad flex to occur without cracking/chunking of pad material. These slots also provide additional "biting edges" for superior pad to rotor contact. Slotted pads are cut with precision gauging by the pad maker. If you attempt to slot your own pads, make a clean, straight cut and avoid getting too close to backing plate. Chances are though, if your pads were not slotted at the factory, they don't need the slot. Rely on the pad maker to make this decision.

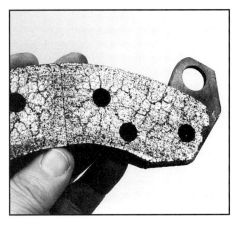

A OEM shape ceramic-metallic pad for showroom stock road racing that was used in a 6-hour endurance race. Multiple heat cracks are normal and accepted for this type of use. Note that each rivet hole was the starting point for many of these cracks, which illustrates why most race pad makers don't rivet their pads.

the big-boy cars, but my point is that pads can make a big difference. Material selection, pad processing and compounding all play a part in formulating a pad that will work under specific conditions.

Pad Hardness/Softness

Generally speaking, a "softer" pad will display a high level of friction at lower temperatures but may fade or glaze at higher temperatures. Soft pads are designed for less-demanding applications where braking isn't severe. Harder pads may offer low frictional properties when cold, but will provide optimum frictional duty at higher temperatures, and will be less prone to fade at high temperatures.

For aluminum rotors, since aluminum is a relatively soft metal, a harder pad needs to be used in order to establish a coefficient of friction that will stop the car.

Pad design and manufacturing is a closely guarded dark world of thermal and frictional engineering, and every pad maker has his own "secret" blend of ingredients and processes to create the best pad for specific situations.

Pad Chunking

One big problem that is always a concern with single- or double-piston calipers is pad chunking or taper-wear. If the caliper features only one or two pistons (in other words, if only one piston pushes each pad), and if the pad is relatively long, under extreme racing conditions the pad can flex to the point where the friction material cracks and can chunk apart. The reason is obvious: if the pad has a single pressure point behind it (one piston), the pad backing plate can begin to deflect as it becomes hot and more malleable. The friction material becomes stressed, cracks start to appear from the stress points, and the material can pop off of the backing plate. Even if the material doesn't chunk, the single pressure point, coupled with a long pad, can easily promote tapered pad wear, especially on a sliding style single piston caliper

that wiggles around during operation. The morale: avoid single-piston or twin-piston calipers that use very long pads. The only time you'll run into this is when the rules demand the use of OEM calipers, since racing caliper makers recognize the dynamics involved, and design their calipers with enough piston "footprint" to support the pad sizes being used.

Pad Slots—If a specific brake setup is prone to creating a lot of pad flex, the pad maker (or the racer) may cut one or two vertical slots in the pad material (one slot in the middle or two equally-spaced slots). This is done in an effort to provide a relief point for stresses that the pad sees when the backing plate flexes. Instead of cracking across a portion of the pad friction material in a random direction, the stress energy is directed at the cuts, thus avoiding deep fractures across the friction material. If your pads continually have a problem with cracking/fracturing that result in the loss of friction material surface area, you might try cutting a vertical slot (maybe 1/16 –1/8" wide) in your pads to see if this helps solve the problem. Make this slot only in the area where the fractures now commonly occur. If you do this, be VERY careful not to nick or cut the backing plate itself!

Another very nice advantage to slotting a pad is that it creates two leading edges for rotor bite, instead of just one. This initial pad bite is probably more noticeable in a lighter, more responsive car like an Indy car or other formula type cars. In heavier cars such as a Trans Am car or a Winston Cup or Busch car, this nuance probably won't be felt by the driver. "Saturday night" racers won't feel this either, so slotting your pads probably isn't worth doing unless you are experiencing major pad cracking problems. Then slotting might make sense from a stress-relieving standpoint.

Even though a rotor or a pad may "feel" or "look" smooth, in reality each features a microscopically rough surface texture, composed of thousands of small peaks and valleys. This microscopic roughness is needed in order to "bed" the pads to the rotor. According to Warren Gilliland of The Brake Man, effective braking isn't realized until 90-95% pad-to-rotor contact is achieved.

Pad Gassing

In the "old days" before carbon-based pads, pad "gassing" was a legitimate issue. As the pads heated under clamping force, the volatiles inside the pad matrix would sometimes rise to the surface and expel a layer of gas that would create a pressure layer between the exit portion of the pad and the rotor. This is the reason that staggered piston calipers were first designed, since a larger piston diameter located at the exit portion of the caliper would exert additional clamping force in an effort to counteract the gas pressure that tried to push the exit portion of the pad away from the rotor. However, most brake experts would agree that considering today's carbon-based pad technology, this really isn't an issue anymore, since the new pads don't "gas" to the extent where a problem-causing pressurized emission is created. Caliper manufacturers continue to offer staggered piston calipers because it doesn't hurt anything, it would be more expensive to re-tool to change the designs (which would make the calipers more

expensive to buy), and because racers would simply be confused if staggered piston calipers were no longer available. As new caliper designs are created, these are usually outfitted with a symmetric piston setup where all pistons are the same size.

Pad Curing/Bedding

Transfer of pad material to the rotor is essential in ANY braking setup. In simplified terms, the object is to have pad material rub against itself. By "bedding" the pads to the rotor, a small layer of pad material is transferred from the pad onto the rotor surface. Once that occurs, the pad contacts a thin layer of its own material that is now present on the rotor surface. Also, this minute transfer of pad material serves to fill the tiny "valleys" that exist in the machined rotor surface, creating a more efficient frictional mating surface. In order to accomplish this, the pads must first generate enough heat to make this transfer possible.

Today's pad makers offer their pads already "burnished." This does not mean that the pads are bedded, as this still needs to be done on the race car. The burnishing process simply cures the pads as the chemical "volatiles" rise to the pad surface and dissipate. Burnishing involves the use of heat to pull the trapped volatiles out of the pad material. Some pad makers use ovens and others use lasers, but the end result is basically the same...to use heat in "curing" the pad material. Depending on how the pads are made, some don't require an extra burnishing step, as the volatiles are evacuated during the pad processing procedures. Simply know that a "burnished" pad still needs to be

This pad is long in shape and was used in a single-piston OEM type floater caliper. Enormous pressure point of the single piston is evident on this backing plate.

bedded to the rotors.

Mystery and misinformation abounds with regard to pad "bedding," mostly the result of bench-racing talk and gossip. All this term really means is that the pads need to be initially "seasoned" to match up to the rotors. The object of bedding is to transfer a slight amount of the pad's material to the rotor surface. When this is done, the result is pad material biting against pad material, which improves the coefficient of friction when the pads squeeze against the rotor.

Pre-Bedded Pads—Some pads are supposedly "pre-bedded," which only means that the pad material has been burnished (heated) a certain degree into the surface layer of the material. This raises the internal resins from the top layer of the pad material to the pad surface, which makes it easier to bed the pads on the rotors. Regardless of any burnishing that has been performed at the factory, the pads still need to be bedded to the rotors.

Bedding With New Rotors—Avoid bedding new pads to new rotors. New rotors require a slow break-in cycle to properly cure a "green" rotor. If new rotors are being used for the first time, they should be seated slowly. Avoid overheating a new rotor. For that reason, it's best to bed fresh pads on used rotors. Break-in new rotors on already bedded pads. If new pads on new rotors, try to use pre-cured pads.

Bedding Procedure—The subject of pad bedding is one of much debate. Everybody has an opinion of how a pad should be bedded, and there are as many opinions out there as there are pad makers and racers. What you want to do is to transfer pad material from the pad to the rotor, and to bring the top layer of resins out of the internal matrix of the pad (if a pad is burnished at the factory, the latter job is already done). Here's a pad bedding procedure that works. If you hear a different recommendation from somebody else, feel free to try it.

1. Make six to eight moderate stops, just to initiate some heat in the rotors and pads.
2. Then make six to eight hard stops, simulating actual race conditions.
3. Finally, allow the pads to cool for about 1/2 hour or so, to drop back down to ambient temperature. At that point, they're ready to be used in racing conditions.

When attempting to finesse your braking system with pad changes/experimentation, don't reduce the pad footprint in an attempt to "tune" your brakes. For instance, a racer may want to bias the car to make left turns, because he feels that the car has too much right-front brake. He may cut the right front pad in half (reducing the pad footprint on the rotor), and, upon testing the new setup, he may think that he "cured" his problem. In reality, all he accomplished was to increase the

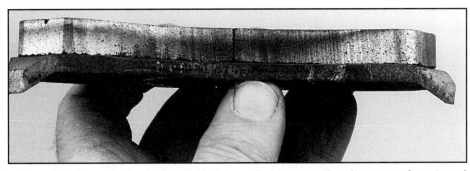

This specially formulated ceramic-metallic (also called a cera-met) pad was one of a set used during a 24-hour endurance road race. The material was highly resistant to cracking and performed with a high degree of frictional performance with virtually no fade. Notice the center slit. This pad was actually made using two separate pieces of friction material. This particular pad saw 12 hours of use before this photo was taken.

right front brake temperature to the point where the right front pads are so overheated that they have faded. If you need to change braking forces at an axle or one specific wheel, use the balance bar and/or proportioning valve instead.

Pads For Processed Rotors

If a rotor has been "processed" by means of cryogenic tempering, or coated with ceramic, for instance, the surface will likely be "harder" which can affect the rotor's relationship with the pads. A "harder" rotor may or may not require a step-up in the pad frictional coefficient. For instance, this may require changing to a "harder" pad.

Whether or not a change in pad compound is warranted depends on a bunch of variables (weight of the car, type of use, track conditions, etc.). For instance, if a steel rotor is ceramic coated (the ceramic acts as a thermal barrier), it is possible that a move to a pad with a higher or lower coefficient of friction may be needed (though not likely). Similarly, if a rotor is cryogenically treated (this makes the molecular makeup of the steel's "grain" more uniform and stable, with a possible increase in surface hardening), it is possible that pad material transfer will be easier or

more difficult to achieve. This might, depending on the performance obtained in track testing with your specific car, require that you move to a higher coefficient pad (to obtain more "grip" on the harder rotor surface).

There are simply too many other variables to make an unwavering statement about this. For the most part, rotor processing probably won't require a change of pad compound, but simply bear in mind that it might. I know I'm repeating myself, but this bears noting. Don't automatically assume that you'll have to change pads if your rotors have been "treated." We must always recognize that a braking system is just that: a system, where one part or set of conditions affects another, and so-on. Car weight, track design (banking, elevation changes, turn length and angle), ambient temperature, brake fluid type, rotor material, pad compounding, pad type, caliper style and size, the affect of heat on fluid and metals, driving style, chassis setup, and more all combine to affect the final outcome of brake performance.

More detailed information on cryogenic and vibratory stress relief is included in this book.

PRODUCT LINE	PRODUCT CODE	DESCRIPTION	APPLICATIONS
HT-9	G	Highest torque friction available. Superior peak feel and initial response. Low wear rate.	Indy Car, World Sports Car, F3000, Group A
HT-8	H	High torque with minimal pedal effort. Slightly less brake response than HT-9. Low wear rate.	Winston Cup, Trans Am, Busch GN, F3000, Group A
Blue MT-4	L	Medium/high torque with minimal pedal effort. Excellent brake modulation. Low wear rate.	ASA, ARCA, All Pro, SCCA, IMSA, Group A, F3000, Showroom Stock
Blue9012	E	Medium torque/20% lower coefficient of friction than Blue MT4. Good wear rate. Good stable pad for ABS. For asphalt cars over 2100 lbs.	ASA, ARCA, All Pro, Group A, F3000
Black	M	High torque with minimal pedal effort. For use in all forms of dirt racing or light asphalt cars under 2100 lbs.	Late Model, Modified, Formula Ford
Black Y5.	J	Medium torque/20% lower coefficient of friction than Hawk Black. Good wear rate. For use in all forms of dirt racing or light asphalt cars under 2100 lbs. Excellent on aluminum rotors.	Late Model, Modified, Formula Ford
HP Plus	N	High performance street material/race-worthy.	Solo 1, Solo 2, Autocross Driving schools
HPS	F	Top of the line high performance.	All street rods & sports cars performance street compound. High torque, low dust, extended rotor life and silent running.

The chart is an example of brake pad compounding/construction based on the needs of various applications. This chart was supplied by Hawk Brakes, and only applies to that brand's pads. Other pad makers provide similar compounding variations designed to suit specific types of racing use. Use this chart only as an example of how pad compounding can be tailored to various types of cars and types of racing conditions.

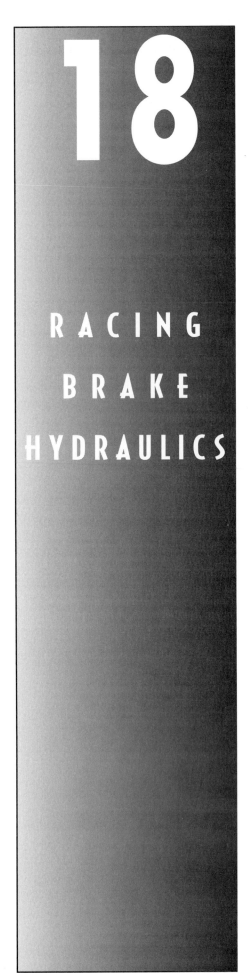

Since the act of recirculating the brake fluid moves fluid from the caliper back to the master cylinder, the system is also self-bleeding. Every time the brake pedal is depressed, hot fluid (along with any air bubbles that may be in the system) is moved out of the caliper, "burping" at the master cylinder fluid reservoir.

MASTER CYLINDER

Several variables must be considered when selecting master cylinder size, including car weight, the weight bias of the car, the tire and wheel setup, brake disc diameter, caliper design and caliper location, caliper piston sizes, brake pedal ratio, track conditions and driving style.

Here are recommendations from the folks at Tilton:

The following principles can be applied toward any type of disc brake system. However, the example given here is based on the use of a brake balance bar. A balance bar is one of the most useful components in any racing brake system for two major reasons: safety and adjustability. By using two brake master cylinders and a balance bar, two separate brake circuits are created. If one should fail due to track debris or a seal failure, the other circuit would still be operational. For fine adjustments on or off the track, the balance bar is used. Gross adjustment in tuning the

system is done by changing master cylinder size. Using single or tandem master cylinders may appear to be a simpler solution, but they are both more complex when trying to achieve optimum results.

The typical force at the front brake pad required for wheel lockup on asphalt is usually between 2400-4000 lbs., while force at the rear pads is in the range of 800-1500 lbs. Although these figures will vary across the wide spectrum of auto racing, they will be used for the following calculations. At the extremes, off-road racers may lock up the front wheels with as little as 700 lbs., while a road racing car with over three tons of downforce might require over 4000 lbs. Brake disc size and material, brake pad material and caliper piston size are all major factors in pad force requirements.

Determining this value for a specific vehicle can be done by monitoring the brake line pressure with gauges. Knowing what line pressures will cause wheel lockup is the first step in optimizing the brake system (bear in mind that rear brake line pressure in a single master cylinder system is always equal to front line pressure unless a brake proportioning valve is installed).

Multiplying front brake line pressure by the total area of the pistons on one side of the front caliper will give the brake pad force required at the front.

Finding Caliper Piston Area

To determine caliper piston area (in.^{2}), use the following formula: A= (piston dia. squared) x .785. For calipers with more than one piston, calculate the area for each piston on one side of the caliper, and then add the areas together. For example, a four-piston racing caliper with 1 3/4" and 1 7/8" pistons has an area of:

A = 1.750^2 x .785 + 1.875^2 x .785 = 5.16 in^2.

If, in this example, this was the front caliper and a line pressure of 700 psi was measured just as the front wheels began to lock up, the force on the front brake pad (clamping force) would be:

F = 700 psi x 5.16 in.^{2} = 3612 lbs. (each front caliper)

For the rear, suppose there is a two-piston caliper with 1 3/8" pistons. Using the same formula, the rear would have a piston area of 1.48 in^2. If a rear line pressure of 600 psi was required to lock up the rear wheels, the force at the rear pad would be 888 lbs.

Since the line pressures have been found, the required force at the brake pedal can be calculated. To do this however, a first guess at master cylinder sizes needs to be taken. Use the table nearby to arrive at this first

PISTON AREA/MASTER CYLINDER RECOMMENDATIONS

Caliper Piston Area (in^2)	Master Cylinder Area (in^2)	Master Cylinder Bore Dia. (in.)
Up to 3.6	5/8	.307
3.6 to 4.2	7/10	.385
4.2 to 4.5	3/4	.442
4.5 to 4.7	13/16	.518
4.7 to 5.5	7/8	.601
5.5 to 5.9	15/16	.690
5.9 to 6.3	1.0	.785
6.3 to 7.6 max	1-1/8	.994

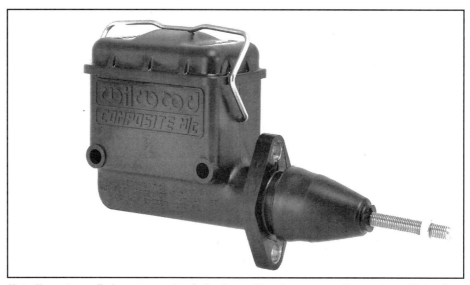

Not all master cylinders are made of aluminum. Here is a composite master cylinder from Wilwood. The plastic composite construction offers benefit in terms of weight reduction. Courtesy Wilwood.

guess, by using the piston area of the front calipers.

Note: While the above chart has merit, it is primarily intended to guide master cylinder bore selection for road race and Indy car applications, where smaller pedal ratios are commonly used. However, in Late Model oval applications, pedal ratios of 6:1 and 7:1 are common. If a 3/8" bore piston is used in the calipers (this gives about 3 square inches of piston area), a 5/8" bore master cylinder will provide a too-soft pedal feel and extended pedal travel for a higher

ratio pedal setup. This will create too much line pressure, causing rear wheel lockup too easily for a late model car (especially on dirt), which can also create engine stalling problems. Road race applications can handle smaller master cylinder bore size combinations in conjunction with lower pedal ratios, for heel and toe style driving. For applications like Late Model, a 5/8" and 3/4" master cylinder setup would provide extended pedal travel and a too-soft pedal, so a larger bore size master cylinder setup would be more

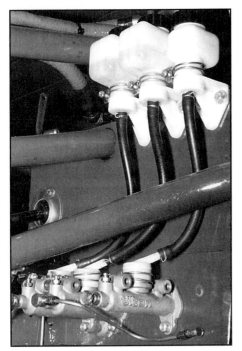

Remote master cylinder setup on a Busch car. Front brake, rear brake and clutch master cylinders are mounted low to attach to floor-mounted pedals, while remote fluid reservoirs are mounted higher for easy underhood access. Keep reservoirs and hoses from sharp edges, hot and/or moving parts. Keep entire area as clean as possible by washing between races. If the entire firewall area is filthy and wet, you won't be able to spot a leak, and fittings will be difficult to locate and service. Also, if lines are disconnected in a dirty environment, debris may enter lines and contaminate master cylinders and calipers. Let the body and interior get dirty if you're too lazy to keep it clean, but you MUST keep the hydraulic lines and components clean for service and inspection.

applicable, such as a 1" and 3/4" or 1" and 7/8" combination.

Since the front caliper has an area of $5.16"^2$, a 7/8" master cylinder is chosen from the table for the front brake circuit. For now, choose a master cylinder a size or two larger for the rear, for example a 15/16".

Master Cylinder Mounting

Whenever possible, always mount the master cylinder as high in the car as possible. If a remote fluid reservoir is used, mount it as high as possible. The object is to keep the fluid

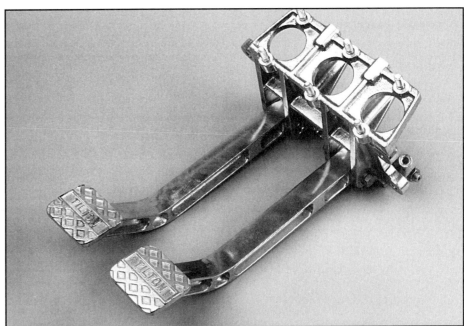

Aluminum brake/clutch pedal assembly. Notice the mounting pedestal is designed to accommodate two separate master cylinders in addition to the clutch master cylinder. Use of two masters, each dedicated to front and rear brakes, is preferred, as this allows the racer to tailor braking bias front/rear via master cylinder bore size.

reservoir as high as possible, with all lines running at a downward angle from the master to the calipers.

It's always best to mount the brake fluid reservoir and master cylinder higher than the calipers, to prevent brake fluid from draining back to the master reservoir, which can deplete the caliper fluid, causing the driver to pump the heck out of the pedal to push the fluid back to the calipers where it's needed. When this mounting layout isn't possible, the use of a residual valve is the answer.

BRAKE PEDALS

With the initial master cylinders selected, now the attention is turned to the brake pedal.

Brake Pedal Ratio

Pedal ratio should be considered to maximize the mechanical advantage of the pedal lever in gaining the greatest brake pressure when the pedal is depressed. The pedal is a

lever, and the pivot point locations affect the effort required to move the pedal and in turn, to pressurize the brake system.

If the pedal ratio is increased, the amount of pedal pressure required is reduced (so the brakes work better with less driver fatigue). Also, as the pedal ratio increases, the pedal stroke will increase as well (the pedal has to move further).

As a general rule, start with about a 6:1 pedal ratio when using a floor-mounted pedal, and a 7:1 ratio for a swing-mount pedal. This may vary 5:1, up or down, depending on the pedal design/brand. The higher ratio (a 7:1 for example) will provide a greater mechanical advantage, so you don't have to push as hard. Brake system manufacturers can make specific recommendations for master cylinder bore sizes that will correspond with certain pedal ratios.

Pedal ratio, coupled with master cylinder bore sizes, represents a "gray" area that needs to be fine-tuned to suit individual racer preference. If the pedal ratio is high (say 7:1 as found in most Late Model oval track cars), a too-small master cylinder bore selection will create a deep pedal with a soft feel. If pedal ratio is lower (say 4:1 to 5.5:1 as found in many road race cars), a smaller master cylinder bore combination can provide the pedal feel a road racer needs when heel & toe operation of the throttle/brake pedals is used. Remember, a smaller bore master cylinder will create higher line pressure. A larger bore master cylinder will create lower line pressure.

Calculating Pedal Ratio—First, the braking effort (force exerted by the braking foot) is assumed. Braking effort values usually range between 75 and 150 lbs. for front wheel lock up (in a panic situation, some drivers can exert up to 400 lbs. on the brake pedal). A value of 120 lbs. will be used in this example.

Now, the brake pedal ratio must be found if it's not already known. This is the distance from the pedal pivot point to the middle of the foot pad (Y), divided by the distance from the master cylinder pushrod to the pedal pivot point (X). The calculation is the same for either overhung or floor-mounted pedals. Typical values range between 4 and 7 (a value of 6.25 will be used for this example).

Example: Y divided by X = 12.0" divided by 2.0" = 6:1 ratio

The braking effort multiplied by the pedal ratio will give the force at the balance bar:

Braking effort x pedal ratio = total force at both master cylinders. In our example, 120 lbs. x 6.25 = 750 lbs.

Since the balance bar is only used for fine adjustment, it is initially set

Pedals can be hung or floor mounted, depending on builder/driver preference or dictated by chassis design. If the pedals are floor mounted as shown in this example, it is absolutely critical to keep the floor and pedal pivots as clean as possible to prevent pedal pivot wear and pedal binding or pedal drag. Especially when floor mounted pedals are used, the driver should routinely wipe his/her shoes on a floor mat or other surface to clean off track or paddock debris immediately before entering the car.

up in the middle of the pedal tube. As the distance from the spherical bearing to each master cylinder pushrod is the same, half of the force of the balance bar is transmitted to each master cylinder (the master cylinders split the load). In this example, a force of 375 lbs. is being exerted on each of the master cylinder pushrods (750 lbs. divided by 2 = 375 lbs.).

Note how this force ratio changes when the spherical bearing moves left or right in the pedal tube. It is this change which directly affects the pressures in the front and rear lines. The balance bar can be used successfully only when the correct master cylinder sizes are being used. It does not have enough adjustment to cure severe brake bias problems.

Pedal Assembly Mounting

The brake pedal assembly must be mounted firmly in the car. In other words, treat the pedal assembly with as much concern as you would treat wheel studs, crankshaft main cap bolts or any other critical part. The

pedal assembly must be mounted as solidly as possible to take the stresses of impact-hits with a feverishly applied foot as the car hurtles towards a tight turn or the bodywork of a slowed or spinning competitor. In other words, don't use sheet metal screws to hang the pedal assembly from a thinwall sheet of steel, aluminum or fiberglass. The pedal assembly should ONLY be mounted to a structural part of the car, such as structural chassis tubing. Use high-strength grade-8 bolts and locking and/or safety wired nuts. Don't take chances with this component. Make the mounting as strong and as rigid as possible.

That brings up another point, and yet another reason that the pedal assembly should be mounted rigidly. If the pedal assembly is mounted to a firewall or floor pan that will flex as the pedal is depressed, even if the pedal box isn't torn loose, even a small amount of deflection will reduce the braking efficiency. When you're using leg muscle to push the hydraulic fluid to the caliper pistons,

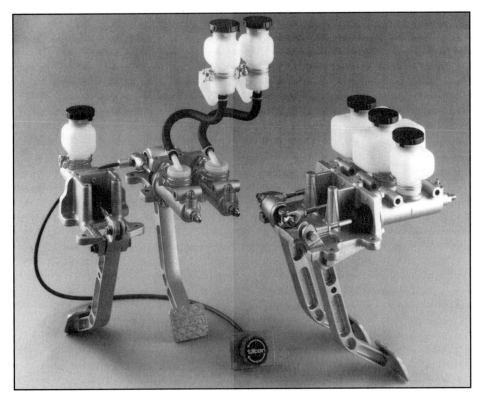

Hanging or "swing mount" pedal assembly examples. Fluid reservoirs can be mounted on the master cylinders or remotely for more convenient access.

any forward deflection of the pedal's mounting base results in lost energy, which means you have to push harder and longer to achieve clamping pressure at the pads-to-the rotors. Braking response can be delayed and excess leg pressure is required to achieve the braking force required. make sure the mounting is solid, so all of the driver's energy output results in positive movement of the braking fluid, calipers and pads. A wimpy-mounted pedal is an inefficient pedal.

Check the brake pedal for free movement. Keep the pivot of the pedal clean and properly lubricated. The brake pedal must be free to return when pressure is released, and the master cylinder pushrod must be allowed to return to the relaxed position. If the internal master cylinder spring isn't strong enough to fully return the pushrod, an external pedal return spring might be needed (first check to make sure the pedal

pivot itself isn't binding or dragging due to dryness, dirt or burrs in the bushing).

If an external return spring is installed at the pedal, the pedal may retract so strongly and quickly that a strain may be placed on the master cylinder pushrod's snap ring (this secures the pushrod in place), as the pedal retraction bangs away at the snap ring every time the pedal is released. To prevent this damage, install an adjustable pedal-stop, and adjust the stop perhaps .005" or so short of the snap-ring bottoming out. In this way, the retracting pedal lever will hit its stop before the snap ring is hit by the master cylinder piston and the internal end of the pushrod.

Be careful not to "over adjust" the pedal stop, which might prevent the master cylinder piston to fully retract. If the piston isn't allowed to fully return when the brake pedal is released, the master cylinder's

primary internal seal may not be able to return past the small pressure relief hole (on a cylinder with an attached reservoir, you might be able to see this small orifice at the floor of the reservoir). If the piston does not fully retract, a small amount of hydraulic line pressure may remain in the system, causing the caliper pistons to push out, in turn causing a slight pad-to-rotor drag. This can quickly overheat the pads and the rotors, and diminish braking performance.

Line Pressure

Now the initial master cylinder choice can be evaluated. Since the force on the master cylinder pushrod is known, multiply this force by the area of the master cylinder to obtain actual line pressure.

Front pushrod force divided by front MC area = front line pressure
(375 lbs. divided by $.601^2$ = 624 psi)
Rear pushrod force divided by rear MC area = rear line pressure
(375 lbs. divided by $.690^2$ = 543 psi)

It looks like both the front and rear line pressures are not high enough to lock either set of wheels (this requires 700 psi front and 600 psi rear in this example), but the balance bar is not very far off. Using these master cylinders would require the driver to exert a little more than the initial guess of 120 lbs. to lock up the wheels (135 lbs. of pedal force). This setup is now ready for track testing to dial-in the balance bar.

Residual Valves—A residual pressure valve is a small valve that is installed in the brake line in certain applications. This in-line pressure

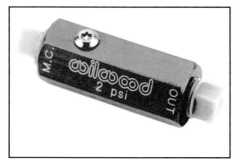

A residual pressure valve is used when the master cylinder is mounted in a lower horizontal plane than the calipers. To prevent the fluid from partially draining the calipers by gravity-feeding back to the master cylinder, a residual valve is plumbed in the brake line between the calipers and the master cylinder. This holds residual pressure in the lines and calipers when the brake pedal is released. Residual valves are offered in two pressure sizes, including 2-lb. and 10-lb. the 10-lb. valves are only used for cars with rear drum brakes, and should NEVER be used on a 4-wheel-disc system! Use only a 2-lb. valve.

Brake fluid recirculating valves should be installed on every race car. Two examples are shown here (on left is an Outlaw brakes unit; on right is a unit from Dan Press Industries, makers of Sierra brakes). A recirculating valve does just what the name implies: it continuously recirculates fresh, cooler brake fluid to the calipers when the brakes are used.

valve retains a minimum brake line pressure to help eliminate excessive pedal travel in both disc and drum systems. The 2-lb. valve is used in disc brake applications where the master cylinder is mounted below the horizontal plane of the calipers, where fluid drainback results from gravity and vibration. This causes excessive caliper piston retraction, and therefore a longer pedal stroke to regain the pedal. The 2 lb. valve prevents fluid from flowing back to the master cylinder without causing the brakes to drag. It maintains 2 lbs. of line pressure when the pedal is released. A drum brake setup requires a 10 lb. valve to compensate for the return spring tension in the drums. Don't use one if you don't have to (since this slight amount of line pressure is always present, with a potential of causing the brakes to drag if the valve has a problem. If however, the master is mounted lower than the calipers, you don't have a choice. Use it but mount the valve where you can

inspect it and easily replace it if necessary. The best place to mount a residual valve is at the end of the master cylinder, where it's obvious and can be seen easily.

Recommendations

1. A larger master cylinder will displace more fluid volume, but will create less line pressure. The result is a harder pedal with more braking effort. A smaller master cylinder will displace less fluid volume, but will create more line pressure (softer pedal with less braking effort).
2. On asphalt, 60-70% front brake bias is a good starting point.
3. On dirt, 55-65% rear brake bias is a good starting point.
4. Whenever possible, be sure brake fluid level is above both master cylinders and the brake calipers, to prevent "bleed down."
5. If a residual pressure valve is needed in the system, use a 2-4 lb. valve for disc brake applications.
6. Small changes to values in any of the formulas presented here can dramatically alter vehicle braking characteristics.

While measuring line pressure with a gauge and using the formulas

presented here are legitimate approaches to determining which size master cylinder is appropriate for a specific application, when you get right down to it, master cylinder selection is a trial and error process. Pedal "feel" and what is comfortable for the individual driver will dictate the final choices.

For Late Models, a good starting point is to use a 1" and 7/8" combination. On asphalt, start with a 7/8" front and a 1" rear, then finish the "dial-in" using the balance bar. On dirt tracks, start by using the opposite combination of a 1" front master cylinder and a 7/8" rear master cylinder, then adjust the balance bar for fine-tuning. If car turn-in and/or pedal feel needs further refining, test other master cylinder in either an up-size or downsize move. Remember, a larger diameter master cylinder will provide less braking force, and a smaller diameter master cylinder will provide more braking force.

BRAKE FLUID RECIRCULATORS

This is a relatively recent introduction that has caught on like wildfire. In an effort to provide the calipers with a fresh, cooler supply of

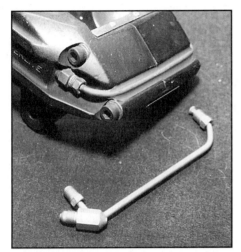

Use of a recirculating valve requires special plumbing on the caliper, but it's no big deal. The brake bleeder screws are eliminated and a special crossover tube with a "T" fitting is installed in their place (this tube connects to the caliper in the same way a conventional external crossover tube is installed). The extra "T" fitting routes fluid back to the recirculating valve.

It may be difficult to see because of the "busy" background, but this caliper is outfitted with a special crossover tube that is plumbed to a recirculating valve. The brake fluid enters the caliper at the center of the inboard caliper body, as normal. The bottom crossover tube remains in place, as normal. The upper bleed screws have been removed, and in their place, a special crossover tube featuring a "T" fitting was installed. Fluid can now exit the caliper and run back to the master cylinder reservoir, self-bleeding itself of air in the process.

The recirculating valve is installed close to the master cylinder. When the brake pedal is depressed, fluid enters the caliper, doing its job to push the pistons/pads towards the rotor. Since the caliper is outfitted with a special crossover tube that also feeds back to the recirculating valve, the hot brake fluid inside the caliper is pushed out and routed back to the recirculating valve and the master cylinder, as fresh cooler fluid is injected into the caliper. This changeover process takes place every time the brake pedal is depressed.

brake fluid at every pedal application, a recirculator continuously circulates the brake fluid through the caliper and back to the master cylinder to eliminate heat buildup that otherwise occurs when the same supply of brake

fluid "sits" in the lines and caliper.

This unit is installed in-line between the master cylinder and calipers. The plumbing path is as follows: from the master cylinder, fluid is routed to the recirculator unit. From the recirculator, fluid runs to the calipers. Fluid then runs through the calipers and out of the calipers (via a special exit tube that is installed at the caliper bleed screw locations), back to the recirculator unit. Fluid enters the caliper in its normal path at the caliper body inlet hole. In order to exit the caliper, a special crossover fitting and tube assembly is installed at the bleed valve holes (bleeding can now be done at the recirculator, or the recirculator may self-bleed by design). Note: the special crossover tube does not replace the caliper's original crossover tube. Remove the bleeder valves from the caliper (on both sides), and install the new crossover tube. The new tube features a T-design, with a third fitting that attaches to the line that goes back to the recirculator.

A brake fluid "cooling" recirculator is a simple device that works wonders. Since the fluid circulates through the caliper, you're less likely to have air trapped in the caliper (since the caliper gets "flushed" with every pump of the pedal). In fact, some recirculator designs self-bleed the system every time the pedal is depressed!

These self-bleeding/fluid recirculator units are available as one-piece units, like Sierra's and Outlaw's, or as two-piece setups like Wilwood's. The Wilwood system (using two small valves the size of residual valves) features one small valve placed in the outgoing line to the calipers and one in the return line from the calipers. Regardless of which unit you choose, they're all small and easy to mount and easy to plumb. Once you try one of these units, you'll never want to be without it. They work great.

Once you've installed a recirculating valve in your brake system, you eliminate bleed screws. Just stroke the pedal, and the system

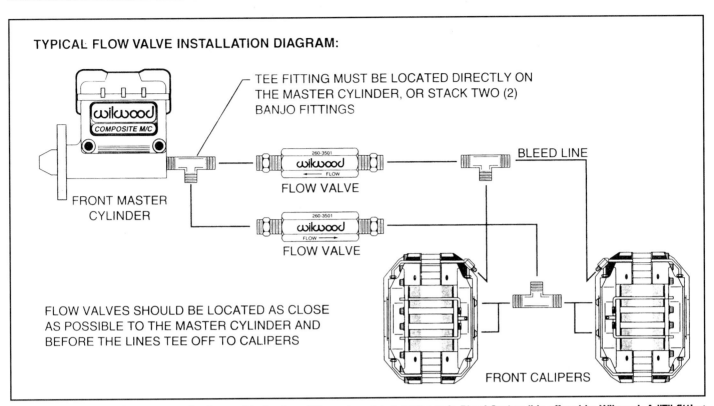

TYPICAL FLOW VALVE INSTALLATION DIAGRAM:

TEE FITTING MUST BE LOCATED DIRECTLY ON THE MASTER CYLINDER, OR STACK TWO (2) BANJO FITTINGS

FRONT MASTER CYLINDER

FLOW VALVE

BLEED LINE

FLOW VALVE

FLOW VALVES SHOULD BE LOCATED AS CLOSE AS POSSIBLE TO THE MASTER CYLINDER AND BEFORE THE LINES TEE OFF TO CALIPERS

FRONT CALIPERS

A brake fluid recirculating system using two residual valves. This system, labeled "Dynamic Bleed System," is offered by Wilwood. A "T" fitting is connected to the master cylinder outlet. As the brake pedal is depressed, fluid runs through the first flow valve to the calipers to push the caliper pistons. By means of a special "T" equipped crossover tube on each caliper, fluid then runs from the calipers, to the second flow valve, and back to the master cylinder. Courtesy Wilwood.

will bleed itself. Air burps through the master cylinder reservoir. Even if you boil the fluid, air bubbles continue to purge from the system whenever the pedal is stroked.

The use of a recirculating valve will benefit any race application, but can be especially useful in road racing endurance applications, where brake pads are changed frequently during a race, and where brake fluid is being regularly topped off. If a caliper becomes "locked up" (where the pistons seize if they cock under full extension when the pads get very thin, coupled with extreme heat levels), and a caliper must be replaced during a race, naturally the system will need to be re-bled. With a recirculator valve in the system, a few strokes of the pedal will self-bleed the system, and the system will continue to self-bleed every time the brake pedal is applied

while on the race track. As far as I'm concerned, no race car should be without one of these wonder-valves.

BALANCE BARS

Some race car applications use two individual master cylinders, each dedicated to two wheels. In order to control the hydraulic push at each master cylinder from a single brake pedal, a "balance bar" is installed between the pedal and the two master cylinders. There are several advantages to this type of setup: brake proportioning can be adjusted by

Balance bar mounted on pedal. Note threaded rod that offers adjustment left-to-right. Rod pivots in Heim ball in pedal center. As threaded rod is adjusted, longer extended side provides less master cylinder travel while shorter side allows quicker travel.

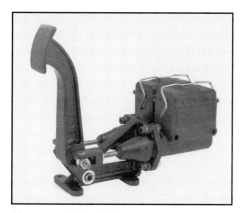

Floor mounted pedal assembly with balance bar. Courtesy Wilwood.

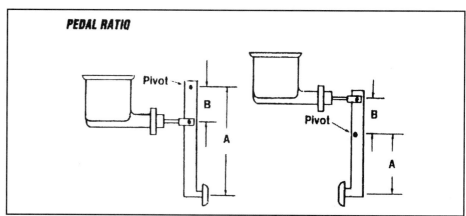

PEDAL RATIO

Pedal ratio illustrated here. Distance A is from center of pedal pad to pivot of pedal; distance B is from pedal pivot to attachment point of master cylinder pushrod. Courtesy The Brake Man.

Balance bar cable allows remote driver-controlled access to balance bar adjustment. This permits quick front-to-rear bias of master cylinders. Cable end attaches to threaded cross-rod on balance bar. Courtesy Tilton.

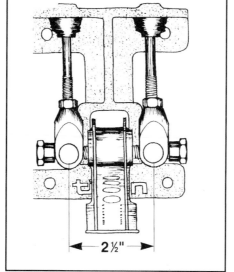

Distance between clevises should be set to match center to center location of master cylinder pushrod points at master cylinders. Courtesy Tilton.

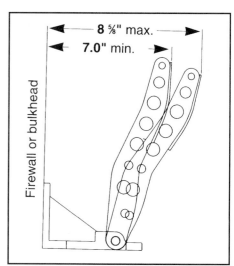

On initial setup, adjust the master cylinder pushrods at the same length. Set the pedal pad at the desired position within the "setup envelope." Floor mounted pedals have a narrow setup window. Courtesy Tilton.

using two different size master cylinders (different size bores) for front and rear brake circuits; front/rear brake balance can be fine-tuned by adjusting the balance bar, to obtain more or less "push" at each master cylinder; and safety is enhanced. Since two separate master cylinders are used, if one circuit (front or rear) fails, you still have a chance of slowing/stopping the car with the remaining circuit.

According to Warren Gilliland of The Brake Man, virtually every race car he inspects has an improperly adjusted balance bar. If the bar is not correctly adjusted, it's impossible to accurately adjust brake line pressures between the two separate master cylinders.

How To Adjust A Balance Bar

First, screw the Heim joints into position on the balance bar to achieve equal spacing (they should be the same distance apart as the master cylinders). The two pushrods should be parallel to each other.

Next, determine which of the two master cylinders will require the longest stroke to fill its assigned calipers. This will be based on master cylinder bore size, caliper piston size and the number of caliper pistons.

You don't need to use a complicated mathematical formula to determine this. Simply look at the master cylinders to see which uses the larger bore, and look at the calipers to see which (front or rear) features greater fluid volume (based on piston diameter and the number of pistons).

Once you know which master cylinder needs the most stroke, you need to adjust the balance bar to bias that master cylinder. Do this by either lengthening the pushrod on the master that requires the longer stroke, or by shortening the pushrod on the master

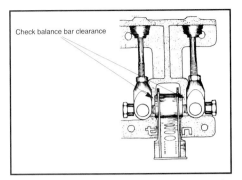

Before adjusting, check that there is adequate clearance at both sides of the clevises, to prevent binding. Courtesy Tilton.

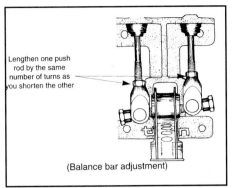

(Balance bar adjustment)

Using a floor-mounted pedal as an example, adjust the master cylinder push rods so the balance bar shift is parallel with the mounting surface when the pedal is depressed. If the pedal position is not to be changed, when adjusting, the length of both push rods must be changed by the same amount. Shorten one pushrod and lengthen the other by the same amount/number of turns. Courtesy Tilton.

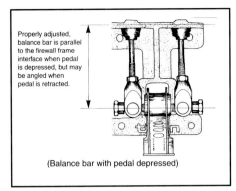

(Balance bar with pedal depressed)

At rest, the pushrods must allow full retraction of the master cylinder pistons. This insures that all residual pressure bleeds back into the reservoir. The balance bar does not have to be parallel to the master cylinder mounting surface with the pedal in the retracted position. Courtesy Tilton.

that requires the least stroke.

It doesn't matter if the balance bar is not perpendicular to the pushrods when the pedal is fully relaxed (pedal not in use). However, it is critical that the balance bar is perpendicular to both pushrods when the pedal is depressed!

To check the operation, install brake line pressure gauges into the bleed ports of the calipers. Dial the gauge to the left and measure the pressure at both front and rear, while holding the front gauge at 1000 psi. Dial the gauge to the right 3-4 turns and measure again. This reading will indicate the pressure differential that you'll have during a race. Record these numbers and re-check after the race.

The use of brake bias gauges are necessary brake "tuning" tools. While they can be temporarily mounted for checking, or dash-mounted in the race car, it is NOT recommended to install these gauges in the car. The extra line plumbing will increase pedal travel, which is something you want to avoid. However, if the gauges are permanently mounted in the car, be sure to install a shut-off valve so pressure will not run to the gauges during a race (again, allowing fluid pressure to expand into the gauges

will "steal" a significant amount of pedal travel).

Once adjusted, it doesn't matter if the balance bar is "crooked" when viewed from overhead. Just make sure that each master cylinder's piston is fully retracted when the pedal is in the relaxed position, to avoid residual line pressure when the pedal is released.

Following are a few pedal operational tips from Wilwood:

1. It's important that the operation of the balance bar functions without interference by over-adjustment. This can occur when a clevis jams against the side of the pedal or the lever, or if

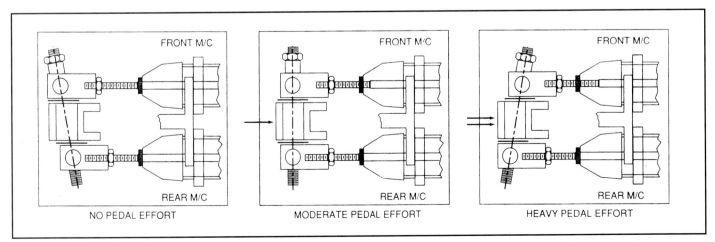

| NO PEDAL EFFORT | MODERATE PEDAL EFFORT | HEAVY PEDAL EFFORT |

The pushrod adjustment shown in this illustration is typical of an asphalt racing application, where large caliper pistons are used at the front brakes and smaller caliper pistons are used at the rear brakes. Courtesy Wilwood.

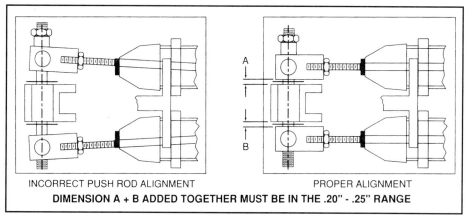

INCORRECT PUSH ROD ALIGNMENT   PROPER ALIGNMENT

DIMENSION A + B ADDED TOGETHER MUST BE IN THE .20" - .25" RANGE

Example of pushrod alignment as viewed from overhead. Courtesy Wilwood.

Knob style proportioning valve allows infinitely variable adjustment, with no "click" stops. Depending on driver preference, either knob style or lever style is a good choice, since either style of valve accomplishes the same task.

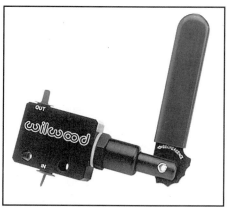

Lever type proportioning valve provides distinct "notches" as lever is rotated. This allows driver easy referencing while adjusting rear brake bias in the car. Courtesy Wilwood.

the bolt hits the pedal bore during any point of travel.

2. Lever movement should be unimpeded throughout the pedal travel. In the neutral position, the clevis ends should have between .20"–.25" total clearance between the clevis end and the side of the pedal. The large washers between the pedal and clevis should remain loose.

3. Make sure that the master cylinder pushrods remain true in relationship to the cylinder during entire pedal travel. Pushrods should not be pushing the master cylinder pistons at an angle.

4. In the non-depressed position, the pedal and balance bar should allow the pushrod of the master cylinders to fully return. This can be checked by feeling the pushrods for very slight

movement, not loose movement. Master cylinder pistons should be against the retaining snap ring (located under the dust boot).

Remember that brake balancing can also be affected by the bore sizes of the master cylinders, caliper piston diameters, and the use of a proportioning valve.

In addition to adjusting the balance bar manually at the pedal assembly, the adjustment can be made by the driver by operating a remote cable adjuster. This assembly allows driver adjustment of brake bias during track time. A cable is routed from the balance bar (attached via a female threaded end to the balance bar) with the other end terminating with an adjustment knob that can be mounted within driver reach. The rotating knob features finger grooves for a non-slip grip, and has a spring-loaded detent to prevent unwanted changes caused by vibrations of a rough track surface. AP Racing also offers a remote knob-type adjuster that features a digital readout display box, which indicates exact position of the balance bar, left of center or right of center.

PROPORTIONING VALVES

A proportioning valve allows the driver or crew to manually reduce

brake system outlet pressure to a specific wheel or pair of wheels in order to adjust braking force. This is a fine-tuning adjustment can make a big difference, assuming of course that the master cylinder sizes and caliper sizes are correct for the application.

Two basic styles are available, including a knob type (as you rotate the knob, you increase or decrease line pressure to the rear brakes, or whatever circuit you choose to select). Most models provide a dial adjustment which is relatively smooth and infinitely variable. Using a Wilwood knob-style proportioning valve as an example, pressure adjustments are available from 100-1000 psi, and provide for a maximum decrease of 57% line pressure. This allows you to fine-tune the front to rear brake balance by reducing line pressure to the rear brakes or one specific wheel position, depending on what circuit it's plumbed into.

The other style features an adjustable lever that allows the driver to make a number of rapid, distinct and repeatable changes to reduce brake force to a specific wheel or pair of wheels (typically this type of unit will provide six or seven distinct adjustment settings). This style

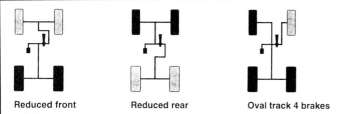

Reduced front
- Rally
- Dirt
- Off road
- Stadium racing

Used when the front tire needs more adhesion for steering, as well as in loose gravel conditions.

Reduced rear
- Road racing
- Street rods
- Trucks
- Tow vehicles

Used to compensate for fuel load or weight changes, deteriorating rear tire adhesion, and brake systems with only one master cylinder

Oval track 4 brakes
- Dirt
- Asphalt

Used to decrease outside front corner braking, which increases turn in and reduces understeer. Used to compensate for track conditions or deteriorating chassis setup.

Oval track 3 brakes
- Dirt racing
- Midget
- Sprint
- Champ car

Used to decrease inside front corner braking, which decreases turn in and reduces oversteer. Usually used on the inside front with twin calipers on the rear.

While a proportioning valve is usually plumbed into the rear brake circuit for rear brake bias adjustment, it can be plumbed into any circuit where the driver wishes to reduce brake pressure for optimum braking and handling characteristics. This chart shows typical effects that can be obtained for a variety of racing applications. For rally racing, dirt or off-road situations, a certain amount of oversteer underbraking may be preferable, so the front circuit's line pressure may be reduced. For road racing on asphalt or cement, rear brake lockup and oversteer underbraking can pose problems, so line pressure can be reduced to the rear brake circuit. For oval track racing on either dirt or asphalt, it's usually preferable to reduce line pressure to the outside front corner (in this type of racing in the U.S., this means the right front). On 3-brake cars used on oval tracks, it's necessary to reduce line pressure at the left front wheel to control oversteer. The proportioning valve can be mounted in any convenient location, including firewall, roll cage tubing, etc. Illustration courtesy Tilton.

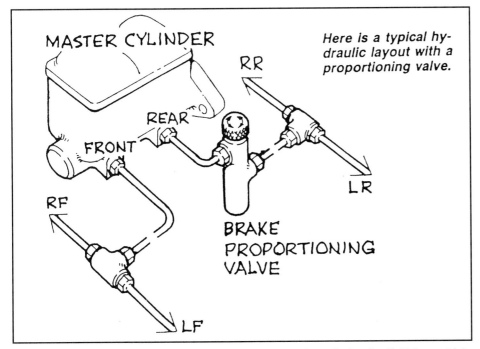

Proportioning valve is plumbed between master cylinder and rear brake circuit. Valve restricts line pressure to a portion of the brake system, typically the rear brake circuit. Illustration courtesy Aerospace Components.

incorporates a cam and lever system and provides a handy feel (the lever clicks into each position) and visual reference for the driver (by noting what position the lever is in, he can quickly increase or decrease brake force to the chosen circuit and quickly go back to the initial setting in a hurry, without wondering about knob position. In other words, sight and "feel" referencing is easier with this style.

Either the knob style or the cam lever style is useful, depending on the driver's preference.

Typical bias setups for different types of racing are as follows:

Reduced front brake force
- Rally
- Dirt
- Off road
- Stadium racing

This setup is used when the front tire needs more adhesion for steering, as well as in loose gravel conditions.

Reduced rear brake force
- Road racing
- Street rods
- Trucks
- Tow vehicles

Used to compensate for fuel load or weight changes, deteriorating rear tire adhesion, and brake systems with only one master cylinder.

Reduced right front brake force (on a 4-brake system)
- Oval track dirt
- Oval track asphalt

Used to decrease outside front corner braking, which increases turn-in and reduces understeer. Used to compensate for track conditions or deteriorating chassis setup.

Reduced left front brake force (on a 3-brake system)
- Oval track dirt
- Midget
- Sprint
- Champ car

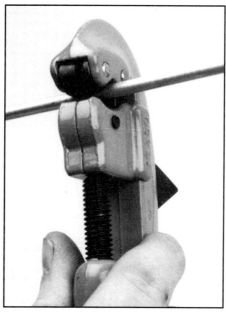

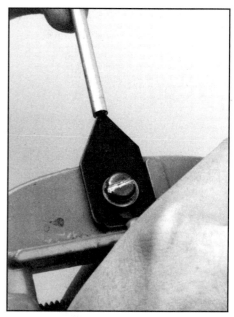

If you ever try to loosen a bleed screw with a "regular" wrench and round the corners off, you deserve the results. Always use a good line wrench when bleeding, and you'll avoid the headaches.

When fabricating hard brake lines, use a quality tubing cutter to cut the line to length. This provides a 90-degree cut that is essential for forming flare. Avoid using a hacksaw, as it's too difficult to obtain a true cut.

After cutting the line, deburr the inside edges and the outside edges. Use a reamer or a V-blade (this may be featured on your tubing cutter) to clean the inside diameter edge. Use a fine metal file or fine-grit grinding wheel to deburr the outer edge. Don't get too carried away. The object is not to remove a bunch of metal. Rather, you want to eliminate sharp edges and burrs.

Used to decrease inside front corner braking, which decreases turn-in and reduces oversteer. Usually used on the inside front with twin calipers on the rear.

BRAKE LINES

Brake lines are made of steel tubing, with flared ends. Two types of flares are commonly used, including double-flares and ball-flares (also called iso-flares). The vast majority used in racing are the double-flare type. The double-flare type features a female "cup" at the flare end, that mates to a male flare at the fitting. NEVER mix flare types! A female flare tube (the double-flare style) will NOT seal if connected to a female flare fitting (by the same token, a ball-flare tube end will not seal with a male flare in the fitting). Never assume that your flares will match. Always check by inspecting the flares closely, especially inside the fitting.

This is critical!

By the way, you can easily create a single flare that simply "bellmouths" the end of the tube, but this type of flare is weak since it's a single wall, and can split over time or as a result of repeated removal. A double flare starts with a male flare, then is "doubled over" in creating the female flare. This provides a tight double-layer flare tip which is much stronger and far more serviceable. Only double-flares should be used.

Flaring Lines

Double-flared tubing can be achieved on one of two ways: you can purchase tubing in specific lengths, already flared at each end (these will feature threaded couplers already installed on the tubing), or you can purchase bulk lengths of tubing and complete the flares yourself. In order to create your own flares, you will need a tubing flaring tool. While a cheap auto parts store flaring tool may

suffice for the backyard mechanic servicing a routine repair, for racing use, do the job right by spending the extra bucks to purchase a really good, top-notch flaring tool. A standard, el-cheapo flaring tool may give you fits because in a percentage of cases, you'll end up with an off-center flare that will not seal. The flare MUST be round and perfectly centered to the I.D. of the tube. In other words, the flare must be concentric. A slightly eccentric flare simply will not seal. You'll have leaks, and the system will suck air.

Ridge Tool makes a professional-duty flaring tool that is excellent (they're at 440-329-4437). This tool allows you to create a centered single flare (you'll still need a flaring kit that includes dies to create the first ball flare). With the tube secured in the tool's 3/16" mounting hole, simply crank the tool handle clockwise. Once

After sliding the fitting over the tube (do this now, since after flaring the tube end, you won't be able to install the fitting), use a die to form the male "ball" flare. This is the first operation in your flaring procedure. To create male "ball" flare, first gage the tube in the fixture by protruding the tube to match the height of the die's head as shown here.

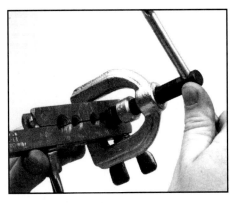

With die in place, tighten tool. Protruding end of tube will form into the die's pocket, creating ball flare.

Next, remove die and use pointed tip of flaring tool bit to push ball flare down, creating final double-flare. This Rigid tool features an eccentric base on its flaring bit, to "walk" around the flare, creating perfect finished flare. Some cheap flaring bits will center themselves improperly and create an off-center flare that is guaranteed to leak. Creating the male flare first, then forming this down into a female flare creates the durable "double-flare" that you'll need. Never rely on a single female flare, as the edges may be too weak for sufficient tightening. A single flare may crack under stress.

the flaring bit creates the final female flare, it senses the pressure when the tool bottoms-out and self-releases (this prevents over-tightening and splitting the flare). The tapered flaring bit is also slightly eccentric at its wide base, which creates a perfectly centered flare, as the taper bit walks around the perimeter of the tube I.D. This is a neat, idiot-proof tool. They're pricey (I bought one for about $100), but worth it.

The procedure in flaring is pretty straightforward. First determine the length of the tube. Then cut the tube using a tubing cutter. Don't cut the tube with a hacksaw or cut-off wheel. After cutting the tube to length, then take the time to deburr the cut edges, both outside and inside. Use a fine metal file to deburr the outside edges, and use a tapered cutter (tapered file, tapered reamer, etc.) to deburr the inside diameter edge. Next, secure the tube in your flaring tool fixture, and use the appropriate sized die to create the first flare, which is a male (ball style) flare. Then remove the die and create the final female flare with the tool's tapered forming bit. The result (providing the tool isn't some cheap piece of crap) is a nicely formed double flare with a female end that will seat against the internal male flare in the fitting. If you've never flared tubing before, take the time to experiment with a few pieces of scrap tubing first. Once you're comfortable with your technique, you'll be ready to start flaring your race car lines. While experimenting, you'll also have a chance to find out how good your

flaring tool really is.

By the way, before you start to make your flare, BE SURE to slip the threaded coupler over the tube first. It's really frustrating to go through the trouble of measuring the line, cutting it, flaring the ends, standing back to admire your work, only to realize that you forgot to install the threaded couplers.

Either steel or stainless steel brake line can be used (stick with 3/16" diameter line for most applications). Stainless line can look really cool if polished, but in the wrong hands, it's also sometimes temperamental with regard to flaring (depending on the temper/alloy makeup, some of this stuff has a nasty habit of splitting at the flare end during the flaring process. Probably the easiest line to use is Everco's Bundy-Flex (sometimes called Bundy-Weld) line. This stuff is easy to bend and form by hand and is highly resistant to kinking (it will still kink if the bend is too tight, but for the majority of the bends you'll have to make, this stuff works great).

In some rare instances, you may want to coil the tubing to accommodate possible vibration or very slight flexing in certain locations. If hard line is being used where a

A completed double-flare. Once assembled to the connection, this female flare will seat against the male angled seat in the fitting or hose end.

potential flex or strain may be possible (such as plumbing from a rigid-mounted location in the engine bay to the master cylinder), you can create a coil shape to provide a degree of "give." This may be handy for those occasions where the master cylinder is to be serviced often, as the coil will allow easier line movement during removal and reinstallation. If you want to form a coil, use the Bundy-Flex tubing, and coil it around a clean pipe, maybe 1 1/2" - 2" in diameter. This will allow you to create a nice uniform coil without kinking the tubing.

For any area of the brake line that is potentially exposed to rubbing or chafing, it's a good idea to insulate the line area with some type of protective sleeve. Rubber or silicone hose or even the split-loom plastic flexible tubing (available at any parts store) will probably work. If you're concerned about brake line chafing, provide it with any covering that will self-sacrifice if rubbed. Do whatever you can to prevent the brake line itself from rubbing through.

Note: When routing brake lines from the master cylinder to the calipers, try to run the lines downhill as they approach the calipers, to prevent areas for trapped air. Air

won't magically remove itself. Let gravity work to your advantage.

BRAKE HOSES

Anywhere the brake line plumbing is required to move along with the suspension, a flexible hose is required. The use of a stainless steel braid reinforced, Teflon-lined hose is highly preferred. These hoses won't necessarily last any longer than a "standard" flexible brake hose in terms of age, but the Teflon lining and stainless braided reinforcement will substantially reduce hose expansion under braking pressure. This results in better pedal feel and a firmer pedal. Because these hoses are highly resistant to pressure expansion, less brake fluid hydraulic energy is wasted. Instead of pushing the hose I.D. larger, the pressurized fluid goes to the calipers where it's needed. NEVER use plastic tubing. ONLY use either approved "rubber" OE type hose or braided stainless, Teflon lined brake hose! Brake fluid plumbing is one area where you should NEVER scrimp in an effort to save a couple of bucks. If the brake hose fails, you can lose a race, lose the car, take out a few competitors' cars or even lose a life. Don't play games with brake hose.

Buy the good stuff, and inspect regularly. If in doubt, replace it.

Hose Routing

This should be obvious, but it's imperative that the flexible hoses do not pinch, kink, or stretch at any time during suspension or steering travel. It's also important that these hoses do not rub on any parts during any point of suspension or steering travel, for two reasons: protection of the hose and protection of adjacent parts. The stainless steel braid that's located on the outside of these hoses can act as a file, and can rub serious holes, gouges, etc. in other metal parts if allowed to rub for any length of time. Pay very careful attention to length of hose and avoid any contact of the hose to other parts and make sure the hose will not be stressed by stretching or crimping or kinking.

Hose & Fitting Recommendations

Standard replacement flexible brake hoses are made of synthetic rubber and reinforced with multiple layers of fabric braid. This type of construction is completely insufficient for today's race applications. Flexible stainless braided racing brake hoses (as those made by Earl's, and similar product

Always keep brake fluid fresh. It's best to bleed and introduce fresh fluid before each and every race. Although frequent flushing with any DOT 3 or DOT 4 quality fluid is certainly better than never servicing the system at all, if you can afford it, you're better off using a high-grade racing brake fluid that will provide high wet boiling point performance. Here are two examples of good brake fluids for any brake application. From left is AP's 550 Racing Fluid and AP's Super 600 Fluid.

made by Aeroquip, Russell & Goodridge) use an extruded Teflon liner in conjunction with a tightly woven high tensile stainless steel outer braid. The Teflon provides a stiff conduit for the brake fluid, working hand in hand with the tight SS braid to dramatically reduce hose swelling under the extreme line pressures used in race car applications. This is the only hose that you should ever use in any race car.

Also, always use a #3 hose. As line size increases, so does the amount of potential hose expansion under pressure, which results in a spongy pedal. Many brake experts agree that a -4 hose diameter is too great for this use. The smaller diameter -3 hose will swell less.

-3 hose features an internal diameter of 1/8" with a liner wall thickness of either .030" or .040". If you plan to assemble your own flexible brake hoses, here's a tip: DON'T. Rather than trying to assemble your own

hoses, it is highly recommended that you order these hoses pre-assembled from the supplier in the length you need, since the hose ends are crimped or swagged for a secure fit.

Some Winston Cup teams have recently experimented with even smaller diameter -2 lines and fittings, as they claim that this boosts the line pressure a bit. This is based on driver feel and preference. As a rule of thumb, stick with -3 hose and fittings.

Citing Earl's specs as an example, a -3 brake hose is rated at a maximum operating pressure of 2,000 psi. The minimum bend radius (this is the tightest you should ever bend one of these hoses) is 1-1/2". Operating temperature is rated at -65 degrees F to +450 degrees F.

When assembling or installing brake hoses, do not use aluminum hoses ends or fittings. Use only steel fittings! Aluminum fittings are soft and can easily be "roached" when you're in a hurry to reconnect your plumbing.

Banjo Fittings—Some fittings are of the "banjo" style (where the hose end features an eyelet shape with an internal groove and fluid orifice). This eyelet is installed to the caliper, etc. with a special banjo bolt that features an internal fluid passage and a side-located orifice. When fluid routes through this fitting assembly, the fluid passes from the hose, through the orifice in the banjo eyelet, through the eyelet's groove path. The fluid then enters the small side-orifice in the banjo bolt and runs through the inside of the bolt shank, into the caliper or other hydraulic part. Banjo bolts allow nice, clean 90-degree placement of the hose end to the mounting location, and they allow a variety of clock positioning due to the round internal

eyelet shape of the hose end.

Whenever installing a banjo fitting assembly, be aware that a crush washer MUST be used on both sides of the banjo eyelet hose end (one to seal between the bolt head and the banjo eyelet, and the other to seal the banjo eyelet to the mounting surface of the caliper, etc.). Always use new crush washers every time you service a banjo bolt assembly, so assure a proper seal! Depending on the banjo fitting manufacturer's recommendations, these seals might be aluminum or copper crush washers, Stat-O-Seals (these are aluminum crush washers that feature a rubber O-ring locked in the washer I.D.), or Dowty seals (these are essentially the same as Stat-O-Seals, but are thicker and smaller in O.D., making them more suitable for certain applications.

Banjo brake line fittings will likely only be encountered in exotic European applications and in road racing showroom stock classes where OEM banjo fittings may be used (Ford Mustangs and Dodge Neons are just two examples). U.S. oval track and drag racers will probably never encounter this style.

BRAKE FLUID

For racing applications, always use a DOT 3 or 4 fluid. However, consider the dry and wet boiling points of the fluid, since the DOT numbers really don't provide the information you need. Use a fluid with a dry boiling point of at least 450 degrees F.

The two most important aspects of a racing brake fluid are compressibility and its rate of moisture assimilation. Compressibility refers to pedal feel...how firm the pedal feels when the brake pedal is depressed (also

Castrol SRF is made in England but is available in the U.S. if you know where to look. It offers outstanding resistance against boiling, and provides a distinctly better pedal feel in many applications. Frankly though, at around $80 per container, buying this stuff is probably overkill for many racers. The most sensible advice is to buy the best you can afford, regardless of the brand. Granted, you want the highest wet boiling rating you can buy, but it's just as important, and maybe more important, to change your fluid before every race. The importance of keeping fresh brake fluid in your race car's brake system cannot be overstressed...it's that important. Yet, many racers completely ignore this issue.

assuming the system is properly bled of air). Different brake fluids can dramatically alter pedal feel, with no other system changes.

Glycol brake fluid is highly hygroscopic, which means that it loves to soak up moisture from the air. Depending on the chemistry of the brake fluid, it can have a high rate of moisture absorption or a low rate of moisture-soak. When a brake fluid is contaminated with as little as 2% moisture content, its boiling point may be reduced as much as 50%, which reduces its racing use to nil. Condensation that occurs within the brake system is probably the biggest

contributor to moisture absorption. The ONLY cure for this is to change your brake fluid often!

We need to talk about DOT 5 silicone fluid in an effort to resolve this question once and for all. Some people love it and some hate it. In a nutshell, DON'T USE IT FOR RACING. The only advantages of silicone fluid is the fact that it won't harm a painted surface, and that the fluid itself is non-hygroscopic (it won't suck moisture from the air). That's why it's popular with restoration, show car and street rod folks. However, in terms of performance, this stuff can cause real problems.

Let me preface these comments by saying that I've used silicone fluid in my own street rods and kit cars and restorations, simply because of the harmless effect it has on a painted fender or firewall if accidentally spilled, so I'm as guilty as anyone else who uses this stuff. The problems, however, can far outweigh the advantages under certain conditions. Silicone fluid can become very unstable at temperature, resulting in a low or ever-changing pedal feel. On the race track, this is obviously not a good thing. As Warren Gilliland of The Brake Man pointed out to me, it's also affected by atmospheric pressure. At higher temperatures, it expands, requiring more pedal pressure and more pedal travel. I'll probably continue to use it in a car that is stored for long periods of time, or in rarely driven restored cars or street rods (even though I know I shouldn't), but as far as racing is concerned, forget it!

If the choice is between dealing with a paint stain on a fender or not being able to stop the damn thing as I approach the end of the back straight

of Watkins Glen, I'll take the paint stain any day.

Regular Changing

Brake fluid is viewed by most racers as a necessary evil. It's slimy to the touch, it can stain a painted surface, and it always seems troublesome to take the time to bleed the stuff. As a result, many racers completely ignore their fluid with the exception of performing an occasional bleed or top-off. The car's brake fluid is probably the most important fluid in the entire car, since without it, that expensive billboard on wheels won't be able to stop, which can spell the end of the race, the end of a promising season, or even the end of the driver's life.

The point we're driving at is simple: CHANGE YOUR BRAKE FLUID ON A REGULAR BASIS! This isn't a joking matter. Aside from the safety aspect (which should be your primary goal in the first place), contaminated brake fluid will crud up your lines, calipers, proportioning valve and master cylinder, causing long-term operational problems and avoidable replacement of expensive components.

Many a racer has chased a soft or low pedal problem by changing pads, resurfacing rotors, adjusting pedal travel, adjusting balance bars, playing with proportioning valves, changing master cylinders, and more, while the root of the problem was simply tired and water-laden brake fluid that boils quickly. Seriously, get into the habit of draining the old brake fluid, flushing the system and refilling with fresh, quality fluid on a regular basis. That doesn't mean once a year, by the way. Plan to change your brake fluid at least several times during the

Use a pressure bleeder, if possible. Two examples are shown here.

season. Ideally, the fluid should be changed before or after every race, especially if you've been racing in very humid conditions. Some racing brake fluid manufacturers even note a maximum lifespan for their fluids (Castrol, for example, recommends that their SRF fluid should not be used for more than 18 months).

The outside air doesn't have to "feel" wet for moisture to enter your race car's brake fluid. Air always carries a certain percentage of moisture (as little as a 3% moisture content can cut your brake fluid's boiling point in half!) and this will wick into your brake system through the microscopic pores in calipers and master cylinders, through seals in the calipers and master cylinder reservoirs, and through improperly tightened fittings. As we mentioned earlier, brake fluid is highly hygroscopic, and it will suck the moisture out of the air no matter how tightly sealed. Your only recourse is to routinely change the fluid. Even after having said this, I know the reality is that most racers still won't do this, but I'm telling you that you will gain a benefit from regular brake fluid replacement. You'll have better brakes and more consistent braking performance at every race if you

perform a one-bottle flush before each event.

While any DOT-approved brake fluid is probably fine for street applications (by the way, street cars need brake fluid replacement at least once per year, but that's another argument entirely), for racing use, stick with high-grade performance fluids that are designed for racing use. That means the fluid should have good compressibility, exhibit a high boiling point rating, and should have a low rate of moisture absorption. Examples of good fluid choices include Brake Man Brake Fluid, AP 550, AP 600 and Castrol SRF. Any of these fluids are good choices. Castrol SRF is the highest-performing and most stable fluid that I'm currently aware of, but it's expensive (to the tune of about $80/2-pint container). While this is a great brake fluid, it simply isn't needed in anything other than a super-hard-stopping application like Winston Cup or some heavy road race endurance cars. For a sprint race, the extra money doesn't need to be spent. For example, at the time of this writing, Brake Man fluid costs about $7 or so for a 12-oz.bottle (this is great stuff by the way, with excellent compressibility and a low rate of moisture assimilation), and the AP fluids run from about $10 to $17 per 16-oz. bottle. Use only racing-quality fluids and change frequently.

BRAKE BLEEDING

Air inside the hydraulic system causes a mushy pedal (or loss of pedal, depending on the amount of air in the system). Remember, you can compress air, but you can't compress fluid. The object is to use a pure fluid transmission from the master to the

caliper pistons, which will operate the pistons immediately with no lag-time that would be caused as you try to compress trapped air.

Bleed your brakes before every single race. Don't assume that just because you bled them in the shop in April, that they don't have to be serviced throughout the season. A regular schedule of bleeding provides two benefits: it provides an opportunity to remove any air that has been sucked into the system during use, and it gives you a perfect chance to freshen the brake fluid.

Bleeding Methods

There are several methods of bleeding available. You can gravity-bleed by opening all of the caliper bleed valves and letting them drain, followed by manual pumping and bleeding, or you can use a hand-held vacuum bleeder tool, or you can use a pressure bleeder. Gravity bleeding or manual bleeding can be time-consuming and messy. Vacuum bleeders are sometimes horrible things to use, since some vacuum bleeder tools frequently leak or fail, and their hoses sometimes love to slip off of the nipples, creating a mess and allowing air to re-enter the system. Some guys love these things, but every one I've tried has caused nothing but problems. The best approach is to use a pressure bleeder.

Pressure Bleeder—A pressure bleeder features a canister with an internal rubber bladder. The lower portion of the canister (below the bladder) is charged with compressed air, and the upper portion accepts the brake fluid. Before using the bleeder, disassemble it and clean the inside of the can and the bladder to make sure all moisture and contaminants are removed. Reassemble the canister and add fresh brake fluid. Then charge the canister with about 30 psi, and bleed the canister itself to expel any trapped air.

Next, connect the pressure bleeder hose to the adapter fitting (the adapter plate/fitting is installed onto the car's brake fluid reservoir). Once you've installed the appropriate adapter to your fluid reservoir, set the bleeder pressure to about 30 psi. Connect clear hose to each caliper's bleed valve and insert the other end of the hose into a clean container partially filled with fresh fluid. Open the pressure valve on the pressure bleeder, and open the caliper bleed valve until you see clean fresh fluid with no air bubbles, then close the caliper bleed valve. Always start with the caliper furthest away from the master cylinder and work your way towards the master. Typically this will involve bleeding the right rear first, followed by the left rear, right front and finally the left front. When using a pressure bleeder, do activate the brake pedal.

Manual Bleeding—If you have to perform a manual bleed, work on one caliper at a time, again starting at the caliper that's furthest away from the master cylinder. Connect a clear hose from the caliper bleed valve and insert the other end of the hose into a clean partially-filled container (this will prevent air from being sucked back into the system). While a helper pushes down and holds the brake pedal, open the caliper bleed valve allowing fluid to escape, then close the bleed valve. Once the valve is closed, the helper can release the brake pedal. Wait 3-5 seconds and repeat this process. Continue repeating the entire process until clean, airless fluid is seen leaving the

EXAMPLES OF BRAKE FLUID SPECIFICATIONS

Brand/Model	Dry boil point	Wet boil point
Brake Man Hi Temp		
577 Fluid.	577 deg. F	300 deg. F
Castrol SRF	590 deg. F	18 deg. F
AP Racing Super 600	572 deg. F	311 deg. F
AP Racing 550	550 deg. F	284 deg. F
Sierra SRP Z-10	570 deg. F	n/a

The dry boiling point is the temperature that new fluid will boil. As the fluid is used, it begins to attract moisture, and will boil at a lower temperature. The wet boiling point is the temperature the fluid will boil at when it contains about 1-2% moisture.

Before using a pressure bleeder, it's advisable to disassemble the unit and thoroughly clean the chamber and bladder. If the unit has been stored for a while, condensation may have built up inside and contaminated the fluid. Make sure it is clean and dry before using.

caliper. Avoid pumping the pedal, as this will only aerate the fluid and make bleeding more difficult. Perform the entire bleeding process at all caliper locations at least twice (once all the way around the car, followed by another complete pass around the car).

Make sure that someone pays attention to the brake fluid reservoir to keep it topped with fresh fluid. Never allow the fluid level to sink lower than 1/2" above the reservoir floor.

After bleeding the system , always check for free rotation of all rotors. If a rotor suddenly begins to drag on the

pads, stop and diagnose the problem.

You may be wondering about the use of a brake fluid recirculator. If a recirculator allows the calipers to self-bleed every time you nail the pedal, why should you have to manually bleed the brakes ever again? Simple: even if you've installed a fluid recirculator in your system, you still need to change your fluid on a regular basis. Granted, a recirculator will bleed air out of the calipers, but you should never use that as an excuse to avoid flushing and refilling the system!

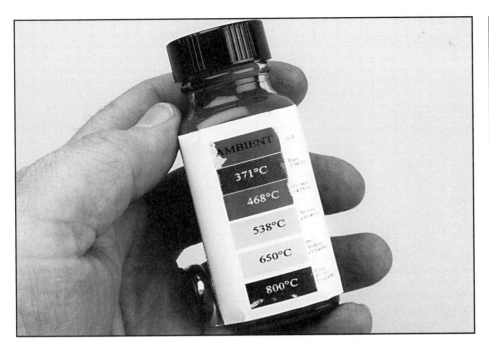

Temperature indicating paint is an invaluable tool for pad selection and brake tuning (choosing master cylinder sizes, determining the change provided by specialty coatings, air ducting, checking temperatures seen by brake fluid, etc.). There are two types of temperature indicating paint available: a multiple-bottle kit (where each paint covers a specific temperature range) and a one-bottle formula. This single-bottle formula sample is from Outlaw Brakes. Once heated, it changes color. Simply compare the color on the rotor to the chart that appears on the bottle's label to determine what level of heat was reached. If a paint kit is used, place individual marks using a variety of temperature range paints. As each paint's target temperature is reached, the paint loses its color. Either method works. Using this sample in the photo as our example of a single formula paint, it's red when exposed to ambient temperature, turns rust color when it reaches 700º F, orange at 875º F, yellow at 1000º F, pale yellow at 1200º F, and gray at 1425º F. This stuff was made in England, so the Celsius numbers are in bold type, while the Fahrenheit numbers are in smaller type on the far right of the label.

TEMPERATURE MONITORING

In any racing application where brakes play an integral part in the vehicle's track performance (road racing, oval track, super speedways, off-road, etc.), it's critical to be aware of the brake rotor temperatures. Knowing rotor temperature isn't "luxury" information that's simply "nice to know." The temperatures that you obtain tell you peak operating temperature, so you'll know which pad compound is best to use at specific tracks and for the weight of your vehicle. Peak operating temperature readings at each wheel can also alert you to problems in the braking system (if one wheel or one axle is working harder than the rest, or if one wheel's brakes are not working

as well as the other wheel locations). This is useful information that will help to diagnose problems, and to aid in fine-tuning the braking system and chassis setup.

Brake pad selection is largely based on rotor temperature. In other words, except for time-consuming trial and error testing on the track, if you don't know what your rotor temperatures are, you can't make an intelligent prediction of which pads to use.

While sophisticated approaches (used in some Indy car or Formula 1 applications) might involve the use of thermal sensors, where information is relayed to on-board data acquisition systems, an economical and easy-to-use approach involves the use of a hand-held pyrometer and temperature indicating paint.

19

BRAKE
COOLING

Use of a hand-held pyrometer will do no good in terms of recording on-track temperatures, but they can still be valuable tools for checking temperatures in the pits, on a relative basis. These can be used to check caliper temperature in relation to rotor temperature, temperature of your master cylinder, etc. This can provide useful information in terms of knowing where to place additional heat insulation or added air ducting.

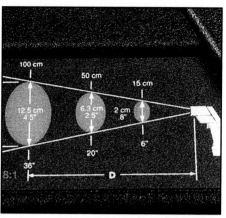

An infrared pyrometer provides an instant reading, with absolutely no waiting period at all. This tool reads surface, or reflected temperatures. The graph on the side shows "read" area at 6", 20" and 36" from target. At 6" away, the read area is .8"; at 12" it is 2.5"; and at 36" away, the read area is 4.5" large.

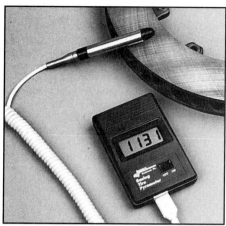

A probe style pyrometer is more useful in reading tire tread temperatures, since the needle probe can dig into the tread compound. While it can be used to measure brake temperatures in the pits, the "ramp" time, or waiting period (before the probe stabilizes) is usually too long for brake component measuring.

PYROMETERS

A pyrometer is a fantastic tool that allows you to check temperatures of a variety of components, including exhaust tubes, cylinder heads, radiators, hoses, calipers, rotors, tires, etc.

Types of Pyrometers

Two basic types of pyrometers are available: the probe style and the infrared style. The probe style features a metal-tipped probe pen that's hard-wired to the gauge. The gauge will feature either a digital or analog readout. The probe style (which is the most common) is used by contacting the probe tip to the surface of the part to be monitored (tire tread, rotor, engine exhaust, radiator hose, etc.). They work just fine and most folks are satisfied with their performance. Specifically for reading tire undertread temps, it's really the best approach, since the probe tip can dig into the rubber and obtain a reading that is closer to the "core" temperature of the tread.

Infrared Type—However, where surface temperatures need to be determined quickly, a hand-held infrared pyrometer kicks butt. The infrared gun will read the surface temperature of any part INSTANTLY. There's no waiting period for the gauge to "ramp-up," while a probe tip soaks up the object's radiated surface heat. The infrared gun recognizes the radiated temperature NOW, with no wait-time at all. This makes it perfect for reading at-the-moment rotor temperatures in the pits. Also, since there's no direct contact between the gun and the rotor, the possibility of accidental burns is reduced dramatically. Every race team, regardless of the type of racing they're involved in, should have an infrared pyrometer. Once you start using one of these toys, you'll wonder how you ever managed without it. Expect to pay about $200 or so for an infrared gun. It's a few coins, I know, but believe me, it'll pay for itself very quickly. You can pinpoint heat-related problems, perform engine and brake diagnostics faster, and it enables you

to establish actual temperature records, so you know exactly what you're dealing with. Buy one and establish a habit of using it.

As previously mentioned, as far as rotor temperatures are concerned, a handheld pyrometer can only be used to check rotor or caliper temperature when the car enters the pits. The problem is that by that time, the rotor temperature will have dropped significantly in comparison to the temperature extremes they experienced during high-speed braking on the track. Don't get me wrong...I think you should still use a pyrometer to check rotor temperatures in the pits, just as a matter of record-keeping.

Once you've captured peak temperature with heat-indicating paint, you can then record surface temperature in the pits with the pyrometer. This comparison will tell you how long it takes for the rotors to cool from peak temperature to X-deg. in the pits. This is useful in that you'll have an idea of how efficiently (or inefficiently) the rotors are dissipating

Applying the paint is easy. Just clean the rotor edge and slap on some paint. If the rotor is vented, be sure to paint both the disc edges and a vane or two. Don't apply paint to the disc face, since the pads will wipe it off. Allow the paint to dry for a few minutes and take the car out onto the track. When the car returns after a few hot laps (or at the end of a race, etc.), yank the wheel off and take a look at the paint. This is the easiest and cheapest way to effectively measure the operating temperature of your rotors, calipers, engine block, cylinder heads, or anything else you want to monitor for temperature. It will provide a wealth of information, which will help in your tuning efforts. For an informed brake pad selection, you MUST know what your rotor temperatures are!

heat. If the race car uses a brake cooling system (such as fresh air ducting), this will also provide some insight regarding the cooling system's operation.

Temperature monitoring can also be accomplished with sophisticated laboratory-grade scientific measuring devices that employ remote thermocouple sensors, but unless you work for a brake system engineering firm, chances are pretty good that you're not going to have access to this equipment. Granted, for precise measurement of operating temperatures on-car or on a brake dyno, there's no better way of achieving the goal. However, unless you're funded by a mega-bucks sugar daddy, you won't buy the equipment or the dyno, so there's no sense in wasting additional space here to provide gobs of information on data acquisition systems that you'll never use. Use temperature paint and a pyrometer, and you'll get the job done.

Temperature Indicating Paint

To obtain in-use temperatures, the trick tool is temperature indicating paint. This special paint (available from several sources) will change its appearance as temperature fluctuates (the material either melts or changes color at a specific temperature, depending on the paint's design), and will remain at a specific appearance that indicates the highest temperature reached. In other words, it changes its appearance as the rotor heats, and remains stable at the rotor's highest achieved temperature, and stays that way after the rotor has cooled. If the rotor achieves, say, 1,000 deg. F in use, the paint will change its appearance that indicates that 1,000 deg. point, and will remain stable after seeing that high temp limit. The paint does not continue to change as the rotor cools, so you have a permanent record of the peak temperature witnessed by the rotor.

Multi-Paint Method—Two types of paint methods are used: the multi-paint system uses a variety of different temperature-limit paints, with each paint capable of indicating a specific temp limit (as temperature increases, one paint mark will change to indicate that 400 deg. has been reached, the next mark will indicate that 500 deg. has been reached, etc.). The paint, when applied, is a certain color. When its temperature limit is reached, the material melts and changes color. For instance, the paint may initially dry to an opaque color (red, etc.). When a specific temperature is reached, the mark will liquefy, and change to a glossy transparent or black. This tells you the specific temperature was reached (if an 850-deg. F paint was applied, and it remains the original color after use, you know that the part did not reach 850 deg. If the mark changed to a glossy transparent or black, this tells you that 850 deg. was reached, etc.).

If this paint system is used, you must apply a paint mark with each temp range formula. After the car comes off of the track, you can inspect the rotor to see which marks reached their range and which didn't, which tells you where the highest temp is. By applying a number of paint marks in a series (spaced maybe 1/2" apart or so), you've in effect created a gauge range. Each paint mark will lose its color as its specific peak temperature is reached. If the second to the last mark and the final dot didn't lose its original color, it's clear to see how high the temperature became. You get the idea. The paint kit will include a reference chart to show specific temperature levels that each specific paint represents when it changes color.

Air ducting to rotor should be aimed directly into center of rotor. Air enters center of rotor, and is pulled through as the vented rotor vanes move the air through to the rotor outside edges. This example shows formed aluminum dual duct that bolts to knuckle.

Single Paint System—The other system uses one single paint formula that changes its hue as temperature climbs, and stabilizes at a certain hue when the highest temperature is achieved. Simply compare the final color of the paint to a reference color chart (supplied by the paint maker, either on the paint bottle label or on a separate chart) to find out what temperature was reached. This style (where one single paint is used) is obviously easier and faster to use, and requires less paint product.

The single-formula type of paint relies on a color change to indicate temperature; while the multiple-formula paint kit type relies on the melting of the paint to indicate temperature.

To cite two examples of temp paint, The Brake Man offers a range of temp paints in specific temperature ratings, from 400 deg. F to 1600 deg. F, in 100 deg. increments (a total of 13 individual paints for each 100 deg. range). Let's say you applied a paint mark on the rotor edge using a succession of paints, including the 800, 900, 1000, 1100, 1200, 1300, 1400, 1500 and 1600 paints. After the race (or test session), you note that the color had melted away from all of the indicators except the 1500 and 1600 marks. This tells you that the rotor reached a peak of 1400 deg. F. A single-paint formula, such as the one offered by Reb-Co, is a light red in color when applied. Once exposed to heat, it changes color. A rust color indicates 700 deg. F, orange indicates 875 deg. F, yellow indicates 1000 deg. F, pale yellow indicates 1200 deg. F, and gray/green indicates 1475 deg. F. The color-matching chart is on the bottle's label for easy referencing.

Regardless of the type of paint kit you choose, the point is to use one! All brake pad compounds are designed to work within a specific operating temperature range. As a result, you really need to know how hot your rotors are when they're in use on the track. Think of temperature indicating paint as a temperature gauge for your brakes. After all, you wouldn't race without a gauge that monitors engine temperature, so why would you ignore (or guess at) the temperature of your brakes? Once you get into the habit of using this stuff, you'll wonder how you ever managed without it. Temp paint is an invaluable monitoring and tuning tool.

Applying The Paint—The paint is applied to the outer edge of the rotor face, between the two friction sides of the disc. Simply wipe the rotor edge clean with a suitable solvent, dry the surface, and apply the paint. DO NOT apply the paint to the rotor disc surface, since the pads will wipe the paint off. Only apply the paint on the outer diameter edge, where no pad contact occurs. The size of the paint mark isn't critical. Just make it large enough for you to easily see and study. In the case of a vented rotor, it's a good idea to apply the paint to both the edge of the disc as well as on one or more of the vent vanes. This provides more surface area of paint to view, and it may reveal a difference (if a difference exists) between disc and vane temperature.

You'd be surprised at how many first-time users simply don't know better, and apply the paint onto the disc faces, only to realize that it was wiped off by the pads.

The temperature indicating paints cover a wide range of temperatures, from about 400 deg. to upwards of 1600 deg. (depending on the paint supplier's offerings). This paint is useful for more than only rotors. It can be applied to caliper bodies, hubs, shocks, engine oil pans, engine blocks, radiators, oil coolers, axle housings, or any area where high temperature extremes need to be recorded. You can also apply this paint to brake pads, but be careful in its use. If you apply the paint to the backside of the backing plate, don't cover the entire surface area of the plate. Just a 1/2"-square dot will work fine. You may apply a small mark on the outer edge of the pad as well, but DO NOT place this paint on the contact face of the pad, where the pad meets the rotor.

By using temperature indicating paints in conjunction with a pyrometer, you can quickly and accurately determine what the rotor temperature limit was on the track, and the amount of cool-down that occurs once the car reached the pits.

BRAKE COOLING

Heat is the bane of all racing

braking. The hotter the brakes run, the more likely they are to fade. Along with monitoring the temperatures, you will have to take appropriate steps to cool the brakes. There are several ways to do this.

Air Cooling

It's almost always a good idea to provide a charge of fresh incoming air to the brakes in an effort to lower and control temperatures. However, two advisory items should be considered with regard to air cooling. Remember that your brake pads are designed to provide optimum performance within a range of operating temperatures. If excessive cooling won't allow the pads to reach their designed operating temperature, you either have to limit the air intake or switch to pads that work within a lower temperature range.

You can't guess about this. The only way to know what effect the air charge has on your brakes is to test using temperature indicating paint. This will tell you if you need additional cooling (chances are you will), and what effect that cooling has on your pad temperature. The other exception/variable to consider is the weather. While oval or drag racers don't race in the rain, road racers do. If the track conditions are very wet, and if the weather is a bit on the cool side, a continuous blast of incoming air may cool the brakes excessively and not allow proper operating temperatures for the pads being used. In certain conditions, it may be advisable to block off the air ducts or move to a "softer" pad that works within a lower temperature range. Again, using temperature indicating paint is a useful tool to determine how rotor temperature is affected by

Note angled vanes in rotor. When cooler air is introduced to rotor center, it channels through the inside of the rotor, between the two disc surfaces, soaking rotor heat along the way and evacuating the heat out of the rotor.

Engine-bay view of front intake duct. This ABS plastic duct is fastened to the inside of the front bumper area, in high pressure area for good impact to incoming air. Flexible duct hose is then routed to the rotor.

specific conditions.

Locating Air Intakes—The fresh air intake should be positioned in an area of clean, high pressure air flow, and the ducting should be routed to avoid sharp bends or changes in duct diameter that might choke the air flow. The air flow should be directed to the backside of the rotor center. In this way, the air will be picked up by the inside diameter of the rotor and sucked through the vanes. As the air is pumped through the vanes, heat is picked up and pulled out of the rotor.

If you have only one air duct per caliper, direct this to the center of the rotor on the inboard side. If you have multiple ducts, it's a good idea to also duct air to the calipers. Direct this to the pad area of the caliper.

In an effort to cool the brakes, you might be tempted to drill a few holes in the rotor hat. Don't do this. Unnecessary holes in the hat can cause a loss of cooling air that would otherwise be directed into the backside of the rotor.

Air Ducting Sizes—When air ducting is needed and is permitted by the sanctioning body rules, a minimum size would involve 3" diameter ducting. Incoming air should be directed to the inside diameter of the rotor. In more severe applications,

such as heavier cars on short-track asphalt or endurance road racers, a second, smaller diameter air intake may be ducted directly to each caliper as well.

Air Intake Scoops—Air intake scoops are available in a variety of shapes and sizes, including round and flush-mounted "NACA" style ducts (NACA ducts feature an imbedded and tapered air path that starts as a narrow slot and widens as it deepens until it eventually channels into the duct hose). These are handy when air pickup is needed on body side panels, where you don't want an air scoop to protrude outside of the bodywork.

Brake Evaporative Cooling

This approach uses small quantities of atomized water that are injected into the inlet of the brake cooling duct. Ideally, the water evaporates before reaching the brake disc, creating the maximum temperature drop before the air reaches the brake caliper and disc (essentially the same principle that road racers experience in the rain, when cool water vapor is ingested into the brake ducts, but in a more controllable and consistent manner). The object is to cool the incoming air intake charge, not to spray water directly onto the disc and

Special ceramic-based heat emitter coating applied to outer caliper body. This helps caliper shed heat outward, pulling heat from aluminum. Ball-milled surface of caliper body not only enhances appearance, but it provides additional surface area for better heat dissipation. Even though the inboard side of the caliper may be heat-shielded with a stainless steel plate and/or a ceramic coating, in a long race heat will eventually soak into the aluminum caliper body. In order to release that heat as quickly as possible, the emitter coating is applied. The application of a heat emitter coating (citing the process applied by Swain Tech Coatings as the example) will shed heat 50% faster than a non-coated caliper.

A whitish ceramic coating is applied to the inboard face of the caliper halves. This serves as a thermal barrier, deflecting rotor heat from the caliper. Especially when used in conjunction with a stainless steel heat shield, the caliper will stay much cooler for a longer period of time. The less heat that reaches the brake fluid, the better the brake fluid works, since it doesn't boil. This coating is sprayed onto the caliper in a special process. The coating is reliable and won't flake off if professionally applied.

Piston bores are anodized. This does not serve as a thermal barrier, but prevents long-term corrosion of aluminum, adding to piston function and reliability.

caliper surfaces. If water is sprayed directly into the center of the disc area, this creates steam, which acts as an insulator. If that happens, you won't achieve the full benefit of the water charge.

This system has been used in a variety of racing scenarios, including IMSA, SCCA and Formula 1, but is generally not legal for use on oval track racing applications. This system uses a pump that is connected to a brake line pressure switch. When the brake pedal is depressed, the pump activates and injects the water. The water is squirted through small atomizing nozzles to create a fine spray that is then ingested through the air duct. Usually, teams will install an override switch so that the system can be turned off when conditions don't require this added cooling.

Recirculated Liquid Cooling

In rare instances (mostly in European and some exotic road racing

applications), a special caliper design may be used that features internal water jackets (AP Racing CP4910 is an example). The caliper itself is internally cooled as a cooling liquid circulates through the internal water jackets, as part of a closed loop system that features an electric pump, a header (pressure/storage) tank, a heat exchanger and a filter. The entire system is plumbed with -4 reinforced hose. A coolant should be used to help absorb the high temperatures (not just plain water). Again, basically any liquid cooling system (recirculator or misting) is not allowed on oval racing vehicles due to sanctioning body rules.

SPECIAL COATINGS

Specialized coatings may be applied for one of three basic reasons: to provide a heat barrier, to speed heat evacuation, or to provide a frictional surface.

Rotors

One of the critical tasks of a rotor is

to absorb and release the frictional heat that's generated by the brake pad's clamping force. The rotor traps a bunch of heat, and the trick is to provide a path of escape for this heat.

In order to release this heat quickly, the rotor relies on a number of factors. Heat is naturally released into the surrounding air. This is handled by both ambient air (the air surrounding the rotor) and by forced-air induction (where intake air is channeled directly to the rotor and caliper).

You'll notice that some rotor discs are vented (where air pockets exist between the outboard and inboard disc surfaces), while others are of a solid machined design. For the most part, vented rotors are used where high heat buildup is expected, and solid rotors are used in applications where heat is less likely to be a factor in terms of excessive levels. As a result, since the braking forces are generally higher in front wheel locations as opposed to rears, you'll generally see vented rotors in front locations and (where peak temperatures are not critically high) solid rotors in rear locations. That certainly does not mean that every rear wheel will feature a solid rotor. If operating temperatures warrant their use, vented rotors will be used at rear axles as well.

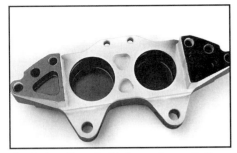

Coated caliper half shown here. Caliper piston bores and bridge faces were anodized, then the body was masked and sprayed with ceramic thermal barrier coating. The coatings (both the ceramic heat barrier and the heat emitter coating used on the caliper outside) work, and are worth the effort.

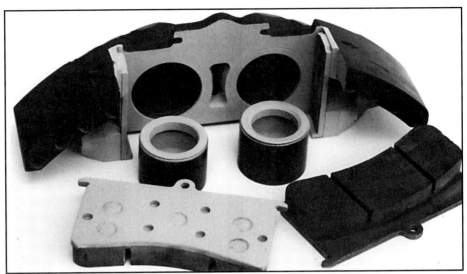

In order to provide heat management, the caliper outer body is coated with heat emitter, the inside faces are coated with ceramic, but this can be taken a step further, by also ceramic coating the piston faces (the side exposed to the pad backing plates), and ceramic coating the backing plates themselves. This provides even more heat barrier layers. In addition, the piston skirts may be moly-coated to provide additional anti-friction properties. Courtesy Swain Tech Coatings.

When a rotor disc is cross-drilled or slotted, the reason is not primarily from a temperature-evacuation standpoint (although slotting or drilling does have an effect, since this provides more surface area for heat release). Rather, the holes or slots serve to reduce rotating weight and in the case of slots, to help "clean" the rotors and pads. Basically, they help to evacuate excess pad dust buildup, which helps to increase pad efficiency.

One method of heat-release is the use of specialized coatings. A heat-release coating (Swain Tech Coatings calls theirs a "black body emitter" coating) can be applied to the vanes on a vented rotor. As heat builds up during operation, hot air is trapped inside the vane openings. While the angled shape of the vane ramps may help to "sling" the heat out as the car runs at speed, this special heat emitter coating speeds the process. This unique coating material (dark charcoal, almost black in color) speeds the release of heat and can dramatically reduce rotor temperature by helping to "sweat" the heat out from the vent holes. Use of this type of space-age coating is becoming increasingly popular in many forms of racing including Trans Am road racing, sports car road racers from

showroom stock classes all the way through the GT categories, NASCAR Busch, Winston Cup and Craftsman Super Truck series, Indy cars and more. The stuff works.

A note regarding titanium rotors: since titanium dissipates heat very quickly on its own, a vented titanium rotor probably doesn't need an emitter coating applied to the vanes. The best rotor material candidates for emitter coatings are cast iron, steel and aluminum.

Calipers

Specialized coatings can also be used on caliper bodies. The inside of a caliper body (adjacent to the pad backing plates) can be coated with a ceramic, while the outer caliper body can be coated with heat-emitter coatings.

The ceramic acts as a thermal barrier, reducing the amount of rotor/pad heat that can leach into the caliper body. Naturally, if less heat reaches the caliper, less heat reaches the brake fluid inside the caliper,

which reduces overall brake fluid temperature. Since the ceramic coating effectively serves to shut-out the heat generated by the rotor/pad combination, the caliper and caliper pistons don't undergo as much dimensional change that would otherwise occur as a raise in thermal level tries to expand the metals. This helps to maintain piston-to-bore clearances inside the caliper.

The heat emitter coating works exactly opposite of the ceramic. While the ceramic coating acts as a thermal barrier, the emitter coating on the outside of the caliper also serves to pull the heat out of the caliper body to the outside air. The combination of ceramic and emitter coatings can make a big difference in reducing the potential of brake fluid boil and in increasing the efficiency of the rotor.

The piston bores and the caliper half mating faces (the bridge connection) are anodized. This does not act as a thermal barrier, but prevents corrosion in the piston bores and at the bridge faces.

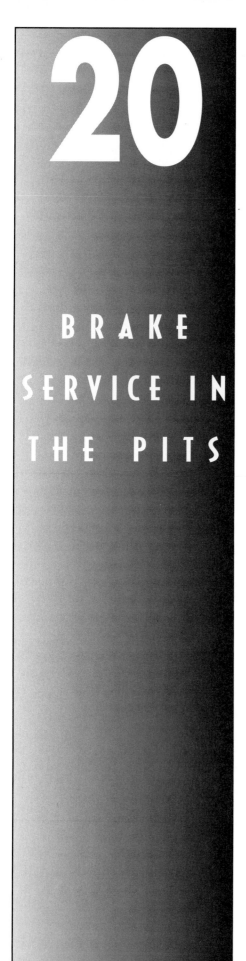

20

BRAKE SERVICE IN THE PITS

Brake are more likely to need servicing during endurance events. Safety precautions must be taken. Those brakes are hot!

By and large, the only type of racing that may require frequent brake service in the pits during an event is road racing, especially where endurance events of 3 hours or longer (up to 24 hours) are involved. Depending on the type of car, car class, weight, type of brakes, driver style and length of the event, it is not uncommon for brake pads to require changes from every 2 hours to every 4 hours, etc.

When pads do need to be changed during a race, heat is the number one obstacle for the crew. The brake system may have experienced temperatures of 1200 degrees or more while on the track, and the rotors and calipers may still be as high as 400 - 700 degrees even by the time the car enters the pits. These high temperatures affect wheel bearings, spindles, wheels, rotors, rotor hats, pads, calipers and fluid, all combining to make working conditions inside that wheelwell very uncomfortable.

When planning your pit stop brake changes, the first order of business should involve the safety aspect of the crew. Eye protection should always be

used whenever servicing hot brakes, as hurried work can cause airborne pad particles, etc. to fly into the crew member's face. Heat protection is paramount. The brake-changing crew must be outfitted with gloves to protect their hands from the hot calipers, pads, etc., but those gloves need to allow enough dexterity to get the job done without being cumbersome. Kevlar gloves, for example, are available in a light-enough weight to both shield the hands from heat and yet allow enough finger movement and "feel" to perform the task. Be aware though, that even a Kevlar glove will not prevent all of the heat from reaching the worker's hands. It simply provides a protective layer to help prevent nasty burns. The other benefit of Kevlar weave is its cut-resistance when working quickly around sharp fender lips, sharp frame edges, etc. The use of Kevlar sleeves is also a very good idea. These cover the forearm area, and provide a thumb hole. Slip the sleeve on first, followed by the glove.

Whenever the crew is servicing hot

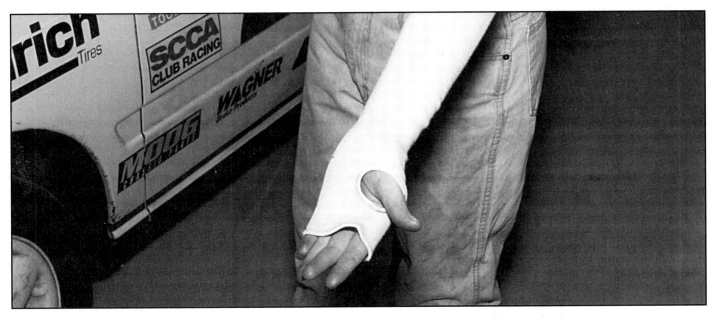

If you plan to perform brake pad changes in the pits, Kevlar arm protectors will reduce the chance of burns and cuts.

brakes, always have at least one crew member standing next to the car with a fire extinguisher (you'd be surprised at how flammable brake fluid can be if exposed to a hot enough surface). Also, always have a metal bucket half-filled with water nearby, maybe next to the pit wall. When a hot brake pad is yanked out of the caliper, it's going to hit the ground somewhere. The danger lies in that discarded pad being tossed on top of an air hose (if it's hot enough, it'll burn through a hose in a heartbeat). When we run a 24-hour race, we always have one crew member whose job it is to keep an eye on where those hot pads go. He wears heat-resistant welding gloves, and picks up a pad when it hits the ground and tosses the pad into a safe container. Usually, this is a metal can or bucket. Once in a while, if a pad (or a locked caliper) is so hot that it's going to create a problem in the pit, it gets tossed into a bucket of water. This tosses a bunch of steam, but as a last resort, it's a good place to dump the darned thing in a hurry. During the first 24-hour race we ever ran, we had a 4-gallon plastic water bucket in the

pits. A hot-potato pad was quickly tossed into the bucket. By the time the pad sunk to the bottom of the bucket, it was still so hot that it immediately melted straight through the bottom of the bucket. The moral is: use only metal buckets.

Always keep plenty of burn cream, disinfectant and bandages in the pits during any race, but this is especially important during a long endurance race where repeated chances of burns are possible.

In terms of spares, this will in part depend on the car's history of brake wear/usage. If you've raced the car in other endurance events and have some degree of experience in pit operation, you can create somewhat of a game plan in terms of how many pads, calipers, etc. you'll need. If this is your first endurance race, always plan for the worst-case scenario.

Bring enough pads to accommodate a complete front brake change every hour, and enough rear pads for a complete rear change maybe every 3 hours. Chances are, you won't change that often, but I've been in situations where changes were needed that

frequently because of an abusive driver.

Bring at least one spare fresh caliper per corner. If you can afford it, bring at least one pair of front calipers for every two hours of race length, and one pair of rear calipers for every four hours of race length. This is especially important if you're running a "stock" car that requires the use of OEM calipers. I've even seen big 4-piston race calipers seize up during a 24-hour race, so don't take anything for granted. Be a boy scout and come to the event as prepared as possible. Nine times out of ten, if you prepare for the worst, the worst won't happen. If you don't prepare for the worst, the worst will happen.

Also, and this is especially important for a 12- or 24-hour race, bring at least one pair of spare front knuckles/spindles. If a caliper seizes up so badly that you can't remove it from the rotor, you can still unbolt the whole knuckle/hub/rotor as an assembly and replace this with fresh stuff. When we prep for a 24-hour race, we always have a fully-assembled front suspension/brake corner ready to install (strut, knuckle, hub, rotor, loaded caliper, brake hose). If you plan ahead with pre-assembled subsystems, you'll save a bunch of time during an otherwise agonizingly long pit stop.

Always consider the heat danger of those hot removed pads and calipers. If you're using an air ratchet to remove caliper bolts, for instance, there's always a chance that the air hose will be dragged over a hot rotor or caliper. To prevent an accidental blow-out of the air hose, install a protective sleeve on the air hose (from the coupler, out maybe three feet along the hose).

Compressed nitrogen is the power source of choice for pit activity. You can rent nitro bottles in a variety of sizes from small manageable 18" high bottles to big 6-ft. monsters. Compressed nitrogen bottles are quiet (no compressor noise to deal with), they eliminate compressor maintenance, and since compressed nitrogen doesn't attract moisture, it's safe to use on your air tools. In order to use a nitrogen bottle in the pits, you'll need a thread-on regulator (to dial-in the pressure you want) and a safety cage for the bottle head (to prevent accidental regulator damage). If the regulator is damaged/knocked off of a charged nitrogen bottle, the 2,000 psi internal pressure will send the bottle through the pits like a cruise missile, killing anything or anyone in its path. Never lay an unprotected nitro bottle in the pits!

If the event is a long one, bring plenty of spare caliper mounting bolts and gobs of spare lug nuts. When the crew is rushing to service the car and get it out of the pit, there's little time to carefully lay caliper bolts and lug nuts out on the ground in neat order for easy locating during reassembly. These fasteners get tossed and strewn around in the flurry of activity, so spares are mandatory. The last thing you want is for a crew guy to frantically look for a lost lug nut, which wastes valuable time. One of the tricks that we use (not exactly high tech, but it works) is to cut a bunch of 4" long pieces of heater hose or garden hose, and stick one lug nut into each end of the hose (with threads aiming outward). The crew keeps a handful of these in a belt pouch or apron pocket. When the wheels are yanked off, the old lug nuts are discarded for later retrieval. When the wheels are reinstalled, the tire changer grabs a loaded hose, starts the threads of a nut onto a stud, flips the hose over, starts the next nut, grabs another hose, etc. This makes quick work of wheel installation, and the pit area is then policed after the car exits the pit.

The same goes for caliper bolts (except for the use of the hose sections). Each brake changer carries a handful with him at all times, so he doesn't waste time looking for the two bolts that were originally removed.

TOOLS/SUPPORT ITEMS NEEDED IN THE PITS

- Burn cream, other first aid supplies
- Compressed nitrogen gas bottle
- Air ratchets
- Air hoses with heat/abrasion protector sleeves
- Kevlar or other heat- and cut-resistant gloves
- Kevlar or other heat- and cut-resistant forearm sleeves
- Water bucket
- Sandpaper
- Brake fluid
- Spare calipers (with pads)
- Spare caliper mounting bolts
- Spare flexible brake hoses
- Spare knuckles/hubs
- Spare rotors
- Spare lug nuts
- Hardened sockets for caliper bolts
- Line wrenches (for fluid line connection at calipers)
- Hammer
- Eye protection
- Heat-resistant apron (to guard upper legs/belly)
- Knee pads
- Fire extinguisher
- Anti-seize paste
- Hardened deepwell sockets for your lug nuts

PEDAL RATIO

RATIO = PPD divided by PRD

Where PPD is the distance from the center of the pivot point to the center of the pedal pad, and PRD is the distance from the center of the push rod to the center of the pivot point.

LINE PRESSURE

LINE PRESSURE (psi) = APF X PR, divided by MCA

Where APF is the applied pedal force in lbs., PR is the pedal ratio, and MCA is the area of the master cylinder in square inches. Line pressure is expressed in lbs. per square inch.

CLAMP FORCE

CF (lbs) = LP X CPA

Where LP is the line pressure, CPA is the caliper piston area in square inches (one side of the caliper only), and CF is the clamp force expressed in lbs.

BRAKING TORQUE PER WHEEL

BRAKE TORQUE (lbs ft) = R X PA X LP X #P X COF; divided by 12

Where R is the effective disc radius in inches (centerline of axle to centerline of pad), PA is the piston area (one side), LP is the line pressure in lbs. per square inch, #P is the number of pads, and COF is the coefficient of friction (contact your pad manufacturer for COF numbers).

RACING BRAKE TROUBLESHOOTING

BRAKES DRAG

1. Bad master cylinder
2. Tapered lining wear caused by improper caliper mounting
3. Residual pressure valve in system where it's not needed, or residual valve with too high pressure
4. System hydraulically locked up by lack of pedal freeplay
5. Weak, deflecting caliper mounting brackets
6. Caliper misaligned at rotor
7. Excessive rotor runout/warped rotors
8. Master cylinder has internal residual pressure valve. Remove valve.

PEDAL DROPS TO FLOOR DURING RACE

1. Fluid boiling (caused by overheat from brake drag; old or inadequate fluid; inadequate air ducting; undersize brake system for application)
2. Master cylinder failure
3. Leak in system (caliper, lines, etc.)
4. Pedal linkage failure
5. Excessive spindle deflection during cornering (causing caliper piston knock-back)
6. Wrong size residual valve (use 2-lb. valve only, and check operation)

PEDAL TRAVEL TOO DEEP

1. Air trapped in fluid
2. Master cylinder too small
3. Pedal ratio too great
4. Excessive spindle deflection in cornering (causing caliper piston knock-back)
5. Warped rotors
6. Calipers misaligned at rotor

EXCESSIVE PEDAL EFFORT REQUIRED

1. Master cylinder too large
2. Insufficient pedal ratio
3. Caliper piston area too small
4. Contaminated pads (oil, grease, etc.)
5. Caliper pistons stuck/frozen
6. Fade caused by incorrect pad selection (if rotors glow orange, don't use soft pads
7. Glazed pads/rotors (replace pads with correct type and sand rotors)
8. Pedal mounted at severe angle (master cylinder pushrod should be no more than 5 degrees off-line of pedal and ideally should be in-line)

OSCILLATION FEEDBACK (PEDAL BOUNCE)

1. Excessive rotor runout
2. Rotor faces not parallel
3. Cracked rotor
4. Loose or improperly mounted caliper
5. Pad lining buildup (welding) on rotors
6. Excessive front wheel bearing clearance

CAR PULLS DURING BRAKING

1. Contaminated brake pad on one or more calipers
2. Sticking/frozen pistons in one or more calipers
3. Wheel alignment (incorrect camber, caster or toe). Examples: too much negative camber on right front will cause car to pull to the left; too little negative camber on right front will cause car to pull to the right; not enough positive caster on right front wheel will cause car to pull to the right; too much toe-out on right front can cause pull to the right.

CALIPER LEAKS

1. Caliper seals old, dried. Replace seals
2. Nick or other damage on piston, or damaged seal

SPONGY PEDAL

1. Air in brake system
2. Calipers incorrectly mounted with bleed screws not in high location
3. Too-small master cylinder
4. Faulty master cylinder
5. Calipers misaligned to rotor
6. Calipers mounted equal to or higher than master cylinder. Install 2-lb. residual valve
7. Excessive caliper flex. Check line pressure, which should not exceed 1500 psi
8. Pedal ratio too great
9. Excessive spindle deflection in corners, causing piston knock-back

BLEEDERS UP: Always mount a caliper to position the bleed valve as close to the 12-o'clock position as possible. Otherwise, you'll trap air in the caliper, no matter how hard you try to bleed the system.

LINE WRENCH: When loosening or tightening a bleed valve or line fitting, ONLY use a specially-designed "line" wrench. This features six sides of contact at the hex of the bleed valve or fitting (partially encloses around the hex to capture all six sides of the hex). This provides a no-slip contact, and eliminates the chances of "rounding off" the hex. Make this a hard and fast rule in your shop. Never service hydraulic fittings/valves/couplers, etc. with a conventional 4-sided open wrench.

BRAKE LINES: Assuming that you're able to mount the master cylinder higher than the calipers, always route brake lines on a downhill angle from the master cylinders to the calipers to avoid creating an air trap in the lines.

BRAKE LINE SIZE: It's recommended to use -3 flexible brake hoses instead of larger -4 hoses. The larger the hose size, the more it will grow under pressure. Hose diameter growth means expansion and a softer pedal.

PAD SPACERS: If you're using very thick pad designs, here's a trick to obtain the longest useable life. As a very thick pad wears, while there still may be plenty of material remaining, the extra clearance in the caliper can allow the pistons to extend further than they should. To cure this, you can use a pad wear spacer (available in 1/8" - 3/16" thicknesses) between the pad backing plate and the pistons. They're cut to match the shape of your pads, and the added thickness helps to insulate the pistons and brake fluid from the hot pads.

PUSH AND RELEASE: When using the brakes on the track, apply them as needed, then release the pedal. Avoid keeping your foot on the pedal when brakes are not needed. Any pedal pressure, regardless of how light the pressure may be, will cause the pads to drag on the rotors. This will prevent the pads and rotors from cooling properly between brake applications. Maintaining slight pedal pressure and dragging the pads can also cause the fluid to overheat and boil. If you have a problem in this regard, install a small indicator light on the dash, wired to the stoplight switch. This will serve as a telltale reminder, letting you know when the pedal is depressed.

LUBE THOSE SEALS: When rebuilding calipers or master cylinders, always lubricate internal parts with brake assembly fluid before and during installation. This will keep seals and O-rings from damage due to dry cylinder walls and pistons.

AVOID HARSH SOLVENTS: Never clean an assembled master cylinder with brake cleaner or carburetor cleaner, since this will dry seals excessively and will cause premature wear and damage.

BLEED PATIENTLY: When bleeding your brakes by manual brake pedal pumping, allow the brake pedal to rise completely at each stroke, providing enough time for fluid to refill the master cylinder bore.

PAD BEDDING: It's best to "break in" new rotors with used, already-bedded pads. This will help prevent rotor cracking and warping, and will help to increase rotor life.

RACING BRAKE TIPS

BLEED EVERY RACE: Bleed your brakes before each race event, and again before the race itself (after practice and qualifying). Replacing contaminated fluid on a regular basis will increase brake system component life.

NO SILICONE: Do not use silicone brake fluid in a racing application. The fluid may foam quickly and cause a soft pedal, and may damage certain seals and O-rings that are used in race systems.

ROTOR PREP: Before changing brake pad brand or compound, remove previous brake pad buildup on rotor surfaces. This will help ensure proper friction material transfer from the new pads to the rotors.

OVAL TUNING: On a typical asphalt oval track application, a rule of thumb is to use a 7/8" front-wheel master cylinder and a 1" rear-wheel master cylinder. A 60/40 front brake/rear brake bias provides a good starting point before further tuning is attempted.

KEEP YOUR COOL: When ducting brakes for added cooling, always direct the incoming air to the inside of the rotor. The rotor rotation will draw the air from the inside to the outside for effective cooling.

SMALLER vs. LARGER: A smaller-diameter-bore master cylinder produces greater line pressure, when using a two-master-cylinder setup. However, on a caliper that features two different piston sizes, the larger diameter piston produces the greatest pressure.

TEMPERATURE CHANGES BIAS: Excessive brake bias can cause rapid temperature rise in a braking system. As temperature rises, bias characteristics can change to the point where the bias loses its effectiveness on the chassis. Using a brake pad with a wide temperature range can help to avoid this problem.

ALUMINUM ROTORS WANT PRESSURE: Generally speaking, when using aluminum rotors, more pressure (as opposed to volume) is required to obtain a more-firm pedal. Downsizing a 1" master cylinder to a 7/8" master cylinder may help.

CHANGE SEALS: Change caliper pistons and seals often. Caliper maintenance can result in several-seasons' use of your calipers.

SIMULTANEOUS BLEED: When bleeding brake systems that use two master cylinders, bleed both front and rear wheels at the same time. This will prevent binding of the balance bar.

BRAKE PRESSURE GAUGE: Make use of a brake system pressure gauge to dial-in your brake bias for each track. A pressure gauge can be dash-mounted or temporarily screwed into the caliper bleed hole. As you test and adjust your pedal balance bar and/or the proportioning valve, the gauge reading can be documented, which will provide you with an accurate method of adjustment. Once you achieve the balance that works best, you can record this data in your logbook. That way, each time you re-visit a specific track, you can quickly adjust brake balance instead of wasting time by guessing and experimenting.

MAINTENANCE: Before each and every race, check for leaks at calipers, lines, master cylinder and reservoirs. Bleed the entire system at least once, refilling with fresh fluid (NEVER re-use the same fluid!). Inspect all of the air ducts for solid mounting and internal obstructions. Check each wheel for free rotation to make sure no pad drag exists.

CLEAN THE PISTONS: Whenever you change brake pads, inspect and clean the caliper pistons. Wipe off the exposed faces and sides with clean brake fluid or a suitable brake cleaner solvent before retracting the piston back into its bore. This prevents dragging debris into the piston seals.

SEAL SERVICE: Replace the caliper piston seals as needed. If the car is raced on a weekly basis, a rule of thumb is to replace the seals at your mid-season point, and rebuild the caliper between seasons. If the car is raced less frequently, plan to replace seals between seasons, or as needed.

DON'T GRIND CALIPERS: Never grind a caliper body to gain clearance between the caliper and wheel or other component. The caliper maker designed the body with a specific material thickness, and grinding can compromise strength and/or might enter a fluid passage. Racing caliper makers try to make their calipers as light as possible while retaining body strength and rigidity. If they could have used less material, chances are they would have done so. If you have a clearance problem, deal with it by changing the wheel, wheel backspacing, using a wheel spacer, etc. Leave the caliper alone!

CALIPER MOUNTING: Remember that the caliper must be mounted "square" to the rotor. If you weld a caliper mounting bracket in place, the heat of the weld can "draw" the bracket (distort), which will misalign the caliper. For example, if the outer pad contacts on the bottom, and the inner pad contacts the rotor on the top of the pad, the bracket has distorted. The bracket must be parallel to the rotor, within .020".

Mike Mavrigian has written technical articles for the automotive industry for the past 20 years, primarily for a number of leading automotive aftermarket trade magazines. His writing and photography work specializes in the areas of internal engine machining & rebuilding, suspension, braking systems and wheels/tires. Mike is ASE-certified and has attended over a dozen automotive parts and equipment manufacturers' technical training schools. An SCCA and IMSA racer, he also operates Birchwood Racing, specializing in road racing showroom stock-class sports cars at both amateur and professional levels. His race shop, located in Creston, Ohio, includes offices, a full race prep shop and photo studio. His hobbies, when time permits, include fly fishing, guitar playing and competition pistol-shooting. He and his wife, Lori, devote the majority of their "spare" time caring for abused and abandoned animals.

Larry Carley is technical editor for *Brake & Front End* magazine, Babcox automotive publications. Over the past 18 years, Larry has written over 1,000 technical feature articles for various Babcox magazines including brake service, alignment, steering and suspension, emissions control, engine performance and electronics. His writing efforts have won eight American Society of Business Press Editor awards. Larry has also authored a number of automotive books including "*The Mechanics Guide To Front-Wheel Drive,*" and "*Understanding Automotive Emissions Control.*" He also writes training programs for many leading aftermarket companies, and is developing computer software "quick reference" programs on a variety of subjects that are of interest to today's technicians. Larry has been ASE certified in seven automotive areas, and has helped ASE develop new test questions for several tests. You can visit his home page on the internet at http://members.aol.com/carpix256

Larry lives with his wife Nina and two children in Clarendon Hills, IL.

OTHER BOOKS OF INTEREST

1,001 High Performance Tech Tips by Wayne Scraba 1-55788-199-5/$16.95

Auto Math Handbook by John Lawlor 1-55788-020-4/$16.95

Automotive Electrical Handbook by Jim Horner 0-89586-238-7/$16.95

Automotive Paint Handbook by Jim Pfanstiehl 1-55788-034-4/$16.95

Brake Handbook by Fred Puhn 0-89586-232-8/$16.95

Camaro Performance Handbook by David Shelby 1-55788-057-3/$16.95

Camaro Restoration Handbook by Tom Currao and Ron Sessions
0-89586-375-8/$16.95

Chevrolet Power edited by Rich Voegelin 1-55788-087-5/$19.95

Classic Car Restorer's Handbook by Jim Richardson 1-55788-194-4/$16.95

Holley Carburetors, Manifolds and Fuel Injection (Revised Edition)
by Bill Fisher and Mike Urich 1-55788-052-2/$17.00

How to Make Your Car Handle by Fred Puhn 0-912-65646-8/$16.95

Metal Fabricator's Handbook by Ron Fournier 0-89586-870-9/$16.95

Mustang Performance Handbook by William R. Mathis 1-55788-193-6/$16.95

Mustang Performance Handbook 2 by William R. Mathis 1-55788-202-9/$16.95

Mustang Restoration Handbook by Don Taylor 0-89586-402-9/$16.95

Mustang Weekend Projects 1964½–1967 by Jerry Heasley 1-55788-230-4/$17.00

Paint & Body Handbook (Revised Edition) by Don Taylor and Larry Hofer
1-55788-082-4/$16.95

Race Car Engineering & Mechanics by Paul Van Valkenburgh 1-55788-064-6/$16.95

Sheet Metal Handbook by Ron and Sue Fournier 0-89586-757-5/$16.95

Street Rodder's Handbook by Frank Oddo 0-89586-369-3/$16.95

Turbo Hydra-matic 350 by Ron Sessions 0-89586-051-1/$16.95

Turbochargers by Hugh MacInnes 0-89586-135-6/$16.95

Understanding Automotive Emissions Control by Larry Carley and Bob Freudenberger
1-55788-201-0/$16.95

Welder's Handbook (Revised Edition) by Richard Finch 1-55788-264-9/$16.95

TO ORDER CALL: 1-800-788-6262, ext. 1, Refer to Ad #583b

HPBooks
A member of Penguin Putnam Inc.
200 Madison Avenue
New York, NY 10016

*Prices subject to change

202